The Mendocino Papers

Bruce Anderson

The Mendocino Papers, Vol. 1
An Informal History of Mendocino County

International Standard Book Number: 1-4196-9014-0
9781419690143

Printed in the United States of America

First Printing: March 2008

Cover design by Lemon Fresh Design
www.lemonfreshdesign.com

for Ling

Digressions, incontestably, are the
sunshine; they are the life, the soul of
reading; take them out of this book for
instance, you might as well take the
book along with them.
— Laurence Sterne

On a chilly March afternoon in San Francisco, at the top of a long flight of wooden stairs leading down to Baker Beach, I look out at the Marin side of the Golden Gate and think of Weldon Kees, poet and original beatnik, who had driven to the Marin end of the bridge on Monday, July 18, 1955, parked in the view lot, walked out onto the bridge and jumped. Another writer, MFK Fisher, said she'd always fought off an urge to hurl herself over the side whenever she was mid-span. Me, too, and I'm not suicidal, and not that these random memories are relevant to the rest of this personal geography, but like most people I can't stop what runs through my mind at certain sites, and this is what first runs through mine whenever I see the inimitable bridge.

As does my most vivid bridge experience ever when I was on the bridge in 1952. As the fog howled through the Golden Gate the hood of my father's lime-green junker of a DeSoto cab he'd bought for a hundred bucks, complete with jump seats between the driver and the princely plush leather of the rear thrones, suddenly flew up and over the side of the bridge. "Jesus Christ!" he exclaimed. "Did you see that?" Couldn't have missed it, Pop. In another memorable commute the old man had run out of gas on the bridge on his way to work then he ran out of gas again on the bridge on his way home. "You again," the tow truck driver had said. "I think you just set a record, buddy." A few years later, as a not so keen teen, I sped across the bridge from Marin to San Francisco one night with a carload of hilarious classmates, right on through the 25 cent toll gate without throwing the 25 cents in the collection basket, careening on into the Marina where a small army of cops jerked us out of the car, shoved us around, righteously yelling that we were "a bunch of little assholes," wrote the driver a huge ticket, took our names, confiscated the car, and told us to get the hell out of their sight forever. "Or else." Or else what? Even then sanctions were mild to non-existent.

The Indians said that San Francisco Bay was once a great inland lake secured at its narrow Pacific mouth by a continuous land mass from Marin to San Francisco. The Indians said a lot of things, most of them ignored or dismissed as myth, but on both sides of the Golden Gate the fractured geology seems to confirm the Indians' long memory of a stupendous earthquake that opened up the Golden Gate to the Pacific, and it is fact that in 1880 to make the Golden Gate safely navigable a huge rock, perhaps the last remnant of the ancient, single land mass that joined Marin and San Francisco, was dynamited out of the channel, its obstructing remnant more evidence that Marin and San Francisco once were one.

And I'm thinking of everything else the bridge means to me, all the times I've crossed it, and the time I crossed it and kept on going to Mendocino County, the least chronicled area of all the United States where I stayed for thirty-four years, a life-time.

But today, looking across the narrow mouth of the bay from Baker Beach, I can almost smell the acacia-sweetened air of the lambent, late winter Corte Madera where, when I was a child, immigrant Sicilians raised cows in their backyards and white Russians shared their home brew vodka with their neighbors. The Sicilians called the Russians Molotov and the Russians called the Sicilians Mussolini, and they all belonged to a volunteer fire department that threw a big 4th of July drunk and barbecue after an intra-departmental water fight between the Corte Madera and Larkspur volunteers with their fire hoses washing each other down Magnolia, not that "negroes" and "mongols" were allowed to buy or even rent property anywhere in the county and could live only in Marin City, the Sausalito shipyard suburb that came with World War Two. And Mount Tamalpais, the serene green sentinel looking down on the accelerating events beneath it, as always, eternally indifferent.

By 1970, the symptoms of the last illness were becoming clear

— class and race warfare, drugs, random violence, the seemingly endless war on Vietnam, feral children, bad feeling everywhere. Name your pathology, it was up and running by '70, busting on up field, eluding all its old tacklers, straight-arming convention, galloping on through the gathering dark. By 2007 there was another endless war underway and new, more ominous symptoms of the rolling collapse joined the old ones — water shortages, mysterious plagues, geologic cataclysms, civil strife, fire and ice.

I wanted out, and north I went, all the way to Boonville, to Mendocino County, the big empty where the remnant Indians had begun their ghost dances in 1870, and what they saw coming was a great cataclysm that would shake the earth free of the white people who didn't know how to live on it, and the great god Taikomol would bring all the Indians back to life for a great restoration of the true people of the earth, while the people who had brought the great sickness down on these true people and their abundant earth would be gone.

I'd been living in a condemned building, teeming with deadbeats, which I more or less managed for Coldwell-Banker in exchange for free rent. It was at Sacramento and Stockton on the Chinatown end of the Stockton tunnel which emitted a round-the-clock cacophony of honking horns, yobs testing their echo voices, the occasional terrified scream. There was a gas station down below and between it and my crumbling building was a nicely-maintained little garden bungalow occupied by a man described by Herb Caen as "man about town, Mathew Kelly." There were mornings when I could look out my kitchen window and watch the dapper Kelly unwrapping a fresh shirt as he prepared for another low intensity day of calls to his broker, lunch at Jack's, a cab ride on up the hill for drinks with Herb, Wilkes and Cyril. I envied him, not so much for his money and his social circle but for his daily fresh shirts, and the expensive bouquets of flowers I could see on his tables. I wondered why Kelly lived there; not that it was an unattractive little house, but it was placed at the mouth of the tunnel and the adjoining gas station and their perpetually toxic stew of noise and vehicle fumes.

In 1769 there had been an Indian sweat lodge, a temescal, at the foot of what became Sacramento Street, and in 1873, the original

7

Grizzly Adams brought his 1500 pound Griz, Samson, to star in Adams's animal menagerie in Leidsdorff Street, since downgraded to Leidsdorff Alley. One day the beast "got out of his cage and took possession of the lower part of the city" before he was trapped in a livery stable and recaptured.

It's 2007; there's a sign in an apartment window in the 100 block of Clement that says, "Return the Presidio to the Mukema Ohlone Nation," the long gone occupants of the 1769 temescal on Sacramento Street. If the ghost dancers were right, all the Mukema Ohlones have to do is wait a few more years, and we'll be gone and they'll be back amid the ruins, and a thousand years from now an Ohlone paleo-seismologist will be scratching his head over the ruins of old San Francisco.

One hundred and sixty years after the Ohlone's temescal, where Sacramento Street runs into the bay, my Sacramento Street menagerie included a large family of industrious gypsies whose men sold transmissions and other hefty car parts out of their living room while their women sold camellias at Fisherman's Wharf. "How ya doin' today, boss," the men would greet me. "You don't happen to need a differential, do ya?" The Gypsies paid their rent in cash, like everyone else in the building, including the "nude girl in the swing" who lived next door with her junkie husband she supported with her naked nightclub acrobatics. Every night she'd swing smiling down out of the rafters out over the yokel's straining eyeballs, packing the place in a time when even faux nudity was considered quite daring. Her husband, in his more energetic moments between dope runs, would beat her up. I'd tell him to stop, they'd both threaten to kill me. It was a weekly ritual with them, but the first time they did it I went out and bought a shotgun. I didn't know yet that dopers never follow through.

When I'd fled north for Mendocino, the Vietnam war went on and on, and amphetamine, heroin, the criminals who sold it, and random homicidal maniacs had taken over the city streets. I'd go north, I thought, a hundred miles north, up into redwood country, up 101 until it was so rural I couldn't see anybody except the people I wanted to see. I'd pass through the rainbow tunnel at the north end of the Golden Gate Bridge, through marvelous Marin, through long gone Sonoma County, to Cloverdale where the invisible green curtain parts and California's last wild country begins, that mysterious vastness of the Coast Range, those thousands of Edenic little valleys that lie between the Sacramento Valley and the Pacific, those miles of mountains and meadows now being sprinkled with gentle people building new lives in eccentric houses they built themselves. We'd drive on through Cloverdale and turn west towards the ocean, me and my odd crew of adult drop-outs and juvenile criminals, and on into the Anderson Valley where the air was clean, the scenery spectacular, land was cheap, and you didn't see a cop or a crook unless you called the former or were the latter.

We didn't know we were in a long tradition of outlaws and mavericks to populate the Northcoast, a tradition that had begun 150 years earlier when the long, lean, lethal sons of Missouri had begun drifting into the vast unsettled land defined by the Sacramento River to the east, the Sisikyou mountains to the north, San Francisco Bay to the south, the Pacific Ocean to the west, all that vast bounty the native peoples had lived contentedly on all those centuries until 1850.

While our staggering collective raised junior crooks on a leased ranch south of Boonville, many of our contemporaries grew pot and threw themselves into great naked piles at solstice boogies at places like the Rainbow commune above Philo, first among Mendocino County's burgeoning collectives, a place Timothy Leary tellingly described as "one of the most successful, upscale hippie communes in the country." Upscale is the keyword here, and can be read as insolence and an oblivious class privilege as expressed by the communard who'd defecate in paper bags he'd leave as gifts in the cars that picked him up hitchhiking. The collective's many other graduates, after a few years of trust-funded rural indulgence in what might be called decadence if their sex and drug bingeing had been conducted more elegantly, more stylishly than slob grunts and casual couplings, re-entered straight society to start-up prudent "alternative" newspapers, run their dubious friends for public office, and to generally begin accumulating the political power they have today on the Northcoast in the me-first-but-love-me politics of the Democratic Party. They all turned out to be as timid, as ultimately conventional as everything they claimed to oppose.

Situated on a ridge overlooking the Anderson Valley, Rainbow would provide Mendocino County with two superior court judges, a movie star named Winona Horowitz Ryder and, of course, several prominent Mendocino County therapists. Other commune grads became professional officeholders who are still entrenched in the Northcoast's better paying political offices.

Less upscale hippies, the ones who preferred not to risk the cops and the annual infestation of city-based pot bandits, dusted off their diplomas, slipped into their "straight people" bon-eroos and came down out of the hills to get themselves public jobs which, in the perennially tight job markets of the Northcoast, are the only jobs that pay college people the kind of money college people think they deserve. The hippies, with a vengeance, re-appeared in the society they'd spent their youths opposing. Or fleeing. But being middle-class and conventionally civic-minded — after all, most hippies never rebelled further than sex, drugs and rock and roll — Mendocino hippies, as loyal as Masons, soon elected other hippies, or hip-symps, to a few low-level offices like school boards; then to some mid-level offices like county supervisor, and before the "rednecks" or "straights" (anybody who supported Little League and the forest products industry) could mobilize their side's vote for a counter-attack, Mendocino County's public apparatus was occupied by the love generation.

One night at a meeting of the Boonville School Board, a re-entered love child, now respectable enough to get herself elected to a position of community trust, told me to, "Sit down and be quiet. You're becoming irrational." Which I probably was, but I remembered her just a few years before rolling around naked at the Albion People's Fair, and here she was judging the rational from the irrational, an authority figure, an educator (as teachers now grandly call themselves), a person to whom I daily entrusted my children. The fact of her was irrational-making, but it was one of many signs that the hippies were successfully inserting themselves into Mendocino County's power slots.

But all of this has happened in little more than two hundred years — from Franciscans to naked hippies, 49er football and the Manson

Family, and I can't help thinking about California as the Indians lived in it, can't help thinking that history suddenly sped up in 1850 and is now hurtling to some place ominous, some place the Indians predicted in their ghost dance prayers when they foresaw the ad sal invaders being swallowed up in great cataclysms and they, the true people, restored to resume living the old way, the harmonious way.

But outside our uncomprehending household on 1969 Sacramento Street, it was getting crazier and crazier.

I was driving a cab the night the Zodiac killer shot Paul Stine to death at the corner of Washington and Cherry streets in Presidio Heights. Stine was murdered on Saturday night, October 11th, 1969, Columbus Day, the day Joe Cervetto, playing Christopher Columbus, waded ashore at Aquatic Part, re-enacting America's discovery.

Cervetto had briefly been interned on Angel Island as a fascist sympathizer at the outbreak of World War Two. Like most Italians who'd admired Mussolini before the war broke out, Cervetto instantly became an ardent American patriot when the shooting started. His family maintains a summer place two miles west of Boonville on Redwood Ridge. In later years, Cervetto was greeted by protesters who pointed out that the discovery hadn't turned out well for the Indians.

When Zodiac and Paul Stine arrived at Washington and Cherry that Columbus Day, a neighborhood assumed to be safe by cab drivers because the wealthy mug us, not cab drivers, Zodiac leaned over from the back seat, wrapped his forearm around Stine's throat while he simultaneously stuck a handgun behind Stine's right ear and pulled the trigger. In a letter to the SF Chronicle accompanied by a verifying piece of Stine's bloody shirt, Zodiac explained that he was collecting slaves for the next life.

That same month a sniper shot out the top light of another friend's cab as he cruised lower Haight Street. The city's more estranged citizens often worked on their night time marksmanship by shooting at cab lights as The Summer of Love devolved into hard drugs and so much street violence that large numbers of young people were inspired to head north for the big empties of Mendocino and Humboldt counties where land was cheap and if it was violence you wanted you'd have to look for it.

I'd known Stine well enough to chat with him in the slow night cab lines out at the airport. It was an unusual group of cabbies. There were under-employed actors, unpublished writers like Hunter Thompson, who was briefly one of us, leftwing radicals, and free-range intellectuals too angry, too alienated for university faculty lounges. We were all passing through, many of us on our way to better paid unconventional work, we hoped. Out at the airport, we'd gather in small groups to talk and argue, mostly argue — about everything, from the endless war on Vietnam, books, movies, the works. We may have been the most high-minded collection of cab drivers in the history of San Francisco cab drivers.

Paul Stine was a graduate student working on his PhD and driving a cab to support himself and his young family while he prepped for the final hurdles. He had two little girls, as I recall. He was smart and a good talker without showing off his grad student knowledge. Everybody liked him. I still think about him whenever I walk past Washington and Cherry where Zodiac murdered him, and I think of that monster lumbering off into the forested end of the Presidio between the golf course and Julius Kahn playground, and on down to wherever in the mostly abandoned military base he'd parked his getaway car.

Zodiac claimed in his subsequent crazy-gram to the Chronicle that the police and their dogs had walked right past where he was hiding in the Presidio's semi-wilderness, but it's much more likely that he went straight for his car down around the old Letterman Hospital with its beds filled with permanently wrecked veterans of the Vietnam campaign, including my Boonville friend, Door Gunner Ray. Ray had done two tours before he was twenty. The second one cost him an eye, and the shrapnel left in his body sets off the metal detectors at airports.

With a bloody swathe of Paul Stine's shirt he'd soon send in to the Chronicle to prove he'd added a cab driver to his household staff for his next life, an assumption that hell allows servants, Zodiac drove back across the bay to his home in Vallejo where many police detectives and Zodiac researchers would become convinced he lived.

Witnesses, described as "several teenagers," heard the shot. They looked out a window only twenty yards away from Stine's last cab and saw Zodiac, a stocky, young-ish white man with crewcut hair and rimless glasses, climb into the front passenger seat of the cab beside his victim where he seemed to fumble with Stine's body; it was later assumed that Zodiac was lifting Stine's wallet and tearing off the confirming piece of Stine's shirt he mailed to the Chronicle to prove he'd done the crime. Then Zodiac casually wiped down the outside of the cab to erase his fingerprints and walked casually off north towards the Presidio.

The shocked teenagers called it in. The police dispatcher inexplicably managed to alert nearby police that the perp was "a Negro male adult." The wrong ID was a nice comment on the times; the dispatcher may have assumed a black thug had done the shooting, but how she'd managed to alert patrol cars to a "black male adult" when she'd been told "white male adult" should have cost her job, but then, as now, city employees are fire-proof.

White man Zodiac was stopped a couple of blocks from the scene by the first police unit hurrying to the shooting. The killer was asked by the cops if he'd seen anything. Zodiac casually replied that he'd seen a guy waving a gun back on Washington Street. The cops, looking for the mythical black male adult their dispatcher had told them to look for, headed off for Washington Street, and Zodiac had a free pass to kill another day.

But Zodiac was a much more remote threat than the many free-range maniacs roaming the streets at the time. And now. Your generic murder-loon gets around on the Muni, not by cab. Cab drivers know that the cops are in full triage mode every night in the midnight hours and that cab robberies, unless they're accompanied by spectacular mayhem, were always low priority calls for law enforcement. The cops sort out the nightly deluge of frantic calls by responding to those that seem most serious. Cab drivers are on their own.

In his memorable psycho-alerts to the city papers, Zodiac used to say he'd like Hollywood to have a go at his memorable public life. I think Mr. Z, forty years on, would be very pleased with the new Zodiac movie, which is so faithful to events it's better than the documentaries on the case. Best of all, it seems to have inspired another round of DNA testing which is likely to prove that a former champion high diver and child molester from Vallejo, Arthur Leigh Allen, was the guy. In 1992, the cops were about to arrest Allen when he dropped dead of a heart attack. He was 58. Paul Stine was 29 when Allen, then 35, shot him to death.

Paul Stine's murder was it for me. I headed north, part of the great urban exodus, the back-to-the-land or, in my case, the out-of-the-city movement. I wanted to get me and mine to a place where the odds of being randomly murdered were not as great as they were in San Francisco, 1969, although I knew that getting a fast pass to oblivion from somebody like Zodiac was about as likely as winning the lottery. But still the every day vibe, as the hippies expressed it, felt ominous. I couldn't have known, of course, that there were more killers per square mile — the miles being adjusted for relative rural-urban population density — in and around Boonville than there were in San Francisco and, taken as a whole, more outlaws and criminally-disposed misfits spread throughout sparsely populated Mendocino County than were proportionately loose in all of the San Francisco Bay Area, many of them making regular commutes back and forth, city to country, country to city.

The Anderson Valley, home of my heart, has gone from the Manson Family, Leonard Lake and Charles Ng, Jim Jones, Tree Frog Johnson, and the Moonies, to Jess Jackson, wine mogul. Measured strictly in terms of all-round civic desirability, Manson-to-Jackson barely ascends from lateral, and Moonies-to-Jackson is a definite come down; the Moonies used to pick up trash every weekend in downtown Boonville, and were known to have painted the homes of the poor. Jackson moonscapes the hillsides for vineyards from which he makes medium-priced booze...

Thirty-seven years after the murder of Paul Stine by Zodiac, I'm back in the city, which is now two cities and a third one under construction in the south sector. The city's true-ist tales are told in the police reports as translated by the city's newspapers, with the city's multitude of writers filling in some of the blanks while the new generations of cyber-mutants flash updates to each other on their hand-held communicators. The big picture is a million little pictures.

It's early March. A sudden hard rain has caught us without our umbrellas. We huddle in the southbound shelter at California and Polk, me clutching my transfer like a worried kid with a note home pinned to his shirt. The bus finally appears, but rather than pull up at the shelter so we can board without getting wet, the driver deliberately stops the bus a dozen feet beyond. A young girl and I exchange amused glances and laugh. Two Asian women react not at all, a young Hispanic male mutters under his breath, a huge fat man in knee length gray shorts inscribed "Michigan Baseball" on one leg lumbers on board and loudly asks the driver, "Why'd you do that?" The driver looks straight ahead, unhearing, uncaring. There's no answer to petty malice, of course, so the fat man, having satisfied himself (and us) with his rhetorical blast sits heavily down in the front section. These seats are reserved for the elderly and the infirm, but the young and firm are often planted in them, as two of the young and firm were that day, both of them mesmerized by their hand-held toys. I was hoping the fat man would plop himself down on them, that they'd have to swim up from his gargantuan buttocks to emerge gasping and so grateful for life that they'd throw away their electronic accouterments and dance off the bus and down forlorn lower Polk, re-born.

But the fat man took up two seats across the aisle from the mutants where he sat wheezing from the effort of climbing the two steps to board the bus, the annoyance at getting unnecessarily wet because of the driver's petty sadism, from getting angry, from now facing the prospect of repeating the experience in reverse order when he got off the bus in the rain because he knew he could count on the driver letting him off in the most onerous possible set of circumstances, away from a shelter in the pond of stopped-up drain. Which the driver did, the fat man's lumbering disembarkation so wary that he was in the puddle and the bus door shut in his face before he knew that the driver had gotten him twice.

Ethnic generalities are impossible not to make on a Muni bus, although almost without exception young people of all races tend to be loud, carelessly vulgar, probably uneducable, utterly vapid, and thoroughly unattractive. We've all been young and stupid, but this crop of under-30's seems uniquely awful in every way, from their laundry bag fashions, complete with tattooed buttcracks, to their cretinous music, even dumber movies, and extreme verbal dysfunction. "Like I said to the fuckin' dude," "Like dude, what the fuck you talkin' about?'" Schools of fish have more individuality. The only kids you see around who look like they might be age-appropriate wholesome are probably very recent immigrants. Or they're home schooled by that tiny minority of parents who know the popular culture and the collapsed public schools for the child destroying evils they are.

The most aggressive Muni passengers are Chinese women between the ages of 60 and 90. They just put their heads down and go, like mini-fullbacks on goal line plunges. You'll feel a soft but insistent pressure somewhere in your lower back and, when you look over your shoulder to see if it's a pickpocket or a perv playing bus rubbsies, what you see and continue to feel is an elderly Chinese woman, or a squad of them, making their head down ways up the aisle. "It's Grandma Fong up the middle! She gets maybe a yard in a huge pile-up of shopping bags and umbrellas. We'll probably need a replay here to see if she got to the back of the bus. But wait! She's still on her feet and still moving, shoving that old beatnik out of the way like he wasn't even there! And Grandma Fong is in for six! How about that, Howie?"

I was on a California Street bus the other afternoon whose black female driver checked the transfers of every boarding white person, me included, while waving all other ethnicities on past. At California and VanNess there was an angry standoff between this driver and a young white woman whose transfer the driver had rejected. Typically, with people piling on through both front and back doors, drivers, even the rare sticklers, don't look at transfers other than maybe a glance at its color to see that it is that day's valid hue.

"You'll have to pay," the driver said to the girl. "This transfer is no good," The girl indignantly replied, "But I just got it." The driver took the transfer from her and looked carefully at it. "It's an hour over," she said. "This is from way early this morning. You gotta pay." The girl continued to say she'd just got it on her previous bus. "You'll have to pay," the driver repeated, this time with some heat.

The traffic light had gone green to red three times while the transfer argument raged. There was an audible groan from the back of the bus. A guy yelled, "Kick her off! Let's go." The driver and the girl were staring at each other when the girl turned and stomped off the bus. The driver would have lingered until she won. As we pulled out, I could see the girl waiting for the next bus, the expired transfer in her hand.

Two hundred years ago all this was sand dunes.

On Divisidero I'm sharing a bus stop with a woman I guess to be roughly in my age group — early AARP. She was dressed in a purple sweatsuit and wore one of those Tibetan wool knit doofus caps on her head with its five or six dingleberry ties bouncing down off it. There was a metal pentagram around her neck, and she carried a pink child's "Hello Kitty" backpack festooned with size-various cartoon cats. I can remember when city women never went anywhere near downtown without their formal day clothes on complete with hats and gloves, and all the men wore suits, ties and fedoras. A large percentage of the old downtown crowd might have been totally crazed in those days, too, but you wouldn't know it looking at them. And you can't know it now, either, in a time when only the truly dangerous wear suits and ties.

This lady, it turned out, wasn't nuts. Or, I should say, contemporary standards of mental health being what they are, she was maybe half way out there given the wacky visual she presented, and given her lack of hesitation in asking me where I was going the instant I walked up. Considering she was asking a stranger a question unlikely to have an interesting answer, and that my destination was none of her business, I replied, but only because I wanted to see if she was as goofy as she looked.

"I'm going to the Castro Theater Noir Film Festival," I said, "to see a movie called 'Cry Danger' with Dick Powell and Rhonda Fleming."

She replied, "I met Raymond Burr once."

I said, "Do you know who my uncle is?" She said no, but looked interested in what I might say.

"He's my uncle," I said.

She laughed.

There have been obnoxious young slobs strewn up and down Haight Street for forty years because the left-lib bloc that controls the vote in San Francisco maintains that public intoxication and living on the streets and in the parks are civil rights. Which is a lot easier than taxing the comfortable to build cheap shelter and to revive the state hospital system for the armies of wounded left out in the cold. The city that knows how simply confines the worst public behavior to Haight Street with its open air drug bazaar at the Stanyan end of the street; an open air thieves market on the north side of Market at 7th; to the Tenderloin where many of the thieves live; to a few blocks in the Mission; and to the adjacent bantustans of Hunter's Point and Visatacion Valley, two neighborhoods far from a smaller ghetto in the old Fillmore area. Most of the shootings in San Francisco occur within these cordons unsanitary.

In the neighborhoods of San Francisco where aberrant behavior is more or less tolerated, areas like Haight Street and the Tenderloin, the crime rates are low because, it seems, every third person is an undercover cop. It's fun to watch the cops work the weekend crowds, cutting the dope dealers and the worst of the street crooks out of the herd as neatly as cowboys culling a herd of its yearlings. But a lot of police effort goes into keeping street crime at a minimum in places like the Haight and the Union Square-Market Street shopping quadrant because both areas draw so many tourists and shoppers, and that effort to confine the worst people to specific areas and out of other specific areas, explains why there's no police time left over to at least try to stem the epidemic of car break-ins and other relatively minor crimes, all of it expressions of the class war gathering steam here and everywhere.

Meanwhile, one and two-person "public interest" and "activist" entities often wield a disproportionate power to stop public good in San Francisco. A proposal to plant trees in the Tenderloin was stopped by a tiny group of lesbians and transgendered whatevers who called the would-be tree planters "a brutal gentrification squad."

When I fled north for Mendocino County in 1970, an unwitting back-to-the-lander, San Francisco, for all its long-distance beauty had, close up, become a place to get away from. Now, in 2007, even the middleclass is getting their houses painted, their hedges trimmed, their children nanny-ied and privately-schooled. Immigrant labor makes a standard of living possible that a few years ago wasn't doable except in the upper levels of the class structure. The other day, as I trudged through the mausoleum-lined streets of Presidio Heights, I overheard a blonde beast say to a guy who could have been his twin, "I always get pocket Mexicans, you know those little guys. They're small but strong as hell."

What we have in the city is a kind of schizophrenia, with many people doing very well served by people not doing well who, of course, include the thousands of unhoused and unhinged wandering around the streets, most of whom should be in lock-up medical rehab facilities but won't be because the well off don't feel much civic obligation these days and the career officeholders are afraid to tax the well-off because the well-off are them. And the streets are dirty, the Municipal Transit Authority, continues as it has for 50 years as a morass of missed schedules, bunched busses, and too many crazy drivers, while street crooks operate in plain view in too many public places, and a small army of skells camp out on the streets and in Golden Gate Park.

The schools?

Every morning a fleet of buses from the Marin Country Day School drives across the bridge to pick up the sons and daughters of the well-to-do for a day of economically segregated classes in Corte Madera. Every afternoon the buses return the students from Country Day to their economically segregated neighborhoods in the northern half of the city The same northern neighborhoods produce the student bodies for the city's many private high schools. Those who can, have fled the city's schools. Why?

One reason is that the city's school board is a collection of babbling fools. The other night the city school board voted to reimburse an un-re-elected colleague for 15 years of travel he claimed to have amassed while toting Frisco's edu-bale. His former colleagues promptly made him a gift of public funds in the amount of $13,747.60 which, by the way, included a junket to Beijing a few years ago. I suppose he went there because San Francisco has a large Chinese population which, in this city, might also be a pretext for tax-paid trips to Russia, Samoa, all of Spanish-speaking America, India, and the United Arab Emirates. The sole no reimbursement vote was cast by a trustee who said she thought the grifter should only be reimbursed for three years travel! The chiseler himself, Dan Kelly, casually pimping his wife and kids, told the Chronicle, "I always knew I was going to ask for the reimbursements eventually, so I kept the receipts. It was really a personal choice and a personal discussion between me and my family."

Who presumably shouted in unison at their patriarch, "If they're dumb enough to give it to you, grab it, daddy, grab it!"

If this is how the city schools manage money at the top, is it a surprise that the racially isolated schools of Hunter's Point don't have basic school supplies?

The mayor? He rides around drunk in his big black limo with blonde bimbos for seat belts. If you can do the job drunk while serially boffing the babes of Union Street, maybe, just maybe, being mayor of this town isn't really a job at all. But Newsom gets over for the same reason that lots of elected hollow men and women get over — millions of people can't tell glib from reality. Anybody who can get a coherent sentence past his or her big white photo-op teeth while wrapping it in chuckles and implied huggsies is on his way to the White House. Or, at a minimum, the San Francisco School Board. Then, again, maybe we can tell glib from reality but settle for glib because the reality is, well, ominous. Newsom and the Frisco School Board are right for the times, though. Give them that.

My friend White Man, when I knew him, was ecstatic at San Francisco's growing Asian population. Chuckling in anticipation of a Tiananmen-like purge of the hundreds of metropolitan irritations besieging him, White Man would say, "When the Chinese take over, and it won't be long now, all the bullshit will be over!" He'd repeat himself about the Chinese bringing an end to all the bullshit, bringing his arm down like a guillotine after each word. "You hear me? No! More! Bullshit! When! The! Chinese! Run! The! Whole! Goddam! Show!"

White Man split apoplectic time between Boonville and the city where he owned a couple of buildings in the Mission District.

He said he was in a constant battle to prevent his Latin tenants from destroying his investment. While White Man's sinophilia left no room for detailed investigations of San Francisco's many other ethnicities, he seemed to regarded blacks as either comic or menacing, Italians as "a bunch of crooks," Jews as "Italians with brains," and gays as "pathetic but great tenants."

No, White Man reserved his fiercest racial opinions for Hispanics, pegging those opinions to his perceptions of the housekeeping habits of his very narrow sample — the occupants of his two exorbitantly lucrative tenements. White Man said that he could walk past a building anywhere in the Mission and know at a glance the national origins of the inhabitants: Nicaraguans were messy and tended to duck out on their rent; Mexicans were scrupulously orderly indoors, total slobs beyond their own portals. White Man said Mexicans felt no compunction about simply airmailing their trash out their windows and into the street. He said Cubans never failed to pay their rent on time but could be dangerous in ways he did not specify. Colombians were a total no-go zone. "They won't pay their rent and they'll kill you if you ask them for it in the wrong way."

White Man also claimed to be a Marxist; he was a gun guy. Need it be said that here was a citizen utterly without irony, a walking contradiction?

"I'm always packin' when I go around my buildings, you can be sure of that," White Man would say, apparently thinking that I'd be reassured that one more crazed individual was walking around the city with a couple of loaded guns down his pants. The only hint of mental illness in his appearance was how fanatically neat it was. Precisely maintained white hair, cleaner than clean Levi's, ironed shirt, shined shoes. (In Boonville shined shoes on a local are seen only at funerals, if there.) White Man's teeming manias were perfectly concealed by the respectable visual he presented. Just by looking at him you'd never know behind that benign, grandfatherly facade the guy was all bombs bursting in air and the rocket's red, red glare.

He'd been married several times. "I just couldn't live with her," White Man would say about his apparently interchangeable wives. "She was totally unreasonable," the man wholly without reason

21

would invariably add whenever he mentioned his love life. More likely the wives had been wafted out the door on White Man's incessant gulf stream of one-way rhetorical gusts. When I knew him, White Man's love interest was a multi-substance abuser who kept herself in a perpetual chemically-induced catatonic state. One day, eating lunch at Libby's, the drug lady suddenly asked me if I had a Muni fast pass because "I need to go to Macy's." That was all she said in the hour I shared her company. Union Square by bus from Philo is an all-day adventure. I guess she thought we were in the city somewhere.

You won't be surprised that White Man was the kind of guy who got very angry when you disagreed with him, even mildly disagreed, as in, "I'm sorry but I don't see it that way."

White Man would go right off.

"Then you're an idiot," he'd say and stomp off.

He was a difficult friend.

White Man liked to drive out to the Coast with me while I delivered papers, and I should say here that I made a sort-of living for twenty years as editor and publisher of the local paper; our friendship, such as it was, probably arose from our shared vintage and, less than more, the same general frame of reference as it played out between 1945-2000. To me, the guy was like muzak. I half-listened to his monologues, only tuning all the way in for the uniquely crazy stuff, like the day he said, "You know what my shrink told me?" I hadn't known he had a shrink, and I didn't know whether to be scared or relieved, so I answered, No, comrade, what did your shrink tell you? (I always called him "comrade" to see if I could rouse the Marxist in him. I never did stir that beast.) "She said I'm on more Prozac than anyone else on her entire caseload!"

What do you say to a confidence like that? Congratulations? Way to go, White Man?

White Man read the New York Times cover-to-cover every day. I've never known a true political nut who wasn't a devout Times reader. I was not surprised that White Man seemed to need the paper even more than he needed his Prozac. He cited it endlessly as the last word on all current events. I once mentioned to him Chomsky's recommendation that the best way to read that paper was upside down, the last paragraphs first because that's where the truth was buried, if there was any truth at all anywhere in the story.

"Chomsky's full of shit!" White Man yelled. "I need the goddam facts, not a bunch of bullshit like you put out in your paper every week."

One day I was arguing with him about fascism, which White Man said had already taken over America. I said it hadn't, and cited the more obvious reasons that the fascisti hadn't yet made their move in the incompetent, deteriorated, haphazardly-policed corporate fun palace we actually do have in this country. Hysterics have been saying that America is a fascist state since at least 1961 when I first parted the political fogs to emerge as a half-assed socialist myself.

I told White Man that while it's true that there are lots of natural-born goose steppers loose in the land, we're not even half-way there. Yet. Anyway, I said, White Man old boy, given your imagined Chinese takeover of San Francisco's municipal management with its No! More! Bullshit! bugles and gongs patrols and summary executions of people who don't pay their rent on time, aren't you kinda fascist-oriented yourself?

"The trouble with morons like you," White Man had said the day of the fascism seminar, "is that you're unable to make simple distinctions; the Chinese aren't fascists; they're orderly."

I hadn't said anything about the Chinese as a people; I'd said China these days looks more like a fascist state than a communist one.

The day after I'd suggested he didn't know fascism from fajitas, here comes White Man with a whole box of books on fascism.

"You assholes" — a visitor to the office was startled to be included — "think I don't know about fascism? You think all these books are just for show?"

I expect any day now to pick up the Chron, and right on the front page there'll be a story about a 65-year-old white guy who went nuts in the Mission, gunning down twenty-five random Hispanics and three Chinese millionaires who got caught in the crossfire. The sub-hed will read, "In Boonville They Called Him White Man."

From the top of the Baker Beach stairs I can see what appears to be a naked man standing with mime-like rigidity at the foot of the stairs. A naked man? A naked man staring out to sea? The odd Triton doesn't stir as I pass, and I can see other naked men at the Golden Gate end of the beach. At the opposite end of the thin margin of sand, children and their young mothers play in the surf. A huge ship called the HaiYan, stacked so high with WalMart cargo containers its bridge is nearly obscured, approaches "the longest single suspension span in the world." I wonder if it might not save Americans endless trips to Costco if we each had a HaiYan container delivered directly to our front doors once a year.

Baker Beach is the peaceful end of the city, the north end, the bridge end, the-way-to-Mendocino County end. From here, everything looks orderly, tritely picturesque in the way of a color postcard, but a few miles to the south and the east thousands of sick people live on the streets of this extravagantly rich city, 150,000 people depend on private charities for their food, and odd behavior, unless it's criminal, doesn't get a second glance from the police or anyone else.

At Ocean Beach later in the afternoon I was watching cops on four-wheelers warn the suicidally oblivious away from a huge, storm-driven surf that had suddenly come up when a male type derelict asked me, "Excuse me, sir. Can you spare a dollar?" I said I was sorry but I didn't have any money on me. "Not as sorry as I am, you Winnebago motherfucker," he said as he scuttled off into a stiff headwind.

That night, in the theater block of Geary, I count twenty-two beggars, most of them men, between Union Square and the California Hotel at Geary and Jones. A police car is parked in front of the theater to keep the skells from molesting the nice people out for an evening of live culture.

Feliz Creek today, where it passes beneath highway 101 at Hopland is, in the summer, a parched expanse of dry streambed that is barely discernible as a water course. Only when it comes alive in the winter as it runs off from its headwaters in the west hills into the Russian River can you get some idea of how crucial it once was to the Indians traveling from Clearlake to the Pacific as they walked west up the seam of the Feliz into the hills separating Hopland from the Anderson Valley, pausing at the Feliz headwaters at the western tip of what is now the McNab Ranch before they walked over the ridge and into the Anderson Valley near Yorkville, and from Yorkville over the last hurdle of the Coast Range mountains to the Pacific. Indians made that annual trek for thousands of years.

There's a spirit rock at the Feliz Creek headwaters, a huge boulder covered with laboriously encrypted symbols the Indians carved into it over the millennia, thousands of years of directions, fertility prayers, perhaps statements of gratitude for the easy abundance enjoyed at the Edenic meadow the spirit rock sits in at the very end of the very western-most road of the McNab Ranch sub-division.

The Feliz Creek spirit rock stopped functioning as a pre-historic message board about the time of the Gold Rush when the Indians were suddenly ripped out of their ancient homes and began to die in large numbers. But on still nights, a mere five miles from interminable 101, it's easy to imagine this paradise as the Indians found it — thick with Feliz Creek's annual migrations of steelhead and salmon, and an unending amplitude of nourishing flora and fauna. And now, below the spirit rock at Hopland, a garish tourist interlude on Highway 101, an enterprise called Real Goods sells unresourceful rich people the expensive technology they think they need to live like the Indians of the Spirit Rock.

In two hundred years California went from Junipero Serra to California Cuisine and the computer. The ad-sals, as Mendocino County Indians called the white invaders, started slow but were soon everywhere, the first of them arriving in Mendocino County to stay in 1848.

The Indians predicted in their ghost dance prayers of the 1880's and 1920's that the ad sals, as the Mendocino County Indians called white people, would eventually be swallowed up in great cataclysms and they, the true people, the Indians, would resume living the old way they'd lived for millennia before the grasping, destructive invaders. The cataclysms are upon us, and are unlikely to spare anyone including, unfortunately, our first peoples.

The Spanish missions established in California late in the 18th century were the work of father Serra, a garrulous fanatic who talked constantly about slipping "the gentle yoke of Christ" over the heads of neophytes, as unyoked Indians were called by the Franciscans, all of whom had been born in Spain. The Indians killed babies born of rapes by the Spanish soldiers who accompanied the missionaries up and down Spanish California from San Diego to San Rafael and Sonoma.

The saving of Indian souls and the training of their bodies in the organized labor that would make the missions prosper was the goal of the missionary effort. Dangling an irresistible amalgam of regular meals and eternal life, with Spanish soldiers standing by to make sure the Indians stayed with the padres when hospitality hour was over, the Franciscans had their first free labor. The religion the Indians already had, complete with one god and an afterlife whose rewards were based on one's earthly behavior, was very similar to the one imposed on them by the padres and their body guards.

Men separated from women, men and women separated from their tribes, many of the Indians of California south of what became the Sonoma-Mendocino county line were soon highly trained serfs whose skilled labor made the missions rich. The missionized Indians spoke Spanish, and had quickly become the fabled vaqueros essential to the success of the cattle-dependent land grant rancheros that had been established in the vastnesses surrounding the missions. Indian women were just as essential to the patrician comforts of the land grant estanzas as skilled household workers.

Heavy handed imperialists that they were, Spain, the monks, and the Mexicans who came after Spain and the monks, at least regarded Indians as human beings with souls worth saving; the Yankees saw the Indians as so many sub-human pests, and would wipe them out in the two murderous decades beginning with the Gold Rush.

The first Americanos to arrive in California in force, the gold seekers of '49, considered Indians as vermin, Mexicans as greasers, blacks as slaves, Chinese as yellow peril, and each other as snakes, but only Indians were killed recreationally. As a government report put it, "Never before in history has a people been swept away with such terrible swiftness."

The missions absorbed Indians, Christianized them, Spanish soldiers and Mexican settlers married them, trained them as ranch hands and domestics, and preferred not to murder them so long as they remained docile and productive. Which they didn't. Early

California history is replete with large-scale Indian uprisings and counter-attacks on the missions and the Mexican rancheros and then the Yankee settlers.

Early on, European, Mexican and Yankee visitors would make the inevitable naked savage observation and then, in the same paragraph, marvel at how well the Indians seemed to do in all sorts of weather, how finely made and attractive Indian basketry was, how beautifully functional their cold weather clothing was. But the civilized men never took the next logical step in recognizing the genius of a people so perfectly at home in the abundance of the world as they found it that they didn't need anything the new world brought with it. One of the more thoughtful European observers did, however, come close to perceiving the root of Indian resistance. "You often hear of civilized men going native and never wanting to return to their former lives, but the desire among primitive people for civilization is non-existent."

Once the Indians south of Mendocino County were thoroughly missionized — or dead — and the padres were confident that these "neophytes" believed that the mission life was superior to life back home with the tribe, the Christianized Indians would be sent out into the outback to bring in their wild brothers and sisters as replacement labor for Indian labor lost to white man disease. By the time Mexico realized that the mission formula — armed proselytization — had created a string of highly prosperous outposts from San Diego to San Rafael and Sonoma, Mexico was inspired to declare independence and the missions privatized.

That was it for the missions, a mere fifty years. California would belong to independent Mexico until the Gold Rush, less than thirty years after the last mission was privatized.

History was picking up speed.

The first mission at San Diego was established in 1769.

Spain and the Franciscan monks ruled California from their headquarters in Mexico City until Mexico declared independence from Spain in 1821.

Mexico loosely presided over California from 1821 until 1850.

In 1834, some eight million more acres of California had become the vast ranches of roughly 800 grantees, reaching as far

27

north as Hopland. A typical land grant was ten square miles. These economically independent, self-sustaining ranchos were empires unto themselves. They grazed thousands of cattle, sheep and horses, and employed hundreds of missionized, Spanish-speaking Indians who made them as prosperous as fairy tale kingdoms.

The Gold Rush began in 1848, and California was a state by 1850 with uncharted Mendocino among its founding counties.

By the time of the Gold Rush, with Mexico exerting what government it could over a Yankee-dominated, restive California, Mexican land grants had been established everywhere in the state as far north as what is now the Mendocino County line. There were two undeveloped land grants in the Ukiah Valley, but only the one based in Hopland was a working ranchero. Two Mexican grandees were given land in the Ukiah Valley but they never established ranches on it. Hopland was as close as the outside world got to Mendocino County before 1850, apart from slave taking expeditions into the Ukiah and Anderson valleys by Spaniards, then Mexicans, then Yankees, which the Spanish soldiers, acting for the missions, had well underway by the late 1700s.

The Gold Rush finished the Indians. The world rushed in so fast that the Indians of Northern California were engulfed, the Mendocino County Indians with them. By 1850, a 150-ton steamer, the Jack Hays, was hauling gold prospectors from San Francisco up the Sacramento River to Red Bluff, and Red Bluff was just over the Mayacama Mountains from what was inland Mendocino County in the new state of California.

While all the Spanish missionizing and Mexican land granting had gone on in the greater Bay Area, Mendocino County slept on, ancient ways unmodified by the missions, and only occasionally affected by missionized Indians. The only reason Spaniards and then Mexicans came north to Mendocino was to capture Indians for slave labor either on the missions or the rancheros spread around the great bay. But when Redick McKee made his long, post-Gold Rush slog from Sonoma to Humboldt Bay in 1851 — nine days from Laytonville to Fortuna alone — to convince the inland Indians to assemble themselves in area reservations, the Indians listened to "the little white father's" pitch then rejected it. As McKee himself put it, "They had seen a few white men from time to time, and the encounters had impressed them with a strong desire to see no more, except with the advantage of manifest superiority on their own part."

McKee was the first Indian agent appointed for Northwestern California. (In an irony of local history it was a man named McKee who played a huge role in the back-to-the-land movement of the 1960s and 70s. The latter-day McKee sold thousands of acres of logged-over Mendocino and Humboldt county land to "hippies" on very easy terms.)

The first McKee's instructions were to protect Indians by establishing reservations for them from Lake County north to the Klamath and Trinity rivers because Indians, wherever white miners and homesteaders had appeared, were being murdered in very large numbers. McKee's mission failed, and the Indians were finished as coherent tribal entities in another decade.

Little White Father McKee, incidentally, on his endless slog north from Clearlake, stopped by the cabin of the Ukiah Valley's first settler, George Parker Armstrong. A member of the McKee expedition, George Gibbs, would write, "We found a small building of logs, or rather poles filled in with clay, and thatched with tule. Its furniture was somewhat incongruous; for upon the earthen floor and beside a bull's hide partition, stood huge china jars, camphor trunks, and lacquered ware in abundance, the relics of some vessel that had been wrecked on the coast during last spring."

George Parker Armstrong! Mendoland's first aesthete!

North of the Feliz land grant estate based at Sanel, as Hopland was then known, the Indians lived as they had for ages, mostly untouched but fully aware, and already wary, of the white civilization mestastazing south of them. The Northcoast Indians weren't "living naked in a state of innocence and ignorance," as an early visitor to Northern California put it; they were merely unaware of the murderous imperialism about to overwhelm them, a people without guile, defenseless against people who were all guile.

No one among the early ad-sals admired the Indians as they found them — perfectly, ingeniously adapted to their world. The newcomers simply wanted what they saw as virgin land for their cattle, horses, hogs, and homesteads; the Indians were in the way. Literally. Their traditional food sources immediately destroyed and disrupted by the settlers' cattle and horses, the Indians tried to live as best they could, begging or stealing from the homesteaders, but there was barely enough food for the settlers let alone whole colonies of disoriented brown people, and the homesteaders, struggling for survival themselves, murdered their desperate neighbors as simply one more obstacle to their success in the new land.

The Yorkville Indians tattooed their young women's chins because the Indians said the tattoos repulsed Catholic slave traders. Descendants of pioneer Anderson Valley families nevertheless wrote that the Spaniards were benign explorers who only wanted to extend European civilization into southern Mendocino, hence dewy-eyed statements like this one: "The visits of these Bueno Hombres with their religion, not greatly unlike that of the Indians, had a lasting impression on the Ma-cum-maks as they lived side by side with their kindly Spanish settlers."

Also in the first quarter of the 19th century, parties of trappers, Russians with their Aleut-Pomo body guards, and French, English and American trappers and mountain men passed through even the remotest areas of inland Mendocino, some of them with their Indian wives and children in contingents of a hundred or so, the children suspended from horses and mules in the woven willow traveling cages that were the car seats of the time. And long before these ghostly parties passed through Sonoma and Mendocino counties, Sir Francis Drake had put in at Marin County where he marveled that a single Indian could easily carry burdens it took two or three of his sailors to lift, let alone move.

By 1840 the Russians had exhausted the sea otters that their outpost at Fort Ross depended on for cash flow and had sold Fort Ross and much of Bodega to John Sutter, the freebooting Swiss who, you might say, was California's first credit card entrepreneur, parlaying his mere signature with Honolulu merchants into an astounding 48,000-acre agricultural community just north of today's Sacramento that Sutter called New Helvetia. Sutter also bought and sold Indians, as did most of the early, pre-Gold Rush settlers the Mexican government gave land and citizenship to.

When the Russians sold out to Sutter and sailed out of Fort Ross just before the Gold Rush, Sutter dismantled the settlement, hauling everything he could use over to his Sacramento estates, first by sea down the coast to San Francisco Bay then up the Sacramento River to New Helvetia and Sutter's experimental farm and retreat, the Hock Farm on the Feather River not far from the Sutter Buttes you see to the east off 1-5. General Vallejo gave Sutter permission to drive the Russians' surplus cattle and sheep through Sonoma east on into the Sacramento Valley. Sutter outfitted his small army of the biggest Indians he could find in the uniforms of Czarist Russia. They were said to be an impressive sight galloping through the Sacramento Valley and, as a fighting force, greatly intimidated the under-manned Mexican garrisons of the Bay Area.

Sutter had fully absorbed the successful formulas for prosperous colonization he'd seen at frontier forts east of the Rockies, which also ran on Indian serfs, and he'd seen the Russians' thriving militarized outposts at Sitka, Bodega and Fort Ross, all of which were also dependent on Indian labor recompensed by free room and board, chits for purchases at the company store, and the coarse cotton Mexican manta shirts the Indians prized. Some Indians liked these arrangements, most didn't.

There were constant Indian rebellions throughout the mission and Mexican occupations, all of them foiled by the genius of General Vallejo who'd made the 6'7" Solano, chief of all the tribes of the North Bay, his enforcer. The giant, and giantly gifted, Solano learned to speak a perfect Spanish and an English superior to many English-speakers. Vallejo and Solano negotiated with dissident tribes when they could, ruthlessly suppressed those tribes with whom there was no negotiating.

By the time of the Gold Rush, enormous and enormously prosperous land grant cattle and sheep ranches checkered the state all the way north to Rancho Feliz at Hopland. The politically nimble General Vallejo served as regional administrator of the vast missionized land grant areas between San Francisco and Mendocino and Lake counties. He called his domain the Northern Frontier.

Indian women married into Spanish and Mexican families, and missionized Indian-Mexican men married unmissionized Indian women, and the new European-American ways of living thus radiated outward into southern Mendocino, mostly from the land grant Rancho Feliz in the present-day Hopland valley.

Rancho Feliz Indians had, since the founding of the vast rancho at Hopland, been related to Mendocino County Indian families in the coastal areas of the county. Ad-sal surnames like Azbill and Lincoln became prevalent in eastern Mendocino County while Indians descended from the Spanish, then the Mexican periods of California, were named Cruz and Feliz and Lopez and Oropeza and Ortiz who still thrive in contemporary Mendocino County.

Steve Knight was one of the founders of the California Indian Brotherhood whose first meeting was convened in Ukiah in the winter of 1926. His was among the most articulate voices in summarizing the transition from Mexican to American rule as it affected Mendocino County Indians:

"Mexican people built no missions up here, so the Indians were allowed to live pretty much as they had been before and after the Mexicans came, and the Indians were given certain areas of land to use to grow things for themselves. They built brush fences around them, had their homes there, planted gardens, had corn and everything they needed to eat on these places. When the Americans superseded the Mexicans the Indians were aware of the change — they seem to have known there was a change — they didn't resent the Americans coming in where there was just a few came in, but finally then the miners came in by the hundreds and by the thousands, then trouble arose between the Indians and the whites. Then the American government sent agents among the Indians to make treaties with them in order to get the Indians on reservations where they might be protected, but mostly to forestall Indian uprisings. These agents came out, made treaties with the Indians, promising them certain reservations. The Indians signed these treaties in good faith. They thought these treaties were final when they signed their name to them — they did not know it had to have the approval of the Senate of the United States, so the Indians were expecting to be moved onto the new reservations, but these new promised reservations were being filled up by white settlers. Then those Indians realized that they had been fooled. But the old people up to very recent times (the 1920s) believed that the government would make some other settlement with them. These treaties were pigeon-holed in the archives of the United States Senate for 50 years. No one ever saw them until after the 50 year term had expired. Someone then dug them up and made a few copies of some of the treaties. When these old Indians were told about the treaties having been recovered from the archives they became very much interested and told the younger Indians about how these treaties were made, by whom signed."

In January of 1848, before his Indian, Hawaiian and Mormon workers deserted him for the gold fields, and before the mobs of gold seekers overran Sutter's thriving estates, California was estimated to be home to 7,500 Spanish Californians; 6,500 foreigners; 3-4,000 former mission Indians living near towns or on ranchos. Wild Indians were not counted in this rough census; no one had any idea how many of them there were in the great unknown between Sonoma and the Oregon territory.

By 1850, the criminal drifters who had not struck it rich in the gold fields began wandering through Mendocino County's untouched magnitudes, much of it perfect country for the raising of sheep and cattle, its empty solitude surprised these first ad-sals; the rest of the state was already mostly claimed. The ad-sals couldn't believe their good fortune, and they weren't about to share it with the people who'd lived there for 12,000 years. The first permanent white residents of the remote mountains and canyons of the Northcoast were killers and outlaws, many of them on the run from the settled areas of the country. The law was a late arrival to Northern California and, I would say from my experience, never has fully prevailed.

As the relentless sons of Missouri staked out Mendocino County's myriad, well-watered little valleys, they shot Indian men where they found them, helped themselves to Indian women, sold Indian children into slavery, rez-ed the Indians they hadn't managed to kill, indentured them, and segregated them for the next one hundred years.

Ukiah's schools were only integrated in 1924. Aggressively opposed by a majority of white residents; the Ukiah schools were finally pried open by court order in 1923 with Steve Knight leading

33

the charge. The rest of the town remained segregated up through the 1950s with a nastiness as mean and low-down as the segregated American South. Indian women could not get their hair done in the town's beauty parlors, Indians were not allowed to try on clothes, let alone purchase them, in the shops of the county seat, Indians could eat only in one Chinese-owned restaurant, and Indians were allowed in one Indian-only section of the Ukiah Theater. Two decorated Indian veterans of World War Two were denied breakfast at the Blue Bird Cafe when they got off a northbound Greyhound. Ukiah wouldn't get all the way color blind until deep into the 1960s.

The cattle, sheep and horses introduced into the seemingly endless valleys of the county instantly denuded the land of the foods the Indians depended on literally for their lives. Their choice was between starvation and death by murder. Or the reservation where you could starve and be murdered. In the decade between 1850 and 1860 the Indian population of Mendocino was greatly reduced, and by 1870 it was a dependent, reservation remnant and a few rancherias on the edges of the acres appropriated by the settlers.

The first white Americans who came to stay in Mendocino County — the Asbill Brothers and Jim Neafus in 1854 — shot an unknown number of Covelo Indians dead when the Indians rushed out to greet them. The white men said they thought the Indians were hostiles and opened fire. That's the first documented interface of the ad-sals and Indians in the county. The ad-sals continued to murder Indians until 1870, the year the Indians throughout the Western United States, including the Indians of the Northcoast, knowing they were finished, first ghost danced their prayer for an end to the ad-sals and the restoration of them, the true people of the fertile little valleys and streams, the people who could live amidst natural abundance without destroying it. 1870 was also the year when there weren't enough Indians left in Mendocino County to provide even a pretext to kill with the old impunity, although there continued to be random attacks on Indians through the 1880s, especially in the wildest parts of the Eel River back country between Covelo and Weaverville.

Like the Asbill Brothers and Neafus, I was also an usurper of sorts when I arrived in Mendocino County in 1970 from San Francisco, barely aware in my preoccupation with the now that I was arriving in a place whose history was largely untold, a semi-wild vastness with a legacy as bloody as any in the country. But unlike the tough, relentless ad-sals of 1850, I was merely one more soft soldier in a small army of the alienated who came to be collectively known as back-to-the-landers. Or hippies. Or the end of the civilized world as it was known in Mendocino County before the hippies.

Some of us, of course, thought of ourselves as white Indians. Mythologized Indians served as inspiration for many rank and file counter-culturalists. As liberals, all of us were Indian sympathizers in generally friendly but specifically unhelpful ways because we didn't know anything about them, didn't even know there were Indians in our adopted homeland of the Northcoast. We knew vaguely the grisly fate of the Plains Indians, the only Indians most of us were aware of, and we were real gosh golly darn sorry it had happened, but we knew nothing about the Indians of Mendocino County, and we certainly didn't know that before the Gold Rush the Northcoast Indians had lived just beyond the long reach of the Franciscan missions, and then when the missions were privatized and absorbed by well-connected Mexicans into their grand land grant estanzas, Northcoast Indians still remained just beyond those Mexicans and their leisurely aristocracies. For a short time, a very short time, Northcoast Indians also remained just beyond the great invasion of American fortune hunters who arrived with the Gold Rush of 1848. (The gold, by the way, that the Argonauts rushed in to find, was mostly found within a 300-mile strip 40 to 100 miles wide beneath a thin crust to depths of 300 feet mostly running along the Sierra foothills. The size of it kept fights over claims to a minimum although there were enough of them, certainly.)

The legendary anthropologist and patron of Ishi, California's last wild Indian captured near Oroville in 1915, the willfully uncomprehending A.L. Kroeber, said there couldn't have been 12,000 and 20,000 Yuki Indians in Mendocino County before the ad-sals descended on them; no, certainly not, and certainly not based on the say so of the few Yukis who somehow eluded the casual murders that began at that very first encounter of Indians and the Asbill brothers in Covelo in 1850.

Kroeber reasoned that because there were only a few Yukis left at the twentieth century's dawn if there'd been as many as 20,000 when the hungry sons of Missouri, many of them the infamous "Pikes" of Pike County of whom some 6,000 came west for gold in 1849, began arriving in 1850, how could there possibly be so few Yukis a mere fifty years later? Kroeber wrote that there was no accounting for the "tremendous decrease" in the Yuki population; no epidemics, no wholesale removals, no prolonged contact with the Spanish mission system that might have reduced a large population to a mere handful of survivors. No, Kroeber concluded, the Yukis must have been a small tribe to begin with, no more than 2,000 he thought. In living deathly fact, it was the sons of Confederate Missouri who killed off Mendocino County's Indians so thoroughly that by 1950 all that remained of the truth of what had happened to them were the haunted memories of old men and women whose grandfathers and grandmothers had told it to them.

Contempt for Indians was still strong into the 1940s, even from crusading liberals like John Steinbeck who, in his epic novel, East of Eden wrote, "And that was the long Salinas Valley. Its history was like that of the rest of the state. First there were the Indians, an inferior breed without energy, inventiveness, or culture, a people that lived on grubs and grasshoppers and shellfish, too lazy to hunt or fish. They ate what they could pick up and planted nothing. They pounded bitter acorns for flour Even their warfare was a weary pantomime."

Farther back, Jack London, whose name appears with his wife Charmian's in an old Boonville Hotel register, was also contemptuous of Indians, had commented, "What the devil! I am first of all a white man and only then a Socialist." To which Mark Twain replied, "It would serve this man London right to have the working class get control of things. He would have to call out the militia to collect his royalties."

The federal government occasionally intervened in what was mostly unrelieved atrocity between 1850 and 1870, by which time the Indians of Northern California had not only been destroyed as coherent tribal entities but mostly destroyed period, the atrocities often being expedited on a cash and carry basis by the Indian agents the feds assigned to the reservations at Covelo, Fort Bragg and east of the Mayacamas near Red Bluff where, in 1865, John Brown's widow settled when the Civil War ended. The widow Brown and her two daughters worked as nurses to support themselves while Salmon Brown, her son with John, established himself as a sheep rancher at Corning. In April of 1865, the Sacramento Union suggested, "If every man, woman and child in California who has hummed John Brown will throw in a dime, his family will have a home." Enough dimes were thrown to buy Mrs. Brown and her daughters a home at 135 Main Street, Red Bluff.

It's safe to say that John Brown would not have approved of California's treatment of its native peoples. By the time Mrs. Brown arrived in the Sacramento Valley, Indians from as far away as Shasta had been herded over the mountains to Covelo in Northern California's very own trail of tears. Shorter trails, watered with just as many tears, led the surviving Indians of Mendocino, Humboldt and Trinity counties to Covelo, not that the trip was optional for any of them. They were collected then driven like cattle to the reservation. This initial mix of different tribes, different language groups, plays out today in ongoing feuds that had their origins in the forced proximity of disparate peoples. The feuds have always worked against the political solidarity that Mendocino County's Indians have needed to defend themselves — still need to defend themselves.

It's one thing to know in the abstract that Indians were murdered almost to extinction; it's another, a kind of double knowledge, to know the specifics. Representative incidents during the initial ad-sal interface with the Mendocino County Indians included:

"I saw a man driving squaws from a clover field inside the reservation; they were picking clover or digging roots; he said he would be damned if he would allow them to dig roots or pick clover, as he wanted it for hay." Deposition of J.W. Burgess, February 28, 1860, Indian War Files.

"Coming home one day a settler near Covelo found a party of bucks and squaws being supplied by his wife with some scraps of food from the kitchen, the bucks sitting stolidly on the grass outside waiting for the squaws to bring them some of the food. The settler went to his corral and released his pack of bloodhounds, and turned them upon the defenseless bucks, encouraging them while they tore the Indians limb from limb in the presence of their squaws." The Horrible History of Round Valley, San Francisco Call, October 21, 1895.

New Year's Day, 1859, as described by a non-participant: "On the first of January, one thousand eight hundred and fifty-nine, a party of citizens came to my house and said that they came to kill my Indians because some Indians had been stealing; I told them that I wanted my Indians to work for me, and they must not hurt them; one of the party stated that they had killed some Indians at Lawson's, and some at Bourne's; Bourne was of the party, so was Pat Ward; four or five of the party were drunk; they told me to pick out the Indians I wanted to work, and they intended to kill the remainder. Not content to shoot Indians living on ranches in the valley, the same group of men went to the reservation the next day and shot another 'ten or twelve' Indians there." Deposition of John Lawson, February 27, 1860, Indian War Files.

Some of the depositions were taken at Round Valley, some at Cloverdale, some at Ukiah. Without them, there would be even less evidence of what really happened to the Indians.

"In coming into the valley on the first occasion I met a man with four Indian boys taking them off, and the third time I came on the trail, I met a man taking off a girl. It is a common occurrence to have squaws taken by force from the place. About a week ago some of the rascals came into the yard, broke open a door, and took squaws that had been locked up by the agent. This was done at night and was witnessed by no white person, consequently I can do nothing." Lt. Edward Dillon, Round Valley, 1861.

"In 1856 the first organized expedition by the whites against the Indians was made, and have continued ever since; these expeditions were formed by gathering together a few white men whenever the Indians committed depredations on their stock; there were so many of these expeditions that I cannot recollect the number; the result was that we would kill on an average, fifty or sixty Indians on a trip and take some prisoners, which we always took to the reserve; frequently we would have to turn out two or three times a week."

— Dryden Lacock, reservation worker at Nome Lackee, Covelo, Indian War Files, 1860.

Item from the Ukiah newspaper, 1862: "The Indian murder. They were only Digger Indians, women who had their brains dashed out the other day, a few miles from town — and old and ugly at that, who had therefore 'outlived their usefulness' in a community such as this. The two Indian men who were arrested on suspicion of doing the horrible deed, after a few days' incarceration, were liberated, it being believed that their guilt could not be shown. Calpella, the old Indian chief, and all the Indians, are positive that the murders were not the work of Indians. It's no matter. The victims were only Indians, and of a tribe that dare not if they would, attempt retaliation. Besides, the bother of an investigation would put the county to expense."

From the Humboldt Times of Eureka about the same time: "Now is the time to rid Humboldt County of this pest. If the people intend to live here and have their interests here they will earnestly take hold of this matter until the last tawny rascal may be taken from the county before having been removed, send him to the happy hunting ground of his race. Make no spasmodic effort but go to work seriously with determination to make the present the last Indian war that we are to be troubled with."

Slavers pre-sold kidnapped Indian children for prices ranging from 50 to 200 dollars each. One Mendocino County pioneer was said to have made $15,000 in a single season of Indian hunting, well over a million dollars in today's money, and a significant fortune in the Mendocino County of the mid-19th century.

The lineage of Mendocino County's first Grand Jury of 1859 would later come to include the Reverend Jim Jones, last of Jonestown, Guyana, foreman of the 1979 Mendocino County Grand Jury. But that very first grand jury assembled in Ukiah recommended that the California state government fund the permanent removal of "the miserable, half-starved creatures prowling about and infesting every neighborhood, greatly to the damage and annoyance of our citizens."

The Mendocino County grand juries of the 1970s, in language as contemptuous as that that Assemblyman Lamar and the Mendocino

County Grand Jury of 1859 had applied to Indians, fretted about the invading, undeserving hippies who were getting free money welfare benefits while they occupied the county's logged over rural land, although real estate sales people were joyous that they'd unloaded thousands of remote acres on the unsuspecting, unprepared newcomers.

When Walter Anderson appeared in 1851 and named the Anderson Valley after himself, there were, at a minimum, some 2,000 Indians living from Yorkville at the southeast end of the valley to Navarro at the northwest end of the valley. The Indians ran Anderson off because white soldiers had just murdered large numbers of Indians, including women and children right on down to infants, on Bloody Island near Lakeport. That the Anderson Valley Indians knew very quickly what had happened forty hard miles to the east is one more indication that the Indians of Northern California were not at all the isolated bands of semi-nomads the early anthropologists portray them as being.

There is no recognition of the slaughter of the Mendocino County Indians by Mendocino County memoirists, although there is the Grace Hudson Museum in central Ukiah dedicated to the memory of a gifted romantic painter who depicted the surviving Indians of the Ukiah and Potter valleys as robust figures of the noble savage stereotype, and their babies as fat, jolly papooses. The museum also has on display the remarkable handwoven baskets crafted by highly skilled Ukiah and Anderson Valley women, the last Indian women to whom the craft, many thousands of years old, had been passed down from the time before the lethal ad-sals. The history of Mendocino County Indians as represented by the museum can be summarized in a sentence: "Once upon a time a happy brown people lived in Mendocino County who were real good at making baskets, and then they weren't here any more."

The Ukiah Indians who survived the first ad-sal onslaughts, along with the remaining Indians of Anderson Valley, disappeared entirely except for a Yorkville remnant which has since disappeared. The Anderson Valley Indians, my erstwhile neighbors, were herded to a reservation on the Noyo River where a stockade called Fort Bragg was built. The soldiers were supposed to protect the Indians from the white lowlifes — "degenerate whites" as they were described at the time — passing through the area, leaving behind syphilis and native corpses. The reservation would also train the Indians in self-sufficiency, the magnificent irony being that the Indians had been self-sufficient for the previous twelve thousand years. A local history describes the Indian's extinction merely as, "The decades following the 1850s were filled with massive loss and continual adaptation."

The rest of the remnant Indians up and down the Mendocino Coast, were rounded up by the Army units and volunteer posses of settlers and force-marched to the new reservation at Fort Bragg, which had been established in 1856, supposedly to protect and train the Indians for self-sufficiency. The area set aside ranged from Noyo to Ten Mile. An inspection for the Indian Department carried out in November of 1858 by Mr. G. Bailey, described the reservation he found: "At present the reservations are simply government almshouses, where an inconsiderable number of Indians are insufficiently fed and scantily clothed, at an expense wholly disproportioned to the benefit conferred... The whole place has an effete, decayed look which is most disheartening."

These days, Fort Bragg and Mendocino have freshly painted, touristy looks; the number of pure mendicants is greatly reduced, but the number of non-dependent "white degenerates" of the drug criminal type is probably proportionately greater than it was in the mid-19th century.

In 1866, the Fort Bragg reservation was closed and its remaining Indians herded east to the one big NorCal catch-all rez at Covelo. When the first elementary school for children of all races was opened in Point Arena where the high school is today, Indians refused to attend because their grandparents remembered that the site was the collection point for the tribes of the area who were subsequently forced first to Fort Bragg, then to Covelo, most of them not surviving the relocations, the most spectacular of which was reported by the San Francisco Herald of December 1859.

"The steamer Sam Soule arrived in Sacramento, says the Union about 2pm Sunday from Red Bluff, having in tow a barge containing between 400 and 500 Indians — the exact number of which we are not advised — including, however, about two hundred warriors from the Pitt river country — the prisoners taken by the volunteers under the command of General Kibbe. They are in the charge of Lieutenant Van Shull en route for the Mendocino Reservation and will leave for the Bay probably today, a vessel having been charted at San Francisco by Gen. Kibbe for their transportation to the reservation…"

Imagine that journey from the Indian perspective. Down the Sacramento River and into the San Francisco Bay where the Indians see the dismaying ad-sal city spreading out over the hills. And then the city ad-sals gathering to gawk at the stunned, disoriented natives on their humiliating barge before they're finally towed out the Golden Gate into the Pacific, and on up the coast to a compulsory home at Mendocino-Fort Bragg.

Mendocino County settlers were able to legally have the Indians who'd managed to elude the first ad-sal onslaughts removed to reservations by the spring of 1858. There weren't very many Indians left by 1858.

J. B. Lamar, Ukiah's first state assemblyman, the first of a long line of Ukiah-area wahoos to hold public office, got all the way behind the Mendocino County Grand Jury's 1859 declaration that "The Indians of Mendocino County are a treacherous, blood thirsty, settler-murdering, and stock-killing people. The state," Lamar thundered on, "should adopt a general system of peonage or apprenticeship for the proper disposition and distribution of the Indians by families among respectable citizens. In this manner the white farmer might be provided with profitable and convenient servants, and the Indians with the best of protection and all the necessaries of life in permanent and comfortable homes. By the adoption of such a policy, most of the Indians now on the reservations and those termed domesticated residing among the whites might be speedily provided for."

Ukiah's determination to enslave the Indians was almost a decade behind the state curve. On April 22, 1850, the new state of California, with Mendocino among its founding counties, had passed into law "An Act for the Government and Protection of Indians," which made legal the "indenture or apprenticeship of Indians of all ages to any white citizen" for open ended periods of time.

Not sixty years later, Robert Renick, born in 1914 at Sherwood (between Willits and Fort Bragg and once the inland route to Covelo) remembers Indians living at Noyo, which was part of the original reservation but had been incorporated into the Union Lumber Company property that runs for six miles along the Fort Bragg coast. In 1937, Renick, an Indian, went to live out on the point, which is today hidden behind Dominic Affinito's garish, oversized, scandalously achieved motel, the North Cliff, erected in blatant violation of state and local law which says no structure can obscure the sea. The North Cliff not only obscures the sea but also obscures what remains of a reservation that once was the unhappy home of 3,000 Indians drawn from all areas of the Northcoast.

"I went to Fort Bragg and lived at Noyo on top of the hill," Renick remembered. "Bought me lumber; I built a shack up there. All them shacks there are what Union Lumber Company pulled down, shacks from logging camps, them houses there. Then when they want the house bigger, Union Lumber Company buy that lumber, build, add-on. So I went along. The lumber company say you could live there the rest of your life. They used to give us wood for the fireplace, wood for the stove. They gave us water. That all changed. We dig our own well, we get our own water. But they put in electricity down there, we got it."

Union Lumber had no legal claim to the land in the first place. It belonged to the Indians. There was a large Indian cemetery on the point dating back to the days of the Fort Bragg reservation which was lost when the lumber company, which founded and ran the town for the next 140 years, buried the Indian graveyard beneath a log deck. More contemporary Indians lie in a recent cemetery overlooking the Pacific. It's surrounded by a white picket fence, scant protection from the relentlessly acquisitive forces which have caused it to come to be as far west as it is possible to rest. Two nearby Indian families are the last of the Indians descended from that first reservation.

From that first reservation at Fort Bragg, the Indians who'd run from Fort Bragg's and Covelo's allegedly protective embraces, drifted back to the only true homes they knew, those serene little valleys with their annually renewed plentitudes of fish, game and edible flora where they were grudgingly allowed to exist on the unused margins of ad-sal land. Except for a small band of Indians in Yorkville who'd been protected by a white rancher and allowed to stay in the valley, there were no Anderson Valley Indians left to return to their traditional homes. They'd been murdered or had died of introduced disease or had not survived their sequestration at Fort Bragg or Covelo. The Yorkville Indians were fortunate in having relatively benign white padrones, but there were so few of them remaining that the padrones, even from their unyielding economic perspectives, could afford to let the few Indian families go on living on the edges of their appropriated lands. Besides, the Indians were good workers, and what padrone had ever refused free labor, especially skilled free labor? This post-slaughter peonage was called "binding out" and was sanctioned by the state's Indian apprenticeship laws as a civilizing process for the Indians. In return for their labor, the Indians received the surplus food their labor had created in the first place, and they got to wear the farm family's castoff clothes.

The remnant Indians lived in small rancherias on the sufferance of the ad-sal usurpers but, in one of the more sanguine local ironies, the ad-sals eventually allowed undesirable pieces of their stolen holdings to be purchased by the Indians and held in common by them for their permanent homes. These rancherias became the basis for today's reservations at Ukiah, Point Arena, Laytonville, Hopland, and Cloverdale. By 1880, Catholic and Methodist missionaries had begun schools for Indians in Ukiah and Covelo; the Catholics had a partially built-in constituency because many of the county's surviving Indians were descended from the Catholic missions of Sonoma County. They were already Catholics. The mission schools were soon taken over by the federal government; over the years, many Mendocino and Humboldt County Indians were also dispatched to distant Indian schools in Southern California, Arizona and Montana where they learned, among other trades, printing.

What I think of as an emblematic house, a house on stilts on Anderson Creek across the road from the Boonville Cemetery, was built in the late 1940s by the Junes, the ranch family who'd come to own the land. An Indian family named Luff, whose patriarch was Frank Luff, a long-time worker on the ranch, spent their summers nearby in a traditional conical Indian shelter snugly built the ancient way from tree limbs and bark. They spent winters in one of the cabins the Junes had erected to house transient hop pickers. Judge June wanted to reward the Luffs for their years of faithful hard work on the June place by building them a more comfortable home, hence the stilt house, which is still there and still occupied by Mexican vineyard workers. Frank Luff's daughter, Alice, was famous for her wizardry at basket-making, one of which Alice called her "hard times basket." It now rests in the Grace Hudson Museum in Ukiah as an example of the craft at its most skilled.

Effie Luff was descended from the Indians who lived on Rancheria Creek near Yorkville, the all-year stream being named after the Indian rancheria located on its banks about where the Pronsolino Ranch is now. The Luffs' children and grandchildren grew up hearing the Luffs speaking to each other in their ancient language and listening to the old people sing the old songs and watching them mourn their dead the old Indian way at the rancherias at Yokayo, Hopland and Manchester. The Luffs were among the very last real Indians of Mendocino County, and you could hear in their sad songs the memory of a people that was just about gone, and was gone when the Luffs died.

Singing the old songs and speaking the old words, the Luffs lived on in the stilt house with their grandchildren on through a terrible day in 1954 when they came home one afternoon and found one of their granddaughters dead. She'd walked home from the old high school just down the road across from Boonville's little red school house and shot herself through the head. No one knew why she'd done it, but the gossip said she was in love with a white boy who didn't love her back. Or couldn't love her back, the times being what they were. The two old Indians went on singing their old songs, sadder now, and speaking their lost language to each other on Anderson Creek until they could no longer care for themselves, and then they went to live with their grandchildren who, in the old way, kept them warm and safe until they were gone, and when Effie Luff was gone in 1975 the last of Anderson Valley's several thousand native people were gone too.

Frank Luff died at age 76 in 1962. He'd been born in 1886 in Ukiah at the Yokayo rancheria. Effie, died at age 87 in 1975. She'd been born in 1888 in Yorkville, and she was the last of the Anderson Valley Indians.

Effie Luff was descended from Rancho Feliz at Hopland. She had married young to a descendent beneficiary of that vast Mexican land grant estate whose boundaries included much of the Yorkville area. Her husband left the land to Effie who was soon driven from it at gun point by a pioneer family whose descendants still live in the Anderson Valley.

Joan Burroughs remembers playing with Violet Renick, a granddaughter of the Luffs. "When I was quite young in the 1940s, I would go with my mother to the hop fields on the farm across the creek from your place near Anderson Creek. The adults would pick hops, my family and all the Indians together. Frank and Effie had a summer house, they called it, built against a dirt bank. I remember most of the way it looked. It was fun running in and out of it with Violet — it was dark and cool — and we were into all their belongings. They had seaweed hanging on the supports across the front and acorn meal stored in containers. The back of the place, against the bank, was covered with bark and blankets and the sides were also covered with blankets or whatever was handy. They spent their summers there when it was hot. They had a large picture of Jesus in their house. Always made me stop and wonder what happened to their god — I guess we know the answer to that one. Frank Luff called me Joans. He was the Pomo chief in the Ukiah area for years.

The Indians of Mendocino County put up a good fight, though, such a good fight that the Army had to maintain outposts throughout Northern California to beat back Indian counter-attacks. A few Eel River Indians called "The Gun Indians" had captured arms and had quickly learned to use them, much to the terror of white settlers in inland Mendocino County. But few of the Indian resisters had guns, and none had horses. Although there were Indians famous for hunting deer by running them down on foot in relay teams, horses could always run faster and farther, and the tough little mountain mares of the ad-sals could go anywhere an Indian could go, and go there faster. Hike into a place you think is so hidden no one has ever been there and chances are very good you're walking on a murdered Indian.

Steve Knight, founder of the statewide Indian Brotherhood and a man of great ability, was predictably dismissed by white 1920's Mendocino County as a mere rabble rouser, but he undoubtedly spoke for most Indians when he described his own wariness around whites:

"Considering that I am an Indian, some people may be curious to know how I might have been impressed by some of the noted people that it has been my fortune to meet. The common Indians belief is that most white people, if not all, are self-seeking, always trying to deceive the other fellow. I think that perhaps I have been afflicted with this same belief only in a modified form. Therefore, in all my contacts with the various kinds of white men and women I instinctively, not consciously maybe, have been in the habit of scrutinizing every one very closely. Then I would make my conclusions as to whether this or that person comes up to the standard that I have set as to what a man should be. With this sort of a measuring stick many a white person, without his knowing, has been silently condemned by me. On the other hand, I have met many men and women of the white race that I admire and respect and also like."

Old settler Walter Anderson of Anderson Valley, a valley whose Indians had simply disappeared to hear the settlers tell it, was stepfather to Henry Beeson, fine saddle maker and Bear Flagger Beeson settled in the Anderson Valley with the Andersons. The family had been forced to retreat to Dry Creek near Healdsburg for a year after their first arrival because the Anderson Valley Indians drove them out. The Indians, putting the lie to anthropology's subsequent assumption that they were unaware and not in touch with Indians outside their own territory, had known within days that the Army had slaughtered a large number of their brothers and sisters in Lake County and probably feared they were next.

Anderson became fleetingly rich off fine horses and hogs, but died relatively young and absolutely broke. The Andersons, and the first settlers in the Ukiah and Hopland valleys, would drive their hogs and horses to Petaluma, then the entrepot for the Mendocino trade to and with San Francisco. It is not known how Anderson managed to lose his fortune, but Mrs. Anderson had died in 1857 at age 52; Mr. Anderson a year later, perhaps out of grief at the loss of his wife, a grief which may have caused him to neglect the horses and hogs that had made his family comfortable in their pioneer home on the edge of the redwood forests, not far from today's bleakly utilitarian high school campus. (The valley's school architecture has devolved from Anderson Valley's first high school, erected in 1915 across the road from the Little Red School House, to its present medium security prison form and function. That first high school was a graceful structure complete with an arched entry and floor-to-ceiling windows set back from the road behind a large lawn. The lawn is still there, the structural grace is long gone. Before 1915, the few valley youngsters who went on to high school after eight years of elementary school in Anderson Valley, boarded in Ukiah or Cloverdale to attend their high schools.)

Boonville's Bear Flagger, Henry Beeson, was the premier saddle maker for much of Northern California whose horsemen. He was descended from perhaps the best horsemen ever, California's pre-Gold Rush Spanish and the Mexicans who lived on horseback before the Gold Rush, and knew their saddles. The great cowboys of Alta California made their way to Boonville to get a Henry Beeson saddle, which he made for years on his ranch just south of Boonville on the wagon track into town where the California Department of Forestry's fire station is now. Beeson is buried in the Babcock Cemetery on a hill off the Manchester Road not far from the Anderson family's first homestead where the road to the coast begins to climb the last of the Coast Range mountains separating Anderson Valley from the Pacific.

The late Wayne McGimpsey was descended from a pioneer Anderson Valley family; the McGimpseys succeeded the Beeson family on the Bear Flagger's old ranch south of Boonville.

"I was born December 3rd, 1918 two miles down the road from Boonville where the CDF station is now. I was delivered by a midwife, Mrs. Tarwater. She delivered most of the babies in those days. Before her, Grandma Stubblefield was the midwife. She lived at the other end of the valley near the old Reiser place. There was never a steady doctor here until quite a bit later. Our ranch, where the CDF is now, was where Henry Beeson had his saddle shop. Made saddles right there. He was the last survivor of the Bear Flag Revolt. I can remember as a kid playing in his saddle shop. He made them the old fashioned way, right there on the trail from Cloverdale to Boonville. The old Beeson place was our place. My father was a sheep rancher."

Beeson would have seen Kit Carson and John Fremont when they rode into Sonoma on their famous way south from the Klamath country, and would have remembered them both as enthusiastic Bear Flaggers. Fremont, more than any single American of the time, was responsible for the annexation of California.

McGimpsey was unaware the Frank James had friends from his home county in Missouri who'd settled in the Anderson Valley. James was known to have visited Boonville soon after the James Brothers' failed great Northfield bank robbery of 1887.

"I don't know if the James Brothers came out here or were ever here, but the Earps were both here. The reason I can say this clearly is because I can prove it. I've got Virgil Earp's icebox. They stayed in a place out at Yorkville and left a trunk there. And all that information is in that trunk, but I didn't have sense enough to pick up the trunk. There were four Earp brothers; the two that were here were Virgil and Wyatt, and they lived out in this valley for a long time. The Earp brothers were very well behaved. Everybody liked them. Caused no trouble. They were just ranchers. (In the 1893 census, Wyatt and Josie Earp are at home at 145 Ellis. Wyatt Earp listed his occupation as capitalist. He was also well-known in San Francisco as a referee for the popular sport of boxing. Earp's life is well-chronicled. There's no mention in the Earp oeuvre that he ever lived in the Anderson Valley.)

"There are Indian artifacts anywhere you want to look. One big burial ground is out on Guido Pronsolino's place. I understand that many local Indians died from diphtheria. There were large Indian settlements in Yorkville, a big one in the Ornbaun Valley; there's a big one right here where the Fairgrounds is, a big one at Philo where the Christmas tree farm is now, and a big one up at the headwaters of the Rancheria.

"I went to work full time when I was fourteen. I was running a ranch — the old Hobson Ranch — with two thousand head of sheep on it. It's all cut up now into little pieces. I rode a horse every day to keep an eye on the sheep. We used poison to control coyotes and bear. Old Newt Ornbaun told me about the time he was running hogs out in Ornbaun Valley and he saw a bear come in there, grab a hog, knock it down, hold it with his paw and eat a ham off it and turn it loose. Whether that's the truth or not I don't know, but they claimed it happened.

"In the early days, I remember the last two drives they made on hogs out of this country. They had dogs that would gather them hogs up and keep them in a bunch. If they didn't stay in that bunch, they lost an ear or they lost part of their nose, or they lost something else. But the dogs would drive the hogs fifty to a hundred in a pack, right to Cloverdale where they were loaded onto train cars. I remember when they used to drive cattle from the Piper Ranch out here on Greenwood to Cloverdale. My dad used to always be in on that drive."

Today, a stern visage, the picture of 19th century rectitude, looks down on passersby from a banner at the corner of McAllister and Hyde, fin de siècle San Francisco. The banner celebrates the adjacent law school, which is named after Serranus Clinton Hastings, born in New York, law degree in Indiana, on west to Iowa where he was Iowa's first congressman and first chief justice, then out to California during the Gold Rush where he became Chief Justice of the California State Supreme Court.

Hastings, through his term as a congressman and founding legal father of the state of Iowa, was already a nationally-connected Democrat when he arrived in California in 1849, looking to add to the small fortune he'd made in Iowa real estate. He knew the Gold Rush also meant a land rush as thousands of Americans made their way into the under-populated state to make their fortunes. But Hastings preferred to look around for likely real estate and legal sinecures rather than pan for gold; and as he prospected for free land he also got himself a seat on California's early supreme court as its chief justice. The Mendocino Indians soon had the judge sitting on them in Eden Valley, near Covelo, which the judge had appropriated for himself as a horse and cattle ranch, remarking that he'd found the place "uninhabited except for some Uka Indians."

The foreman of Judge Hastings' Eden Valley ranch was a Texan named Hall, "Texan Boy Hall" as he was known in the Covelo area, and a giant at 6'9" and 280 pounds, a doubly intimidating presence to the Indians who were still trying to adjust to the lethal unpredictability of ordinary-size white men when they first encountered Texan Boy, a recreational Indian killer who showed up with the first wave of white settlers in the Round Valley area in the middle 1850's, and may have killed more Indians than any other single American, including Kit Carson, the generally recognized champ.

While Hall ran Judge Hastings' ranch in Eden Valley, Hastings built himself a big house at Benicia in Solano County, a remove which would later lend the judge what he seemed to think was plausible deniability when his foreman became a little too notorious for his freelance retaliatory rampages against the Indians on the judge's behalf, and the judge reluctantly let him go; an indiscriminate baby killer, after all, was an unseemly sort of employee for chief justice of the state supreme court. Texan Boy, though, soon got a paid job killing Indians with Jarboe's Eel River Rangers.

Indians had been casually murdered in every part of Mendocino County since the Gold Rush. According to California's 1850 Act of the Government and Protection of Indians neither murder nor rape were crimes. Every year saw new and larger expeditions of both settlers and Army units sent out to kill them. But Judge Hastings, Texan Boy Hall and Walter Jarboe, in California's first public-private partnership, managed to convert dead Indians to cold cash in expeditions against the Indians of the Eel River drainage, from Covelo to Hayfork, public funding arranged by the judge because the Eden Valley Indians killed his horse, a black stud stallion the judge planned to use to start a herd of quality animals much in demand in the rugged back country that was then all of Mendocino County.

"A little more than a year ago, Hall of Eden Valley employed 13

Indians in place of pack mules to go and pack loads from Ukiah City to Eden Valley, and promised to give each one a shirt in payment; the distance, I think, is about 40 miles. The Indians commenced complaining at not receiving the shirts, and he, Hall, whipped two of them, to keep them quiet; he said he never gave them the shirts after he whipped them." (Indian War Files)

Indians, when there was a shortage of horses and mules, were often forced into service as foot teamsters.

A Covelo settler reported in 1857 one consequence of Indians as human pack trains:

"About three hundred died on the reservation from the effects of packing them through the mountains in the snow and mud. They were worked naked, with the exception of deer skins around their shoulders. They usually packed fifty pounds if able; if not able, a less load."

In retaliation for not getting their shirts from the judge and Texan Boy, the Indians, knowing exactly on whose behalf Texan Boy was acting, killed Judge Hasting's $2,000 stallion.

At the time, no one in Mendocino County was in danger of drowning in the milk of human kindness, but Judge Hastings and Texan Boy Hall were extreme even by the frontier standards of 1856 although the competition was keen. A San Francisco Examiner of 1899 interviewed a Covelo rancher named Jackson Farley in his home, noting that Farley's walls were decorated with "dozens of Indian scalps." Farley, the newspaper said, "has scalped more Indians than any other person on this coast, and has his trophies to prove the fact." Farley was a Jarboe Ranger, but at the time of the massacres the names Hall, Hastings and Jarboe were the most frequently recurring. Texan Boy was called "Monster Hall" in an Army report by Lt. Dillon who'd been assigned to protect the Indians of the Round Valley reservation. The lieutenant was unable to stop the terrible trio of Hastings, Hall and Storms from repeatedly violating the reservation and the Indians in the surrounding hills. Dillon said Hall was the worst he'd seen with a Van Duzen river man named Larrabee running a strong second.

In retaliation for the death of Judge Hasting's stallion, neighboring rancher William T. Scott would testify, Texan Boy got up a gang of his friends and "commenced killing all the Indians they could find in the mountains; when Hall met Indians he would kill them. He did not want any man to go with him to hunt Indians who would not kill all he could find, because a knit (sic) would make a louse. Mr. Hall said he had run Indians out of their rancherias and put strychnine in their baskets of soup, or what they had to eat."

Scott related another incident when Hall, having killed all the adult males among a group of Yuki Indians he'd encountered near Covelo, took some women and children into his custody with the apparent aim of taking them in to the reservation at Covelo. "I think all the squaws were killed because they refused to go further. We took one boy into the valley, and the infants were put out of their misery, and a girl ten years of age was killed for stubbornness."

But Judge Hastings was still unhappy about the Indians killing his stallion, and he seemed to consider Texan Boy's random revenges inadequate payback for the loss of his horse. The judge wanted all the Indians of inland Mendocino, Humboldt and Trinity counties permanently gone. On July 11, 1859, the judge called 16 Covelo-area settlers together who all signed a declaration selecting "Walter S. Jarboe as Captain of our Company of Volunteers against the Euka Indians." Hastings ordered Jarboe to "chastise" the Indians.

Jarboe's ensuing chastisement was rather broadly carried out. He and his rangers, assisted by Storms' contingent of Paiute Indians, and with Texan Boy Hall leading the early morning charges, in one summer's work the Eel River Rangers almost succeeded in emptying the entire Eel River drainage of Indians, from northern Lake County on up into the Hayfork and Weaverville, (also then known as Faggtown) areas of what is now Trinity County, chastising on into the next life every Indian they encountered.

The Indians didn't have the horses and the guns possessed by their enemies. Jarboe and Hall and their Rangers would typically ride down on Indian rancherias at dawn, slaughtering men, women and children right down to infants. The only casualties the white warriors suffered was an occasional non-combat injury unrelated to their one-way war. Bows and arrows were no match for dragoons, and certainly no match for Chief Justice of the California State Supreme Court.

California's early taxpayers got their money's worth from Jarboe, a man so admired by the early settlers of Ukiah they would make him their first sworn peace officer because Jarboe knew how to handle Indians, having radically reduced their populations and pauperized into dependency those who managed to survive him.

In January of 1860 Jarboe billed the state of California $11,143.43 for five month's chastising, state compensated chastising being pretty much a warm weather affair. A big part of the bill was compensation for the beef that fed the Indian hunters; the beef came from Judge Hasting's ranch at Eden Valley. If the steer dressed out at, say, 400 pounds, the judge and Jarboe turned in a claim for 600.

The legislature, seemingly aware that they were dealing with both an efficient Indian killer who was also a chiseler, paid Jarboe $9,347.39 which the legislature said represented "payment of the indebtedness incurred by the expedition against the Indians in the county of Mendocino organized under the command of Captain W.S. Jarboe in the year 1859."

The newspapers of Northern California regularly urged extermination of the Indians, so when news of large scale murder drifted out of the seemingly infinite recesses of an area larger than some states, an area which is today bordered by I-5 to the east and 101 on the west, Clearlake to the south, and the Trinity mountains to the north, they were blithely reported as body count estimates followed by announcements of horse races. By the end of the Civil War, and certainly by 1870, the Indians were finished. They'd fought back as best they could, but they'd been hit so hard and so fast they were finished as coherent tribal entities before they could mount an effective, unified counter-attack.

Judge Hastings, attorney, jurist, rancher, real estate developer, and mass murderer is memorialized as the University of California's Hastings School of Law, San Francisco. Pioneer Ukiah appointed Walter Jarboe its first law enforcement officer; and a man named James Jarboe is contemporary America's domestic terrorism section chief for the FBI. He told Congress in February 2002, that the Animal Liberation Front (ALF) and the Earth Liberation Front (ELF) have "become the nation's most destructive domestic extremist groups," committing "more than 600 criminal acts in the United States since

1996, which resulted in damages in excess of $43 million."

Which may or may not be histo-genetic linkage, as may or may not be a very large Covelo horseman named Hall, as in Texan Boy Hall, who is presently confined to the state hospital at Napa.

A New Age entrepreneur calling himself TimoThy is trying to buy Eden Valley to convert it to an "Earth Village, a sustainable community" featuring "a straw bale roundhouse" and cabins for TimoThy's followers that would be called "earth arks." For $33,000 you can buy in.

Funny thing is, Eden Valley fully sustained a hundred people for 12,000 years before Judge Hastings and Texan Boy moved their horses and cows in on those self-sustaining families and killed them for the sin of resistance.

Jarboe, Ukiah's and Mendocino County's first peace officer, died in March of 1865, maybe of a heart attack, maybe from apoplexy. He was an apoplectic kind of man, the kind of man who would sputter and hyper-ventilate at so much as a suggestion that Indians might be human beings.

In 1860, Jarboe had married Cynthia Winchester of Napa County and settled down in Ukiah where he functioned as justice of the peace, his credentials for ruthlessness having been established by his unresisted, sneak attacks on the Indians. Ukiah admired him, and Jarboe became Mendocino County's first law enforcement professional.

But Jarboe's bride was a liberal. After her husband's death the widow Jarboe sold her place in Ukiah to a fellow named Robert Hildreth, an extreme ad sal even by the bloody standards of the time. Hildreth, also a semi-retired Indian killer who'd ridden with Jarboe's Rangers, thought the sale included Jarboe's Indian slaves, but Mrs. Jarboe, who may have been trying to restore some karmic balance to her husband's bloody memory, had released the Indians from their painful servitude before the sale to Hildreth was final. Hildreth hated Indians but he knew he needed them to do the heavy lifting on his old friend's ranch.

Hildreth was very unhappy. He thought the deal included free labor. Hildreth was so unhappy that on a sweltering day of August, 1865, spotting one of the liberated slaves near his new property, grabbed the man, tied his hands behind his back, coiled the rest of the rope around his saddle horn and yelled "Giddyup!" Hildreth's horse spooked, throwing Hildreth but continuing to drag the Indian a good distance, wrenching the Indian's arms off at the shoulders before Hildreth could finally grab the animal's reins.

This atrocity was too much even for pioneer Ukiah. Shocked onlookers complained, and their eyewitness accounts of Hildreth's atrocity made their way into the Sacramento Union of August 19th, 1865. Hildreth was never charged, of course, because Indians had no legal standing to either complain or testify, but Hildreth;s reputation in Ukiah's polite society suffered somewhat.

Ukiah's determination to enslave Indians was almost a decade behind the state curve. On April 22, 1850, California passed into law "An Act for the Government and Protection of Indians" which made the "indenture or apprenticeship of Indians of all ages to any white citizen" for open ended periods of time.

Before the onslaught, the Indian population of the Round Valley region alone was variously estimated conservatively at 5,000 Indians on the low end to a high of 20,000 if you kept counting up to the Yuroks of the Klamath and the mountain Wylackis who lived from the Mattole to Alderpoint to Hayfork. There may have been more people living in the wild country north of Sonoma than the much less resourceful people who live there now in that rugged country limned by I-5 and 101. All estimates of Indian populations before the ad-sals descended on them range from high to low, but there were lots of Indians in every part of Mendocino County except in the redwood forests. The Indians moved through the redwoods quickly; it is said they believed the woods to be haunted and the dwelling place of bad spirits.

It is impossible know the precise number of Indians murdered in the bloody pioneer years between 1850 and 1870, but there were many, and most of those remaining were slaves or periodic slaves confined to the reservation at Covelo, a place described early on as a "paradise for white outlaws." White outlaws had descended on the Indians, and with fluid numbers of Indians now confined next door to them on the Covelo rez, Indians continued to die of murder, venereal disease mostly inflicted by rape, and starvation.

The county's Indians who eluded both casual and deliberate murder became the property of the ranchers who gave them uncultivated areas of their back forties for their rancherias. The Indians could stay so long as they worked for the rancher.

The following report appeared in 1872 summarizing the stabilized situation at the Covelo reservation:

Round-Valley Agency. — The Indians belonging to this agency are the Ukies, Concons, Pitt Rivers, Wylackies, and Redwoods, numbering in all 1,700. The number has been increased during the past year by bringing in 1,040 Indians collected in Little Lake and other valleys. A reservation containing 31,683 acres has been set apart per act of April 8, 1864, and executive order of March 30, 1870, in the western and northern part of the State, for these Indians, and for such others as may be induced to locate thereon. The lands in the reservation are very fertile; and the climate admits of a widely varied growth of crops. More produce being raised than is necessary for the subsistence of the Indians, the proceeds derived from the sale of the surplus are used in purchasing stock and work-animals, and for the further improvement of the reservation. Several of the Indians are engaged in cultivating gardens, while others work as many as twenty-five or thirty acres on their own account. The Indians on this reservation are uniformly quiet and peaceable, notwithstanding that they are much disturbed by the white trespassers. Suits, by direction of the department, were commenced against such trespassers, but without definite results as yet; the Attorney-General having directed the United States District Attorney to suspend proceedings. Of this reservation the Indian Department has in actual possession and under fence only about 4,000 acres; the remainder being in the possession of settlers, all clamorous for breaking up the reservation and driving the Indians out. The Indians at this reservation have shown no especial disposition to have their children educated; and no steps were taken to that end until in the summer of 1871, when a school was commenced. There is now one school in operation, with an attendance of 110 scholars. These Indians have no treaties with the government; and such assistance as is rendered them in the shape of clothing, &c, is from the money appropriated for the general incidental expenses of the Indian service in the State."

One hundred and fifty years later in front of the Alderpoint Store, not far from where the gun Indians met to plan counter-attacks on Covelo's murderous pioneers, an Indian is sitting in his pick-up truck. He's drunk. The Indian was born in Garberville and raised up in the hills near Zenia. A man with two large, well-groomed poodles walks past his truck heading for the store. "If I had a fuckin' dog like that I'd fuckin' commit suicide," the Indian says, taking a suicidally large swig from a fifth of whiskey.

My connection to the heavily Southern, heavily pro-slavery, heavily pre-disposed to violence, heavily sensitive to the slightest insult perceived or actual, heavily prepared at all times to kill with a gun, a knife, by hand, my connection to the wild people who settled the Anderson Valley and the rest of Mendocino County, is specific.

My great grandfather on my mother's side was a Quantrell raider, as confirmed by St. Louis Republic, Sunday, the week of April 20, 1900: "The death of John W. Major, born in Clay County, Missouri," was reported in The News which went on to report that the obituary had also been carried in the St. Louis Republic. The News went on: "John W. Major, who was buried at Chapel Cemetery, near here, Hillsboro, Illinois, was well known throughout this section of Illinois as one of Quantrell's men. In the Civil War he served as companion-in-arms to the James and Younger brothers. So great was his reputation as an expert horseman and crack shot with the revolver that when the G.A.R. held its celebration at Coffeen, Mr. Major was invited to give an exhibition. He complied, and his skill, even in advanced age, astonished his old neighbors. Mr. Major was among the best citizens of the state, and no man possessed more of the confidence of the people. After the war he applied himself systematically to business, and was so successful that at his death he left his widow and two children in very comfortable circumstances. The Lost Cause was always to him a memory of sadness and his heart was always warm for his friends of the Confederacy. Yet he accepted the defeat as final, and so lived that he attached to him the veterans of the Union Army, as well as the general public and his death was regretted by all who knew him."

My grandfather had married Major's daughter, Chloris. He said of his father-in-law, "the reason he was said to be respected was that people were afraid of the old crook." Major had not approved of the marriage, which may account for the hostility of his son-in-law. The James brothers and Quantrell's guerrillas were a 19th century version of a criminal gang on horseback, subsequent romanticizing of them aside.

Major's name appears on the great memorial Confederate cenotaph at Vicksburg, Mississippi. He often visited his good friend Frank James at James' ranch in Texas where he'd buy a horse or two from James for his farm in Southern Illinois. The old boys knew their horses. They rode them and they raced them. Major always said Jesse James was crazy, the kind of man who'd kill another man "just to see him die," that Frank James was a restraining influence on his brother. It is Frank James' name that appears on an old guest ledger of the Boonville Hotel.

So many Missourians settled in Mendocino County before, during and after the Civil War that the county was a kind of long distance extension of the old neighborhoods back home, the same neighborhood my ancestor Major was from. When Frank James had come out to the Anderson Valley to lie low with his old friends and neighbors from Clay County, Missouri, after the James' gang's famously failed attempt to rob a bank in Northfield, Minnesota, he was, in a sense, coming home.

My mother was born in Hillsboro, Illinois, an hour from St. Louis by car, less than that from Vandalia, the western, frontier end of the national road Jefferson built to speed settlers west to what was in 1810 the jumping off place for everywhere west of the Mississippi. Young Abe Lincoln practiced law in Vandalia, often traveling north to his home in Springfield through Hillsboro where he frequently spent the night. When my mother was a child, there were men and women still alive who remembered seeing Lincoln in Hillsboro.

Hillsboro was also home to Ben Blockburger, founder of the tiny town of Blocksburg deep in the wild mountains of Humboldt County not far from where Trinity, Mendocino and Humboldt counties meet at a place almost as untamed today as it was then. Blockburger bilked the area's sheep and cattle ranchers out of their combined wealth, having convinced them that he would buy all their wool right there in Blocksburg then go out into the outside world and get them a much better price for it than they could get individually. Blockburger disappeared with the money, leaving behind his Wylackie wife Bonnie and the little outback town he'd founded. Contemporary America's premier cage fighter is from Hillsboro, too, perhaps an indication that that part of the country still produces tough people much like the untamed men who found the obscure fastnesses of hidden, uncharted Mendocino County so much to their barbarous liking.

Among the people heading west when Jefferson's dirt track of a national highway opened in 1812 were my mother's family, people called Edwards, and probably related to the iron-haired politician John Edwards, because like him my mother's Edwards came from North Carolina.

Ralph Edwards, "like all the Edwards he had the gift of gab," an early television game show host, was an Edwards from the Edwards Priairie farms close by the Hillsboro of Marshal Winn, Ben Blockburger, my mother and, today, America's cage fighting champ. It is alleged by descendants on the maternal side of my family who are intent upon family grandeur, there were Witherspoons and other founding fathers deep in my mother's branch of the family. Whatever their lineage, though, the Edwards had hit the road in 1812, lighting out for the territory which then began at Vandalia, Illinois.

The Edwards stayed and prospered a few miles from Vandalia. The fertile area near Hillsboro is still called Edwards Prairie. The Edwards founded the first church in Montgomery County and married into a family called Hickman who, it was only vaguely mentioned anecdotally by ancient aunts, had their origins in either Kentucky where there is a town called Hickman or Tennessee, where there is also a town called Hickman. There are many black people surnamed Hickman, although there is no evidence that our Hickmans were ever prosperous enough to own other people.

The Hickman and the Edwards branch of the family, my grandfather's side, fought with the north, although at least one pair of Hickman brothers, forever afterwards estranged, fought on opposite sides of the great conflict. And on my mother's side there was John Major, regionally famous trick shot artist, horseman,

Quantrell Raider, and boyhood friend of Jesse and Frank James; Major fought with the South as a guerrilla with Quantrell.

Grandmother had been Chloris Major, 16, when she married my grandfather, Percy Hickman, 30. Her father did not approve of the union and never again spoke to his son-in-law in all his long life although they lived within twenty miles of each other.

Percy Hickman, my grandfather, refused to join the Klan when it dominated Hillsboro, and he sided with the anarchists and other independent radicals against John L. Lewis's United Coal Miners. Mother Jones, revered by coal miners, is buried forty-five minutes from Hillsboro at Mount Olive. A passion-free magazine bears her name these days.

Southern Illinois, then, was a crucible in the 20's and 30's for wildly disparate political impulses. Percy Hickman had gone to work in the Hillsboro mine as a boy, but was moved up top when his first child was born to mind the mules that pulled the coal cars out of the pits. Black people lived out by the lake in a ramshackle neighborhood known, of course, as "Nigger Town." There had been black people in Hillsboro forever who were, of course, comprehensively suppressed. The Mississippi was just down the road. On the St. Louis side was slavery, on the Hillsboro side semi-slavery.

A black maid popular with the Hillsboro elite was murdered by her husband in 1925. He'd chopped her into little pieces, placed them in a trunk, and had attempted to send her remains to her family by train to Chicago. Blood seeped from the trunk as it awaited dispatch at the Hillsboro train depot. The robed Klan, marching past my mother's childhood home with torches blazing, carried the doomed man past the Hickman home on their way to the town square where they hanged him minutes later. Percy Hickman stood out in front of his house watching the pointy-capped parade flow eerily towards the lynching tree still standing outside the Montgomery County Courthouse in downtown Hillsboro. Hooded men called out, "Join us, Percy, join us." Percy told his terrified family, "I'll kill any man who steps one foot onto my place. I know who they are. I can tell them from their shoes." They strung up the maid killer from the hanging tree in the middle of Hillsboro, Illinois, right there in front of the courthouse, right there in the middle of the Jazz Age.

Everett Sharkey "Shorty" Rawles, a Mendocino County old timer, left behind diaries that said as a boy he'd been told that Frank James stayed in Boonville in the mid-1870's, hiding out from the Pinkertons who were after him for the James Gang's failed Minnesota bank robbery. Rawles said James lived with Jeff Clement, brother of the notorious Little Arch Clement of Quantrell's raiders. Little Arch became infamous for the murder of unarmed federal soldiers at Centralia, Missouri, on September 27, 1864. The James boys were from the same area of Missouri, Clay County, as most of the Missouri settler families in the Anderson Valley. Cole Younger may also have visited Boonville in the 1870s. The James brothers' preacher father had disappeared into the California gold fields near Placerville. There were so many Missourians in the Placerville area a street in that town is still called Missouri Flat.

It's still said around Boonville that it was Missouri people, who'd settled in Anderson Valley up in the Peachland area, who held up a stage on the Ukiah road when it was little more than a dirt track maintained by a man who charged travelers a toll to use it, hence his old dwelling, then and now called the Toll House beside what is now called Highway 253.

It was a warm spring day in 1897 when James Rose of Anderson Valley set out from Ukiah atop the afternoon stage from Ukiah. Rose's boss, F.D. Berryhill, owner of the stage coach was aboard, as was J.R. Barnett, a prosperous Anderson Valley pioneer. Barnett carried $146 in cash. Roughly seven miles southwest of central Ukiah at a then densely wooded area where there'd been another holdup not long before, two men carrying rifles stepped into the road from behind a tree, pointed their guns at Rose and told him to rein in the horses and stop. Berryhill and Barnett were sitting behind Rose. Barnett immediately reached into his pocket for his money, hoping to drop it under his seat where it might be overlooked by the gunmen. The bandits, assuming that Barnett was reaching for a gun, shot him dead. Rose threw out the three express strong boxes the stage was carrying, and the coach was waved on by the bandits. Posses combed the area for more than a week without finding a clue that so much as revealed a directional hoof print. Boonville people always suspected that that questionable Missouri family living in Peachland, not more than ten miles northwest of the robbery, was responsible.

Black Bart, assumed to have committed several stage coach robberies in Mendocino County, had presumably retired by 1897 when he was released from San Quentin and, the newspapers of the time inform us, "was never heard of again." He wasn't the only stage robber roaming the Northcoast. A Ukiah school teacher was another one, but he went unnamed; the school teacher was a rumor spread by stage drivers who always knew more about the bandits than they told the front office.

Bandit's Rock on the Willits Grade is still known as the Black Bart Rock because the dapper bandit stepped out from behind it at least once to hold up a mail stage. The famous highwayman knocked over 28 stage coaches between 1875 and 1883, traveling on foot for thousands of miles from the Sierra to the Coast Range to plunder stage coaches in Calaveras, Sierra, Plumas, Yuba, Butte, Shasta, Sonoma, Mendocino, and Trinity counties. Seven stage robberies in Mendocino and Sonoma counties, all of them committed up and down what is now highway 101, were attributed to Black Bart who was later revealed as Charles E. Boles. An old myth said that ranch wives in Mendocino County would always set an extra place at the dinner table for the famous bandit so he wouldn't rob them.

Boles had style. He never fired a shot even though he was shot twice himself, never took passenger's money, was especially gallant to women and, at two robberies, left class conscious poems indicating he felt he was kept down by "you fine-haired sons-of-bitches" who lived grand urban lives like Boles lived when he was flush after a successful hold-up.

The infamous highwayman often ate with the cops at a bakery on Kearney Street when San Francisco's Hall of Justice was located on Kearney. His energetic rural walking tours for the eight years he was known to rob stage coaches provided Boles with an inconspicuous but luxurious living. When he had it. When he didn't have it he went out and got it.

An evidentiary lapse on the usually meticulous bandit's part led to his arrest. The confident Boles, perhaps enjoying the irony, was invited to the San Francisco offices of Wells Fargo on a pretext unrelated to stage coach hold-ups. Once securely inside the bank's headquarters, Boles was invited to explain to a large audience of cops and bank dicks why a handkerchief with his laundry mark was found at Bear Mountain in Calaveras County where Wells Fargo had been hit by Boles for Boles' biggest score ever — $4,100 in coin. Boles said, "You got me, boys." Black Bart Boles served five years in San Quentin — 1883 to 1888 — and disappeared. It was rumored that Wells Fargo pensioned him off. The bank was always suspiciously confident that Boles had retired.

Thirty-three years after Texan Boy's recreational murder of who knows how many Covelo-area Indians, and the surviving Indians reduced to peonage in their own land, horsemanship and its recreational stepchild, horse racing, remained Mendocino County's number one sport. Nobody was better at both than vivid Jack Littlefield, an inland buckeroo, as Mendocino County's cowboys were called in the 19th century, whose outsized verve had made him a legend in the Yolly Bollys before he was thirty.

Littlefield's was a mixed legend. On the high end Littlefield proved he was the best horseman in all of Northern California when he outraced Frank Feliz in the great Lake Mountain downhill dash of May, 1892, an amazing contest marveled at for years afterwards and never attempted since. On the low end of his fame Littlefield was regarded as a horse thief and a cattle rustler, although the people who put the knock on him were unknown in the moral heights themselves.

Right up until the dawn of the 20th century the wild country from Covelo north to Weaverville was outlaw country; it still is, some would say, but the ruthless, fiercely independent, sons of confederate Missouri who claimed inland Mendocino, Humboldt and Trinity counties beginning in 1850 remained free of all authority long after the rest of the bordering counties had settled into a tranquil mercantilism. Inland, though, the seemingly endless mountains and their infinite little valleys were home to men and women who depended on the horse, the gun and themselves, and a world of woe was all yours if you crossed them. Jack Littlefield was their archetype, a man who outdid these untamed people at what they did best — riding, shooting, fighting, and keeping enough cattle and sheep alive in the grudging terrain to scratch out a living.

Littlefield wasn't merely an unequaled horseman, he was also an undefeated fist fighter among people who were as quick with their fists as they were with their guns. And he was a great romantic who once deliberately lit a match to illuminate himself in the winter's dark so the outraged father of a fifteen-year-old girl Littlefield was courting could crank off a fair shot at him. Dad missed, the girl yielded and Jack Littlefield grew larger than life, his exploits enlivening dinner table talk from Ukiah to Weaverville. Everyone had heard of Jack Littlefield before the great race; after the great race people were talking about him in Portland and San Francisco.

Round Corrals sat on the top of a mountain east of Spy Rock. It was the site of inland cattle round-ups and the post-round-up rodeos where the buckeroos sorted out just who could do what from the top of a horse. In this wild land dominated by tough men who made their hard livings in the saddle, the rodeo competition was stiff. These boys knew horses, and they could ride and rope with any cow puncher in the world, and Littlefield beat them all. Nobody could ride like he could, except maybe Frank Feliz.

Feliz was foreman of the Doc Merritt ranch and the son of Fernando Feliz, the Spanish-descended grandee who owned Sanel Rancho, the vast Mexican land grant ranchero at what is now known as Hopland. Feliz, like Littlefield, was a great horseman and all-round cowboy with a Littlefield-like reputation for daredevil riding. Their fellow buckeroos thought that Littlefield and Feliz were about even in horsemanship with the consensus difference between them being that Feliz was an "honest citizen," while Littlefield, popular as he was, was generally regarded as the proverbial "outlaw with a heart of gold."

Feliz said he was confident that he could beat Littlefield down the side of Lake Mountain, and doubly convinced he'd beat Littlefield for the five hundred dollar cash prize. Never one to turn down a challenge, Littlefield quickly agreed to race Feliz. Both cowboys agreed that anybody could steer a fast horse around a race track, but how many would even consider running a horse full-out and straight down the side of a very steep, mile-long hill over and around natural obstacles which could have killed horse and rider if either man or beast were to miscalculate in the slightest?

Feliz had the pick of the very best horses on the Merritt ranch. Littlefield rode up to Hayfork, Trinity County, where he bought what was described as "a fine little chestnut thoroughbred mare." The riders were ready, mountain people were gathering, buckeroos from as far away as Red Bluff to the east, Weaverville to the north, Lake County to the south, and Eureka to the west wouldn't miss it because they knew legend was in the making.

The two contestants agreed that the starting point would be the corral on the top of Lake Mountain, the finish line the Eel River far below. From the corral the terrain almost immediately fell off into a very steep half-mile before the hillside became strewn with boulders and treacherous gulches "full of fallen trees and gopher holes," not to mention intervals of stunted oak and madrone broken by clumps of manzanita. First man who got to the river through this fearsome downhill obstacle course would be the winner.

They were off! The two buckeroos plunged down from the ridgetop, their amazingly agile horses making their own paths as their riders whipped them to run even faster down the hill, weaving like equestrian running backs through the trees, around the boulders, Littlefield and Feliz, neck and neck to the river where Littlefield arrived ahead of Feliz only by the length of his heroic little mare, her shoulders torn from their sockets at the finish line where she rolled over and died, her bones becoming something of a local landmark where they lay on that Eel River sandbar for several years afterwards.

The site of this astounding event is, these days, part of the Dean Witter family ranch, still a working cattle ranch. Witter used to have his own railroad car that would be uncoupled near Island Mountain deep in the Eel River Canyon when Witter rode up in it from San Francisco for respite from the stock market. He'd be met by a ranch hand driving a horse and buggy and taken to his ranch house on the ridge overlooking the river.

The splendid Littlefield didn't live long after the great race. It was his outlaw reputation that got Littlefield murdered a few years later by the infamous King of Round Valley, George E. White.

White had become convinced that Littlefield, a former buckeroo for White, made a good part of his annual living by rustling White's cattle, which was a clear case of a very large, very dark pot calling Littlefield's beige kettle black. White, from his palatial home in Covelo, had thundered this threat about Littlefield's alleged thefts of White's cattle: "Why don't you do up those goddamned sons of bitches up there."

Added incentive for Littlefield's murder was Littlefield's ability with his fists; Littlefield had twice beaten White's toughest buckeroo, Joe Gregory, in all-out beat downs, and had also beaten Gregory for the affections of Indian Mary, the most beautiful girl in Covelo. And none of White's buckeroos could ride a horse like Jack Littlefield could ride a horse. Littlefield had them all beat every which way.

And then they beat him the only way they could, from behind in a group ambush. White's gunsels, Joe Gregory eagerly among them, on September 27th 1895 on the old trail from Covelo to Weaverville, shot Littlefield in the back and, to make sure he was dead, boldly hanged him just off the trail in plain view in what the newspapers of the time called "the bitterest quarrel of all the west" and "the only deadly feud in California." Not content to have him gone, during Gregory's and White's subsequent trial for the Littlefield murder, as Gregory rode north from Covelo, Gregory dismounted at Littlefield's lonely grave on the Weaverville trail and, beginning to urinate on it, said, "I guess we'll give him something to drink. Drink that you goddam son of a bitch."

The press post-mortems were kind to Littlefield.

"Littlefield's chief handicap was his reckless bravery. He was so innocent of underhand methods that he never suspected them in others. He was constantly warned against ambush, but he would only laugh. He was afraid of nothing on earth. He was a king among vaqueros, would go where other men did not dare for cattle, was marvelously swift and sure with a reata — a lasso length of leather with a wooden handle that was lashed out with whip-like speed and precise effect — and a dead shot; he was more centaur than horseman. The last time he passed through Covelo from Ukiah he had come sixty miles in seven hours without change of horses and, scarcely stopping, went into the mountains. Reckless, brave, fearless, he had a heart in him as big as an ox. Many a man in these hills owes him for his keep through a long winter. It is true that at times when he came to town after a long spell in the hills, he would drink and get noisy, and that he only went to church for the fun of shooting out the lights, but as for Jack Littlefield taking a shot at an enemy from behind a tree, it is impossible."

George White died June 8, 1902 at age 71. The San Francisco Examiner was less kind to White.

"White's name has been more or less associated with the history of Mendocino County for more than 50 years, and for a greater part of that time, no one was more feared, no one more implacable in his hatreds and no one more swift to seek revenge. He was owner of a vast tract of land in and near Round Valley, and he gathered some of the roughest men about him that ever pulled a trigger. As far as is known the only person he ever shot with his weapon was himself, when he fell on Montgomery Street in this city and sent a ball through the calf of his leg. He affected long, high-heeled boots, and his swaggering air of a bad man, to which his height and angular appearance lent picturesque aid. In the early days he had many quarrels with neighboring cattle men, and those who ventured too close to Round Valley never got away again, though no one was ever found who would tell what happened. In this way several men met sudden death."

Before it was finally over, the Weaverville trial of Littlefield's killers had bankrupted Trinity County. White, the shot-caller, was acquitted; Joe Gregory and several others were found guilty of second degree murder and sent to San Quentin. Gregory died there at age 38, probably of tuberculosis. He's buried in the Covelo cemetery.

White's nephew, John Sylvanius Rohrbough, was White's heir. He was 43 when White died. Rohrbough had falsely testified that Frankie White was unfaithful to White, testimony he had to give or face disinheritance. John was compelled to remain silent when his uncle's hired perjurers testified for White that his nephew had been seen sneaking in and out of Mrs. White's bedroom, thus falsely establishing her alleged infidelity and just as falsely securing White's fortune for the Rohrbough family still prominent in Mendocino

County today and after whom the recreational complex on South State Street, Ukiah, is named.

The great hippie political takeover of Mendocino was still a few years away from the summer day in 1971 when we established our raucous brood in Mendocino County's serene summer hills, not far from the unsuspecting hamlet of Boonville where, on a memorable night soon after we'd arrived, we got our first lesson in the psycho-pathology of the pre-pube criminal, the immutable psycho-pathology of the pre-pube criminal.

The delinquents occasionally acted like the children they were, and when they did we were reminded that as demented as their behavior often was, they were still kids, chronologically considered. One of the few wholesome, age-appropriate exertions we could get them to make was night hikes, and even these excursions couldn't be too strenuous; the delinquents wouldn't do long uphills so we had to plan the walks as if their crippling mental wounds were also physical handicaps.

None of them had ever been any place that wasn't paved, let alone been taken out at night for a non-violent walk to explore the non-neon world. So there we were strolling along under the moonlight disturbing whatever nocturnal fauna there was to disturb when a frog suddenly appeared on the path before us. In one instinctual leap, six delinquents jumped out to stomp the amphib flat.

"Why'd you do that?"

The frog killers stared back with "we-did-something-wrong?" looks on their faces.

There's no cure for the frog stomping personality; it's either jail or a career in law enforcement.

All day every day, and long into the night every night, we fought to maintain a semblance of order, or "structure," as the theoreticians of delinquency called it, but in reality, even on our best days, all we accomplished was damage control. Every waking hour was a struggle to keep the little nutballs from harming each other or from destroying our leased premises; there was no time left over to steer them in the direction of functional citizenship, which we, being products of the great turmoil of the sixties, weren't much committed to ourselves.

The delinquents were quick to exploit the contradictions.

"You tell us not to smoke marijuana and you smoke it." Etc.

Yes, we were wholly unprepared for our hopeless task. Worse, we lacked practical skills, such as the crucial one of large-group food-prep, itself a full-time job in our harried circumstances. We could hardly take time away from the exhausting supervision of the delinquents to grab a peaceful bite ourselves, let alone prepare three hearty nutritionals every day to all of them. Of course as idealists one of our sub-delusions was that if we served wholesome foods instead of the negative food value fuel preferred by the delinquents, the delinquents might at least be less energetically delinquent.

Wrong.

Tofu or deep fried tacos, the delinquents remained delinquent.

We called down to the employment office in San Francisco for a full-time cook. We knew we'd be lucky to lure anybody north for a job slot like ours so we euphemized the position as "Live-in organic cook for rural child care center. Free room and board."

A job counselor said she had just the couple for us with just the right experience. "But," she added ominously, "Scott and Emily are different."

"Different," as applied to the generic American citizen of 1970 was already an infinitely elastic descriptive, having come to include everyone from freeway killers to people who deliberately wore mismatched socks.

But our job offer was far from ideal employment, what with guarding the knife drawer from underage psychos while trying to prepare three healthy meals a day in a primitive country kitchen three hours north of San Francisco.

Desperate, we hired Scott and Emily sight unseen. We were getting two cooks for the salary of one, the job lady assured us, and our eager new employees would arrive the very next day by Greyhound.

They did, too.

The first chef off the bus was a large, shirtless man with a weightlifter's upper torso whose shaved head looked like a topo map, scars forehead to nape. Wherever the guy had been, he'd been there often, and he'd been there head first without protective head gear. And he'd obviously had regular access to a serious weight pile.

Chef Scar Head, his eyes averted, ignored our extended hands and welcoming grins as he dismounted the Greyhound, but he did grunt what could have been interpreted as a greeting.

Behind him appeared a plump woman of about 30. She was togged out in a granny dress and an old-fashioned wagon train bonnet. She greeted us with what sounded like, "bok-bok," but could have been "awk-awk." Either way the sound seemed as non-committal as her mate's grunt. Mrs. Scar Head either had a serious speech impediment or she was crazy. Assessing her entire presentation, from her mid-19th century outfit to what we hoped was a speech impediment, we assumed Emily was at least as far off as her man, Scott, the world's strongest cook.

Last to appear was a little girl of about six. The child was togged out in a pink chiffon party dress and wore shiny black pumps on her fat little feet. She looked like she was going to a birthday party, circa 1950. We hadn't expected the child, but she merely punctuated what we already knew was the huge error of hiring her parents.

The Greyhound spent the night in Fort Bragg before it returned southbound through Boonville the next morning. The odd family would be with us over night. Looked at objectively, the Scar Heads weren't that much wackier than we were, and besides they'd just arrived. Just because they looked nuts didn't necessarily mean they were nuts. Hell, if you went only by appearances, half the population of the valley looked like they'd benefit from face time with a mental health professional.

Scott and Emily's luggage consisted of a bulging backpack lugged by Emily, and a two-foot square metal ammo box toted by Scott. The family traveled light for people who'd taken on a live-in job.

The child's parents, our new cooks, hadn't introduced themselves other than Mom's cryptic "bok-bok," so we weren't surprised that they never did identify their daughter, who was also non-verbal in the manner of her mother. When we greeted the child, she replied with a cheery "wook-wook."

We would call her Little Wook-Wook and her parents The Bok-

Boks. We certainly didn't need three more disturbed persons added to our volatile population of marginally competent adults and junior criminals. But here they were, and a deal was a deal. It might even work out. Maybe they were just shy.

The two-and-a-third chefs climbed into our van for the six-mile trip to the ranch, Scott gripping his ammo box, Emily soundless beside him, the child on her mother's lap, attentive to the country scenery.

Assistant chef Emily responded to our attempts to get some recent work history out of her with affirmative "bok-boks." We couldn't speak bok-bok but were encouraged that bok-boks seemed affirmative. Chef Scar Head ignored us. He stared straight ahead, his big hands cradling the ammo box. The little girl, spotting some sheep, sang out, "wook-wook."

When we arrived at Rancho Loco, Emily tossed the family backpack into the indicated cabin and, still without speaking, all three Bok-Boks walked on into the kitchen for an introductory tour of their work site. The Bok-Boks always moved single-file, like a family of Dyaks on a jungle path: Scott and his ammo box, then Emily, Little Wook-Wook bringing up the rear. Two of us fell in behind the child, wondering why we were following our employees rather than leading them.

At our appearance in the shed-like mess hall, the delinquents, as usual raucously arrayed around a battered pool table, went silent. Children who have been raised on the violence principle — force or the threat of it to get what you want — know at a glance who's dangerous and who's not. The delinquents knew in their estranged bones that the big scary-looking guy who'd just walked through the door could and would stomp them at little or no provocation. He wasn't just another harmless, neo-hippie doofus like the rest of the so-called adults at this rural juvenile hall; no, the new cook presented a clear and present danger to all living things, as randomly hazardous as any two-legged predator roaming their old neighborhoods in San Francisco and Oakland.

"Settle in, look around, meet the boys," I grandly invited the cooks without meaning it, hoping that Scar Head's unspoken menace didn't manifest itself in tangible trouble before I could get the Bok-Boks back on the southbound 'hound the next morning and to hell outtahere.

Ignoring all attempts at communication, Scott and Emily began throwing open the doors of the storage shelves hauling pots, pans, cooking sheets, and number ten cans of government foodstuffs down out of the cabinets. They soon had a pizza assembly line set up with Little Wook-Wook at the finishing end where she was soon diligently sprinkling a concluding garnish of olives on the pre-oven product. The Bok-Boks had produced institutional pizzas before, and we knew that the institution probably had bars on the windows.

There were soon four pizzas in the oven and a dozen more ready to go, way more than even our dedicated junk food eaters would down in a week.

I asked the Bok-Boks to stop making pizzas. Then I asked them to please stop making pizzas.

The Bok-Boks went on making pizzas.

I knew something very weird had kicked off.

A delighted delinquent yelled at me, "Whatcha gonna do now, big boy?"

I knew I couldn't handle Scar Head one-on-one and my colleagues, still high on The Summer of Love, were all committed to non-violent conflict resolution — doubly, triply committed to the path of the Mahatma when they saw Scar Head. I'd thought about trying to get the drop on the big psycho with a two-by-four but worried that (1) the board would bounce off his head and then be used to beat me to death, (2) the mayhem would reinforce "inappropriate behavior" in the delinquents. I was, after all, a role model.

Forty or so pizzas later, our new cooks had started in on what became an even five hundred bulgar and molasses cookies the size and texture of frisbees. (We'd been baffled by bulgar, the wheat-like grain we'd vaguely associated with 19th century Russian novels. We had bags of it but no idea how to make it into anything we could eat.)

On the cooks cooked.

Little Wook-Wook, exhausted by her long bus trip up from the city, then her task as pizza garnisher, then arranger-of-endless-cookies-on-tinfoil, stretched out on the cement floor and went to sleep. With piles of pizzas and cookies surrounding the unconscious Little Wook-Wook where she lay at her laboring parent's feet, she could have been a living shrine to the junk food gods.

Her parents soon moved on to more complicated dishes in what had become a full-on cook-a-thon; it wouldn't end until there was nothing left to render inedible.

The delinquents had been mostly silent for the show, happy at the subversion, but wary because they couldn't quite fit it into their precocious portfolios of aberrant adult behavior. After a couple of hours of serial food prep, and as delighted as they were at our impotence in the face of the crazy cooks, the delinquents wandered off to bed, pleased with the day's events.

When we returned to the cafeteria in the morning, Scott and Emily had the countertops covered with dozens of congealed fried eggs, some forty meat dishes assembled from the mysterious contents of cans labeled "U.S. Government Beef," and they'd blended every available vegetable into gallons of home brew V-8. Little Wook-Wook slumbered on where we'd last seen her the night before, the center-piece of the junk food shrine.

Every pot, every dish, every possible container had been deployed in an all-night cook-in. Or cook-off. Or nut-off. Scott and Emily had transformed a month's larder into unappetizing piles of whatever it was now, food maybe. A kid muttered the consensus opinion: "No fuckin' way I'm eatin' this shit."

Still not a word out of the Bok-Boks, not even a bok. And here they were, day two, casually posed in a calamity of dirty pots and pans calmly smoking post-culinary cigarettes.

We called the cops.

The delinquents, energized at the mere possibility of violence, and silently jubilant at the chaos of the overnight food frenzy, now eagerly anticipated Scar Head's interface with law enforcement.

In the Anderson Valley of that time, law enforcement consisted of a young resident deputy, George Simon, occupying his first cop post. Inevitably, the deputy was locally known as, "Simple Simon," although like the rest of us, his gifts seemed securely in the middle of dull-normal range.

Deputy Simon was soon on-scene.

We explained that two city screwballs had cooked up all our food, that we'd fired them because they wouldn't stop cooking and now they wouldn't leave.

"I'll be damned," the deputy said.

His game face on, deputy Simon strode authoritatively up to Scott, who still lounged at the sink with a cigarette. He and Emily were looking off at a kitchen wall as if it were more interesting than the arrival of the cop. Little Wook-Wook was on her feet, fully awake. She peered out at the deputy from behind her mother's billowing skirt.

"You've got to leave," the deputy said, without the usual cop preliminaries like, "Hi. How are you today?" And so on through the appraising protocols until the showdown demand for the perp's identification. Given Mr. Bok-Bok's obvious potential for effective instant violence, we thought deputy Simon had been recklessly bold.

"These people want you out," the deputy said.

"No, we don't," yelled a delinquent.

Scott, cradling his ammo box, stared silently back at the deputy. Emily issued a defeated-sounding, "bok-bok." Little Wook-Wook continued to peer out at the deputy from behind the ample pioneer cover of her mother.

The deputy repeated himself.

Scott, Emily and Little Wook-Wook, like three deaf mutes, gazed back at him.

We anticipated the worst.

A three-minute stare down ensued until the cooks, communicating in perfect sync in ways we couldn't see or hear, suddenly strode rapidly past the startled deputy, past us equally startled spectators, and into their nearby cabin, Little Wook-Wook slamming the door behind her.

"He's probably got a gun in that ammo box," a delighted delinquent speculated.

"I hope he does," shouted another.

"I've got a gun, too, don't I?" Deputy Simon said, dramatically unholstering his .357 as he walked to the Wook-Wook's door.

"Come out of there. Now!" the deputy yelled at the door.

Silence.

"You," the deputy ordered me, "get that two-by-four and stand over there. Knock the shit out of that nut if he comes out of there with a gun."

The delinquents, beside themselves with anticipatory joy, eagerly moved uphill of the cabin for theater-seat viewing of whatever came next.

It seemed to me that the deputy's orders were tactically defective. If Scar Head came charging out of the cabin, gun (or guns) blazing, the deputy and I were arrayed so closely on either side of the door that I would have hit the deputy in the head with my two-by-four while he simultaneously put a big hole in me with his hand cannon.

For the next several minutes there wasn't a sound from inside the cabin. The two-by-four, which I held over my head in "knock the shit out of" mode, grew heavy. I was soon leaning on it like it was a crutch. The weight of Deputy Simon's .357 caused him to shift it from hand to hand where it was usually pointed straight at one of his feet.

The deputy whispered to me, "I'm tired of this bullshit. You better go in there and have a look around. See if you can talk to them."

Entering a small, dark room occupied by a deranged weight lifter seemed more in the deputy's job description than mine. Besides, wasn't it wiser just to wait them out, let them make the next move?

As we debated cabin-extraction tactics, the Bok-Boks burst out the door in their habitual single file. Sure enough, the deputy's gun was pointed directly at his foot, and I was so startled I stumbled backwards, my two-by-four uselessly clattering behind me on the cabin porch.

Looking straight ahead, our two-and-a-third food prep specialists set off for the west hills at a fast walk, a very fast. walk. Any faster and they'd have been jogging.

We stood speechless at their retreating forms, Little Wook-Wook's pink chiffon party dress vivid against the summer's golden browns.

The delinquents cheered. The Bok-Bok's flight promised to

prolong the drama, now approaching its sixteenth hour. Of course the show would have been a lot better if the deputy had cranked off a couple of rounds at the Bok-Boks' departing forms, but the Bok-Boks did appear to be leaving and gun fire was not called for.

But what could the cooks be thinking? What was their plan? The road to Boonville or San Francisco was to the east, not west, but Scott, Emily and Little Wook-Wook were headed in the opposite direction from Highway 128, headed into the rough, the back country. There wasn't anything or anybody until the blue Pacific, thirty-five miles away as the crow flew or the psycho walked.

None of us authority figures, and certainly not the deputy, were inclined to hot pursuit. We all watched the odd trio move at Sherpa-like speed up the first steep slope, marveling at the pace and apparent endurance of plump, bonneted, retro-matronly Mrs. Bok-Bok and Little Wook-Wook in her party pumps. The patriarch, we knew, had the double strength of the furiously insane. He could walk to Manchester and back without breaking a sweat because, in his teeming mind, he was the wronged party. He and Mrs. B. had been hired to cook, he'd cooked, she'd cooked, and then they'd been fired for cooking. It didn't make sense.

We anticipated the worst. Maybe the guy would wait until we'd made a Safeway re-supply run; then the three of them would come back down out of the hills late at night and cook up all our food again. Or maybe Scott would come back by himself and strangle us all in our sleep, one at a time, and stuff our remains in number ten cans, the ones marked "U.S. Government Beef."

Had the Bok-Boks done this before? Had Scott and Emily and Little Wook-Wook descended on other outback youth camps, cooked up all the food and then fled into the hills? Maybe the Bok-Boks were some new kind of cult, a secret sect of gastro-vandals! Why not? There were eccentrics of every description moving into the hills of Mendocino County in the early 1970s, many of them seriously whacked. And now there were two more screwballs in the hills — three more — if you didn't feel like cutting Little Wook-Wook any slack. And, at that point, I didn't.

The Bok-Boks didn't leave.

They haunted us for the next month. The delinquents left food for the Bok-Boks at pre-arranged drops designated by Scott and the lead delinquent, who'd been sneaking off to meet Scott ever since the Bok-Boks had taken off into the hills.

For several weeks, always at daybreak, we'd see the fugitives far down Rancheria Creek, the year-round stream that split the sprawling ranch's 320 acres before it met Indian Creek west of Philo to form the Navarro. During these long-distance morning sightings Little Wook-Wook was a faint pink blotch against the tree line, mom a larger cloth ball, and dear old dad, shirtless and ominous even at two miles.

We'd shout out long, echoing hallos at our estranged cooks; they'd look up; then, still as a family of deer, gaze back at us for long seconds before they'd turn from the stream and disappear into the woods — Scott, Emily, Little Wook Wook, single file.

We were besieged.

Our fugitive cooks were lingering in the hills to creep us out. Or worse.

Scott's liaison man, the lead delinquent, denied that he was feeding the Bok-Boks, but his smirk gave him away. The Bok-Boks could easily spend the whole summer in the hills so long as they were fed regularly, and they would be fed regularly given the help they were getting from our treacherous band of 602's. (602 is cop code for juvenile offender.)

We didn't know if Scott was hanging around to get revenge for his firing or if he and Emily hoped to make one last sneak attack on our kitchen to cook up our replenished supplies, frying up a hundred secret eggs, baking dozens of clandestine cookies, laughing at us as they rattled our pots and pans.

Then we didn't see them for a week, then two weeks, and we knew they were finally gone.

When Scott, Emily and Little Wook-Wook had first run for the hills, deputy Simon had suggested to his high command in Ukiah that the Sheriff's Department mount a full-scale manhunt for the three fugitives.

"That's child abuse what they're doing to that little girl," the indignant deputy argued, "making her sleep out in the hills. And I'm sure whoever that Scott guy is he has a gun in that ammo box and a whole bunch of priors to go with it."

A manhunt was summarily rejected by the sheriff.

"If we start trying to run down crazy people in the hills of Mendocino County we'll be doing nothing else," he said. "There's an army of them out there. Besides that, from what you say about them, those people sound like they're deaf and dumb, handicapped people. Leave 'em alone, for Crissakes."

If there weren't enough lunatics lurking in Mendocino County's vast hills to make up an army, as the Sheriff had declared when he nixed a manhunt for the Wook-Wooks, there were certainly enough in plain view for a platoon. The Manson Family was in and out of Anderson Valley, pausing long enough to sell local kids their first marijuana, and topless Manson girls had some of the pillars of the community spending long hours on a lonely hill overlooking the Family's ragged, rented house near Navarro, their binoculars sweeping the wooded property for thrilling glimpses of bared breasts, fleeting butt cheeks.

And Kenneth Parnell, with his kidnapped catamite, Steven Stayner, was established not far away in Comptche in the first of his many rentals up and down the Mendocino Coast. Parnell had moved north from Santa Rosa to Comptche, then to Point Arena and finally to a remote house on the Piper Ranch, halfway between Manchester and Boonville. And all that time not a single school required the child's bona fides, not a single teacher was curious about the child's life away from school, and if a single neighbor ever wondered about the true nature of the relationship of the middle-aged motel desk clerk and his "nephew," that neighbor kept his skepticism to himself.

Tree Frog Johnson was already solidly established in the Boonville area, staying with his sanctioned catamite on the property of a back-to-the-land family in the hills a few minutes west of Boonville. Johnson was a much more visible public presence than the reclusive, peripatetic perv, Parnell, who worked as a night clerk at motels on the Mendocino Coast and, when he was arrested, night man at the Palace Hotel in Ukiah. A black man in his early thirties when he appeared in Boonville with the small white boy, Tree Frog was immediately embraced by the counter-culture as a sort of wise man cum naturalist.

Tree Frog's silent companion, Alex Cabarga, hadn't been kidnapped; he'd been turned over to Tree Frog by his parents, Ted and Diane Cabarga. Tree Frog and the abandoned little boy lived in a half-finished cabin on the property of the Colfax family of Boonville, three of whose home-schooled sons went on to Harvard. The Colfaxes' said they supported themselves by raising goats, but most of their neighbors supported themselves by growing marijuana.

David Colfax is now a Mendocino County supervisor. Before that he spent twelve years on the Mendocino County School Board. He has always said he had no idea that his tenant preyed on the small boy with him, and was just as unaware that Tree Frog preyed on as many sons of the counter-culture as were put within molesting distance of him. Boonville counterculture people can claim they didn't know that Tree Frog was a walking evil, but that opinion doesn't explain why the hippies "shunned" Tree Frog when they finally got the terrible news. Shunning was supposed to be a kind of internal exile, but the hapless, undefended Cabarga, instead of being retrieved from a childhood of terror and forced sex, was shunned right along with his captor.

The Boonville hippies shunned Frog all the way to Albion, a 30-minute hop from the Anderson Valley, where Tree Frog and his diminutive sex slave lived in Tree Frog's step-van at Albion's "alternative" Whale School. Tree Frog and Cabarga camped out at the Whale School for another year before they moved to San Francisco where, months after kidnapping an East Bay child named Tara Burke three months before her third birthday, they were finally arrested.

With Tree Frog the lead story on television and newspapers everywhere in the country, Alex Cabarga, now 19, was described by Chronicle columnist Art Hoppe as "soft-featured and slow-eyed" when he appeared in court on kidnapping charges. Cabarga's formative years, like Steven Stayner's, had been spent in the hills of Mendocino County with a sexual psychopath.

But Cabarga was 9-years-old when his parents turned the boy over to Tree Frog because, she said, the boy needed a father, and who could be a better dad than this guy? It was Alex Cabarga at age 17 who, as always doing what Tree Frog told him to do, had run out of Tree Frog's step-van and snatched little Tara Burke from her parent's car at a shopping center parking lot. The little girl's parents had left her in the car with her 9-year-old brother. Cabarga tapped on the window, telling the 9-year-old that his mother wanted him. When the kid opened the car door, Cabarga grabbed his little sister and ran off with her. An 11-year-old boy, also a kidnap victim of Tree Frog, was able to escape the van. This boy, indentified as Mac, went to the police.

Cabarga's mother, Diane Cabarga, writing as if she were an innocent bystander, would write: "If the tragedy of my son's life, his arrest and conviction for kidnapping and sexually molesting 2-year-old Tara Burke, has any purpose at all, it may be that it will help to focus public attention on a social problem which has reached a magnitude that is beyond belief. In 1982 in California, the Department of Social Services received 119,000 reports of cases of child abuse (and, of course, there were many more unreported cases). A large percentage of these involved sexual abuse, most of them perpetrated by a family member. Usually, by the child's father, step-father, or by a close and trusted friend of the family, a baby sitter or a teacher.

"While Alex's case is extremely unusual in many ways, there are certain aspects which are classic. Luis Tree Frog Johnson, who already has been sentenced to 527 years in prison for his offenses against the little girl, was a trusted friend who was accepted as a surrogate parent for Alex from the time the boy was nine years old. Not until their arrest the day after Alex's 18th birthday, on December 18, 1982, did we discover that he had been sexually molested and beaten up all of that time by Tree Frog.

"Our son's case is but a sensational example of this very widespread problem. For one thing, it brings to light the fact that men and occasionally women are seducing and raping both boys and girls at very early ages, as early as infancy. Secondly, it demonstrates how hidden the sexual relationship can be, both from other family members and from members of the community. There are signs to indicate the problem exists, but they are subtle and one has to be aware of the syndrome before being able to recognize them. Unfortunately, we were not.

"When an adult, especially a trusted parent figure, has sex with a child (called incest), he is using the power of his size, age and respected position to betray the child's innocence. One of the first noticeable signs in the child is the change from a free, outgoing innocence to a withdrawn, fearful distrust. The offender always makes the child swear not to tell anyone, which is obviously necessary to protect his crime from being discovered as well as to allow the acts to continue. In addition, there is the psychological manipulation used on the child to create guilt and to arouse a binding sense of loyalty. The child is soon totally under the control of the adult, and has lost his or her will and self-esteem to such an extent that the child feels completely helpless and trapped. Children will rarely admit what is happening even when a loved and trusted parent or teacher tries to find out what is bothering them."

Tara Burke was with Tree Frog and Cabarga while all three were in and out of the Whale School in Albion, a counter-culture enterprise at the center of the so-called Albion Nation. Nobody said a word. Never, ever would a true hippie go to The Man, so Frog was just doing his thing, as was at least one more child molester at the Whale School who serially molested a young, loosely supervised pre-teen girl over a period of years. When that child's stoned parents tardily discovered that the nice photographer who was so kind to their child was not the disinterested teacher they'd thought he was, instead of having him arrested, they settled on a long-term financial settlement, the matter being resolved "within the community," as the hippie propagandist Beth Bosk would later describe the crime's resolution.

As it happened, I had a step-van for sale back in the time of The Frog. It had been given to me by a social worker who thought maybe I could drive my delinquents around in it. But I could never get it to run, and I wanted to get rid of it before it became a permanent part of my front yard. I put it up for sale. Tree Frog came to look at it.

I would see Tree Frog around Boonville on his under-sized motorcycle, the little white boy riding pillion behind him. I didn't know who they were, wasn't much interested in who they were. So many unusual visuals presented themselves in those days that this improbable couple was simply one more among the passing parade. And in this case, to ask who they were was to risk accusations of racism.

"What's strange about a black man and a little white boy?"

Nothing cabrones, but que pasa? Is he the step-father or what? Looks like a weirdo to me, and not a man to be in charge of a small boy. Which was judgmental and extremely uptight, as moral equivalence was called then.

I put the step-van up for sale in the Anderson Valley Advertiser, the weekly newspaper I bought for $20,000 a few years later.

A man called to say a friend of his wanted to look at my step-van. Two men soon appeared, one of them a standard-issue longhair, amiable, pleasant. The other was introduced simply as Tree Frog. He was an unimposing, silent, dark, Latin-looking man with a round face, a long pig tail and quick, furtive movements that kept me from looking at him straight on. Years later when Tree Frog was arrested I was surprised to read his description as black, but I wasn't surprised that his real name was Luis Johnson.

The white hippie did all the talking while Tree Frog examined the van. Tree Frog never said a word in the ten minutes he and his pal were there, never so much as looked in my direction. Studiously avoided looking at me. Later, when I saw the white hippie downtown, as Boonville's bar, market and post office was called, I asked him if his friend was some kind of mute. "No, he just doesn't like straight people. He never talks when there're straights around."

Several years later, the city detectives investigating the Tree Frog case came to Boonville with a portfolio of photos of nude children, many of them Boonville kids, the rest of them, I supposed, from the Mendocino Coast. The cops spent a couple of days in Boonville attaching names to the pictures, then they went out to the Whale School at Albion where they were denied access to the property and where nobody would talk to them about the man who had undoubtedly preyed on their children, too.

Mass murderer Leonard Lake had just been evicted from the collectively-owned Greenfield Ranch north of Ukiah where he'd managed to unnerve even the loosest of the do-your-own-thingers with his morbid sex talk of whips, chains and girls tied up in dungeons. Lake was expelled from Greenfield when he rented a small bulldozer and had begun to excavate a presumed sex bunker like his final abattoir in Calavaras County. Arriving in Boonville with his pal Charles Ng, the first Chinese psycho killer in American history, Lake became the Anderson Valley Volunteer Fire Department's recording secretary, the dishwasher at the Boonville Hotel, his wife Cricket a teacher's aide at the local junior high school.

Where there is now drug-fueled debauchery stored in books and newspaper archives, history was once wholesomely memorialized by the Indians in their spirit rocks, the Rain Rock, Squaw Rock, and there was the Arrow Tree, unremembered now by any living person and the tree itself long gone, but it was a mile east of Korbel, which is six miles east of Arcata, an ancient redwood noted by the first white men to pass through on their way to the Trinity gold fields.

For thirty or forty feet the Arrow Tree looked like a giant porcupine because of the hundreds of arrows shot into it over many hundreds of years by many hundreds of Indians. Indians said that way back, when time was young, coast tribes were at war with the tribes who lived in the hill country. There was a great battle with untold losses on both sides, with the hill tribes getting the worst of it. The carnage was so great the Indians vowed never to repeat it. Ever after the redwood became the border between the coast people and the hill people, and the tree, because of its significance as both boundary and a symbol of the bloodshed preceding the boundary, sacred.

Whenever Indians from either side passed the tree they shot a commemorative arrow into its soft bark. At first the arrows may have been real war arrows, but within the memory of the last Indians who knew its history, they have been merely sharpened sticks. Gradually, the original significance of the tree was partially lost sight of, and it became more and more an altar for worship and a place of prayer for the last Indians able to remember it as it was. And then the tree died and Korbel became the site of tree worship of a much less reverent type when timber executives erected a combined lodge and rumpus room not far from where the Arrow Tree had stood all the way back to when time moved slowly.

The Rain Rock sits on the Trinity River in Sugar Bowl Valley four miles from Hoopa. At not more than four feet in diameter, the Rain Rock is hardly noticeable. It was called the "Rain Rock" when white people became aware of its importance to Indians, who called the smallish boulder Mi, or Thunder's Rock. The Indians believe a weather spirit has its home in and around the stone which, when it's unhappy with the Indians, calls down killing frosts on Hoopa's gardens or prolongs the rains until it floods or withholds them to bring on drought and famine. When some natural or human catastrophe affects the Indians, the Indians believe the spirit inhabiting the Rain Rock is angry with them, and that only a mandatory feast which everyone must attend at the site of the rock will restore order to the world. Announcing and accompanying the feast, fires are built in the canyon as a kind of illuminated path to the Rain Rock where a final fire is kindled to cook the food for the appeasing banquet. After the people have eaten, and the remnants of the feast have been burned, the priest makes a prayer for temperate weather as he sprinkles the sacred rock with water in which an incense root has been mingled.

According to legend, probably a legend that had its beginning among the pre-Gold Rush Indians, a Sanel Indian maiden named Sotuka jumped from the top of the foreboding Squaw Rock while holding a great stone, landing, as she'd hoped, on her faithless lover, Chief Cachow and his new bride who were sleeping below, killing the three of them. Squaw Rock, some local liberals claim, is a vulgar reference to female reproductive organs, but its mammoth stone bulk looms so large beside the Russian River between Cloverdale and Hopland that stories about it seem inevitable. "Squaw" may not be as vulgar as some people claim, but given its prevalence among the first ad-sals it can hardly be said to be endearing.

Comparably famous Indian landmarks are everywhere in the Redwood Empire. Few of them are remembered, but wherever the landscape suddenly becomes startling, you can be sure it was as significant to Indians over a much longer time than the Golden Gate Bridge has been significant to us.

And there was Blindman, a monument of sorts himself. It was still 1971, and we'd just moved to the Mathias Ranch six miles south of Boonville with an overwhelming load of juvenile delinquents. It was always a relief to get away from Rancho Loco for an evening of fast pitch softball and beer drinking in Cloverdale; normalcy, more or less. Because we were still young enough to want to play ball games, and were unaware Boonville had a team of its own, we hooked up with some softball-playing hippies who put three of us on their team in the Cloverdale fast pitch league.

We were the worst team in the league; not for lack of trying, but lack of a whiz bang pitcher. With a good pitcher, a squad of paraplegics can be dominant in fast pitch softball, but our two guys, hard as they worked, got ripped good every time they went out there. We had the best post-game funnsies of any team in the league, though, because hippies were still fun in '71. A few years later hippies were scrambling for respectability, pretending it hadn't happened, and hippies, like fast pitch softball, were over.

Those dusty, hot Cloverdale summer nights were made even more memorable by Blindman, aka Bob Wright, the legendary umpire. Blindman was a chunkier version of Popeye. A man in his middle sixties, he had Popeye's jut jaw and he had Popeye's comic pugnacity, not that Blindman at all saw himself as a comic figure. He saw himself as authority, the authority when it came to baseball and all the sub-species thereof, from Little League to softball to American Legion baseball.

Blindman was Cloverdale's umpire. There were summer days when Blindman would be behind the plate all day and well into the night, calling balls and strikes for Little Leaguers in the morning, Pony Leaguers in the afternoon, softball games in the evening. And the guy was no kid. Try umpiring baseball games all day from about nine in the morning until nine at night in a Cloverdale summer. Who would want to do it for maybe ten bucks for two hours in a hundred degree heat? Blindman, whatever his deficiencies as final arbiter, was there, omni-available.

The man had absolute confidence in his judgment. He never hesitated to stick his authoritative jaw into the faces of incredulous ballplayers, and there he was with all his tools, his whisk broom, shin guards, chest protector, face mask, even a rule book he would condescend to consult from time-to-time, invariably interpreting a dispute in ways not even implied in the rule. He wasn't off on every call, of course; if he'd been consistently off even his round-the-clock availability wouldn't have saved him. Most of the time he was, well, acceptably bad behind the plate. You could count on him to miss about one in every ten pitches, but when he missed one he missed it big time, head-slappingly big time.

"Jesus, Blindman, where was that one? Are you kidding?" Blindman would blandly reply, "It caught the corner, for chrissakes. You never seen a breaking ball? Quit belly achin' and get back in the batter's box."

Blindman would make a preposterously bad call against a family man's little leaguer in the morning, an astoundingly bad call against the guy's pony leaguer in the afternoon, and here he was the same night calling some real doozies against the guy himself in a fast-pitch game.

Around town, Blindman was Blindman, not Mr. Wright as his age might entitle him to be addressed — certainly entitled him to be addressed by children if they knew him by his right name. And even Blindman's wife, a silent, wraith-like presence in a corner of the grandstand who'd often been observed laughing as the love of her life was deluged with spectator insults, was known as Mrs. Blindman. Blindman was Blindman to everyone from little kids to gaffers and gaffettes in walkers. You'd hear a kid who looked like he was about five greet Blindman with a merry, "Hi, Blindman" to which Blindman would distractedly but instantly reply, "How ya doin', sonny."

Blindman had umpired two generations of Cloverdale ballgames. There were grown family men who were telling Blindman stories from their ballplaying days as their incredulous children were walking back to the dugout on a Blindman-called third strike that the kid couldn't have hit if he'd swung at it from the top rung of a step ladder. And if the kid so much as glanced quizzically back at Blindman as he made his puzzled way back to the dugout, Blindman would say something like, "If you're gonna play this game, kiddo, you better get used to risers." Blindman had somehow seen the ball in the strike zone before it had taken a sudden, Blue Angel-like hundred degree climb so steep it had eluded the leaping catcher's glove. But that was the old riser ball, by god, and Blindman knew it when he saw it.

There were days when Blindman had to be the most verbally abused senior citizen in all of California. Americans have never been shy about denouncing an umpire regardless of his age or physical condition, and abusing him in the most vulgar way. "For Christ's sake, Blindman, you're the first guy I've ever seen who could get his head all the way up his ass and suck his thumb at the same time!" To which Blindman, as always infuriatingly, serenely confident, would blandly reply, "I call 'em like I see 'em." And that one would evoke, "That's the goddamn problem, Blindman, you can't see 'em!" In three contentious minutes, Blindman might absorb more verbal abuse than most people suffer in a lifetime. But he loved baseball, he was always available and, you could say, he had the perfect judicial temperament. So far as Blindman was concerned, he was Solomon himself in shin guards and chest protector. Nothing anybody said ever bothered him.

Blindman worked all the games by himself, too, meaning that his most famous bad calls weren't over balls and strikes, which come and go almost subliminally. Nope, Blindman's most memorable calls were like the one he famously made one hot summer night during an otherwise forgettable game.

Now, those of you who have played or watched fast pitch softball know the ball gets up to the plate real fast, typically getting from the pitcher to home plate at between 90 and 100 miles per hour. At night, under weak lights like Cloverdale's, the ball seemed to get to home plate even faster.

A man of about 40, a little too old and more than a little physically past it for a game this fast, squared around to bunt, and here came the pitch at a good 95-per, a hard, round projectile coming straight at his crotch with the speed of a Civil War cannonball when it struck the man squarely in his unprotected pills. The batter went down like he'd been shot. Everyone froze in an "Oh, no!" moment. The downed man's wife came flying down out of the stands, screaming, terrified.

We surrounded the wounded ballplayer in a worried clump. The guy didn't move for many seconds. He looked like he was dead. He finally stuck both hands protectively into his groin and rolled his legs into a fetal cringe, groaning, his face gray, pain tears running through the home plate dust on his agonized face.

Blindman had been standing nonchalantly off to side, apparently unconcerned. Someone said, "We better call an ambulance." Some one else said, "It's on the way," and sure enough we could hear a siren. Just then, Blindman, jostling his way roughly through the crowd at home plate, leaned way down between the injured man's grieving wife and directly into the injured man's face and yelled "Yer outta there! Out! You! Are! Out!"

There was a stunned silence. We all stared at Blindman. It wasn't computing. It couldn't be that Blindman was telling the injured man that he'd made an out. This was an injury accident scene, no longer a ball game. This guy might be crippled for life! Maybe totally impotent! Someone asked in a weak, shocked voice, like someone who'd just overheard his father making a pass at the widow at a funeral. "Wha, Wha, What are you doing, Blindman.?"

Blindman, unperturbed — the wronger he was the calmer he got — replied, "The batter's out because he didn't try to get out of the way of the pitch. That's the rule. If you get hit on purpose, you're out. He's out." And then Blindman, just as the ambulance crew hustled up to the downed man, shouted, "Play ball!"

We were shocked speechless. But Blindman's bizarre ruling had brought the dead man back to life. He was rolling around in the dirt of home plate moaning, "No, no, no, Blindman," as if fearing the heartless ump might pounce on him again. Somebody laughed a disbelieving laugh as everyone else commenced a barrage of insults, the kindest of which was, "You're nuts, Blindman."

Months later, I happened to stop in at the Cloverdale Bakery, a known Blindman haunt. Blindman was lecturing another old guy on, of all things, the danger of the international communist conspiracy. If a platoon of heavily armed Vietcong had at that moment come jogging through the door, Blindman probably wouldn't have noticed, and if he had noticed he probably would have thought they were an American Legion team from Chinatown. But I liked the idea of Blindman as global strategist; I was happy he had a life away from the ballpark.

Blindman's second most memorable move came later that night

during an extra-inning game that didn't start until 9:30 because the previous game had also gone into extra innings. A heavy fog had rolled in. It was cold and damp and the fog was so thick the outfielders were barely discernible from the stands. They looked like ghosts out there. Blindman was calling his third game of the day when we kicked off. The game was replete with arguments, walks, minor injuries, and other time gobblers. We were still playing at midnight. We wouldn't be able to drink beer after the game because the bars would be closed by the time Blindman had made his last bad call and we'd called it an exhausted night. The score was something like 17-16 with our team on the short end as usual when we came up for our last at bat. It was a quarter past the witching hour. We'd started playing on Wednesday night and now it was Thursday.

We loaded the bases. With two outs a guy hit a long fly ball that was barely visible in the thick mists of left center field, but a dim form appeared to be circling beneath it, an easy catch, a can of corn as they say, when suddenly the lights, never particularly illuminating even on clear nights, went out. The night had gone black. Everyone was suddenly invisible. There were yelps, thuds and curses as guys careened sightless around the base paths, running into each other. The lights magically snapped back on. All eyes went to the power box behind home plate, and there was Blindman with his hand still on the lever with a huge grin on his face. "You know," he explained, I've played ball all my life and I've umpired thousands of games, and I've always wanted to do that."

Marshal Winn, originally from Hillsboro, Illinois, home of Ben Blockburger, the Humboldt County swindler, and my mother, not a swindler so far as is known, was postmaster at Philo for many years before and after World War Two. Winn was locally famous for the tunnel he hand dug from the back porch of his house on Ray's Road out to what he seemed to think would be a get-away tree line. Winn was convinced that he needed an escape route if the Japanese came ashore at Navarro-by-the-Sea, jogging up 128 to Philo where they would bayonet him and Mrs. Winn before they moved on to Boonville to similarly dispose of the Boonville Postmaster, another representative of the federal government.

Fortunately for Winn, Japan's geo-tactical considerations had not included the Anderson Valley, but out on the coast near Point Arena, a Japanese family who had developed a prosperous little farm north of town was nearly lynched in 1941. Joe Scaramella, immigrant, autodidact, faithful reader of the Appeal To Reason and the poor man's encyclopedia, the Little Blue Books produced by the great socialist Julius Haldeman out of Girard, Kansas, would become a county supervisor, and the only vote against Sonoma County's appropriation of Mendocino water stored behind Coyote Dam as Lake Mendocino.

Scaramella and a Presbyterian minister talked a Point Arena mob out of harming a terrified Japanese family in the hysterical days following Pearl Harbor. The Japanese farmer was accused of signaling offshore countrymen through a radio that Joe Scaramella had sold him. Joe told the mob, "It's a radio-radio, a receiver, not a transmitter." The Japanese family left Point Arena, and no more is known of them, but they left alive, leaving behind their little farm, too, which their mercenary neighbors appropriated and went on farming as if they'd developed it themselves.

My mother remembers living on "milk and potatoes for weeks at a time" during The Great Depression. The hard times and the war years combined to propel her first to nurse's training in St. Louis then she and a friend, with their new credentials, departed the Midwest for the most glamorous place they could think of, Honolulu, where my mother met my father, Mr. Suave, with his white dinner jackets and surf board.

"We went to Bernstein's Fish Grotto on Powell Street after the trip out from Hillsboro by Greyhound bus," my mother remembers. "It was 1936. We were met in San Francisco by a Hillsboro lady, Helen Lippard, who took us to Bernstein's Fish Grotto on Powell Street. We stayed at the Pickwick Hotel at the Greyhound station before taking a ship to Los Angeles, which then went on to Honolulu.

"I met your father, I think, on a blind date. He took me to the Royal Hawaiian to dance, but he didn't take me to dinner first. I should have known…" her 90-year-old voice trails off. "As you know, I believe in the spirit world. Your father visits me often. He's always sitting down, of course, but he wasn't a bad man, just lazy. He never got over being a rich man's son."

She leaves the only seated ghost in the history of ethereal visitations to return to that fatal first date at the Royal Hawaiian.

"The dance floor was right on the water. I almost stepped into the sea when I saw Cary Grant while I was dancing near the sea wall."

Marriage soon followed the dinnerless dance, and the unsuspecting couple commenced life together in pre-war Honolulu.

"We lived in Manoa Valley at 3495 Alani Drive, above the Chinese cemetery. People used to steal the food the Chinese left out on the graves of their relatives. Your father was eleven years older than me and had been married to a woman named Edie. I bought a hat from her at the department store in Honolulu and didn't even know it. Your father met her at the University of Washington when she saved his life when he got a cramp while swimming in Lake Washington. Edie was from Seattle. After your father, Edie married a man named Stuart who worked for the San Francisco Chronicle and they lived on Telegraph Hill. In the early 1930s your father and his mother lived on Hilligas in Berkeley while Mr. Anderson [my grandfather] worked in Manila. They then all moved back to Honolulu where they rented a house on the beach at Waikiki."

My mother always called her father-in-law "Mr. Anderson." He was a "Mr. Anderson" kind of guy, with his every day suits and strict Presbyterianism. He'd correct our careless American grammar and rap our knuckles with his butter knife if we reached too far across his dinner table. Mr. Anderson was a large, handsome man whose photo in full kilt regalia appears on the cover of a book called, "The Scotch in the Hawaiian Islands." He was, it seems, a great thunderer whose rumblings were seldom accompanied by lightening. Two of his three sons became premature hippies, doing an early about face from their father's old world work ethic and, as adults, were never known to appear in a church except for the occasional family wedding.

Mr. Anderson had done so well so quickly as a single man in old Honolulu that he sent home to Edinburgh for a bride rather than choose one from among the resident, upper crust haole Presbyterians who saw him as Triple-A husband material. One of the few surviving anecdotes about Mr. Anderson had him demanding of his imported wife when she returned from a beauty parlor session with her fingernails painted a wicked bright red, "Remove that nail polish at once." "I will not," she replied, and she didn't.

The coal miner's daughter thought she'd hit the mother lode with my father, a man who commuted to college in Seattle during The Depression on the luxury liners Lurline or Matson, who sent his laundry home by the big boat to have the family's Japanese maids do it the way he liked his laundry done. When he first encountered the mesmerized nurse fresh from Hillsboro and the Great Depression he told her that all the clothes he owned were white dinner jackets and swimming trunks. He swam all day, danced all night, although in theory he was employed by the Honolulu Police Department where his duties seemed nebulous to the point of non-existent. We have an old photo of my uncle doing a handstand on a surf board as he rides a wave in to Waikiki. The Anderson brothers spent a lot of time at the beach where as boys they sold photos of themselves doing surfboard tricks to tourists.

My father soon had five children with the Hillsboro girl, and paternity and his inability to work for long at one job, meant hard times for us all, but he labored on, and never did descend the social scale to the depths achieved by his brother, Bob, a drunk by age 14 and a scandalous presence in Honolulu from that age on who mortified his respectable parents with one public escapade after another until his death by drowning during a drunken fight in downtown Honolulu in 1968.

Uncle Bob was profligate by any standard. In his early 20's he married a comparably well-placed young Honolulu woman in a large society wedding that drew the cream of pre-war Hawaiian society. He was so drunk when he finally appeared for the ceremony that his best man had to hold him upright for the recital of vows. Immediately after fumbling the gold band of holy matrimony onto his bride's finger, Uncle Bob took off, bypassing the reception, which in any case he'd already ruined, to continue his drunken debauch downtown with companions more to his liking. When his distraught bride appeared in the marital bower later that night she discovered her betrothed in bed with the Hawaiian maid. One consequence of that day's startling events is that I have twin first cousins I've never seen. They are said to live soberly staid lives in Los Angeles

As their marital warfare evolved from occasional skirmishes to a one-way campaign waged against my father outside all known rules of verbal engagement, my mother would inevitably drag Uncle Bob out as her opening salvo.

"Your grandfather, Mr. Anderson, was a very nice man, but your Uncle Bob..." My father would interrupt. "Now, Ruth, we really don't need to hear that again."

Undeterred, Mom would proceed with the full recital of Uncle Bob's catastrophic wedding, with heavy bore side shots at "Mr. Suave," as she called my father. Her monologues always implied that her husband had dragged her into a white dinner jacket sordidness "a dumb cluck like me from a little town in Illinois" was not only unprepared for but had somehow been dragged down by. She'd proceed on through the lengthy catalog of my father's deficiencies, perceived and actual, before segueing into a vivid account of some random horror she'd seen that day at her nurse's job in the emergency ward. "This little homo came in with a light bulb..." And my father would say, "Now, Ruth, do we really...?"

The marriage of the surf board and the RN endured until the San Francisco beatniks set America free in 1955.

The old girl became even less inhibited once she was liberated from her marriage, and became an absolute verbal menace in her golden years when she would blurt out some terrible insult then duck behind a self-diagnosis of senility. "Oh, don't mind me. I'm just a crazy old woman."

My father assessed his married life, "The day I got the final papers my hemorrhoids cleared up."

A binge drinker well into her eighties, downing a fifth of Old Crow in one more or less eight hour sitting a couple of times a month, Mom would rest her liver then do it all over again. When I finally refused to buy her whiskey "because Old Crow might finish off the old bat," Mom denounced me, her first born, as "a chickenshit" and "a prick." Like all drunks, though, she always found a way. If I didn't get her the Old Crow, someone else would.

In between bottles, in a technically sober condition, if there was another person in the room, she could be counted on to serve up an audible feast. I would half-listen for the choice cuts, of which there was always a virtual banquet. When an evening television news segment showed a lesbian couple getting married at San Francisco City Hall, "Gran," as we'd all come to call her, probably because by then she was so unmotherly it was painful to call her mom, blurted, "O my god how disgusting!" She paused. "Well, on the other hand, maybe it's a good thing that homely people have each other," wrapping up with, "Are people getting uglier, or are there just more ugly people on television?"

I would find myself trying to unravel one of these Zen knots when she would rattle off another one, "You know, my mother had the smallest kidneys the doctor had ever seen." The beauty quotient among the general population seemed about the same as it had always been, but I wondered what the size standard was for kidneys. I wondered if my genetic heritage included small kidneys, wondered if, as my prostate puckered, small kidneys would force me into Depends.

When her personal hygiene became a health hazard to her, and an olfactory assault on us and my brother-in-law's house, I began to pressure the old girl to bathe.

"That's it. I'm leaving. I can be a bag lady; of course I'll need a raincoat and maybe a small tent. And you, you dictator, do you think you're doing me a big favor living here with me? Out! Leave! Now! I'm not cut out for gratitude. You see me feeling grateful, shoot me. My problem is I'm just too damn old."

If she didn't smell so bad, it was a temptation to just get her a half-pint of whiskey every day and let her disintegrate into her chair until both became a kind of geriatric puddle, but I didn't want to go to jail for elder neglect.

There were nights when Gran didn't even bother to totter off to her bedroom, fifteen steps from her funky throne, but she usually made the trip because I could hear her radio all night tuned in to the talk shows. "Bob in Gold Beach. What's on your mind tonight, Bob?" And Bob would answer, "If everyone in this country could carry a gun right out in the open people would be a lot more polite, that's for sure." I wondered how much she slept with these lunatics bellowing into her pillow.

Bathing is a problem for the elderly. Their bodies have collapsed.

They hurt all the time. It's a major effort for them to get in and out of their chairs, to get to the bathroom, to get to the table to eat, to get anybody to talk to them like the adults they once were, to listen to them, to sympathize. But bathing is the Mount Everest of elder care. Why isn't there a mini in-home car wash for the aged, in one end, out the other, a scented talc falling on them like a light snow?

Because there are Mexican immigrants like Myrna, a large, strong, commanding woman who earns her way cajoling the recalcitrant elderly into letting her treat their bed sores, wash their hair, clip their toe nails.

Myrna asked, "What is your mother's name?" Ruth, I said. We call her Gran.

"Now, Root," Myrna would say, "Root, you are going to take a shower now." I don't want to take a shower, Gran would say, but Myrna would already have hoisted her out of her festering chair and half way down the hall to the shower as my mother was still vowing she had just bathed the day before "When you busy bodies were out doing whatever busy bodies do when they aren't tormenting old ladies."

The elderly don't get this crazy, this difficult in Mexico, and the Indian elders of Mendocino County are still treated with great respect by their tribes.

A wacky relative had presented Gran with a realistic replica of a deer head. You pushed a button on the thing and its lips moved as Frankie Lane sang "Mule Train," and then Johnny Cash belted out "Ring of Fire." My mother loved "Buck," as she called the singing replica. Buck was mildly amusing that first hour of Christmas day, but a hellish instrument of torture thereafter, which my brother-in-law never quite got around to mounting because we knew it would be harder to disappear it from a permanent position. So there it was, Buck the singing buck, propped up against a wall at the extreme right of Gran's chair-bound viewshed. Two or three times a day she would demand, "Play Buck for me."

I'd say, "I'll hit the button for you but don't make me stick around to listen to it again."

"You've always been a stick-in-the-mud, haven't you?" she'd say. "Not a fun person, a real Gloomy Gus. No wonder you've always gotten in so much trouble, with your attitude like it is."

One day I moved Buck so I could vacuum the floor, forgetting to put the beast back in Gran's line of sight.

"Buck!" she suddenly screamed. "Where's Buck? Goddamit, did you take him downstairs because he makes me happy?"

"Of course I did," I said. "You know the house policy. Anything makes you happy, out it goes!"

And she'd laugh, which meant she was still more or less with it. But she used her advanced age and physical decrepitude to lash her keepers, and maybe her regular eruptions of quivering anger kept herself from going gently into that final talk radio night.

My sister Jean would visit for a few days every couple of months. Jean lives in Fort Bragg. She's disabled, an epileptic, a person two saintly Fort Bragg doctors, Glusker and Graham, have kept alive through thirty years of physical catastrophes, Dr. Glusker's mother was a secretary to Trotsky in Mexico. Another Fort Bragg woman is the daughter of a former Secretary of Defense. She threw herself off the old Noyo Bridge but survived. Mendocino County's connective tissue often seems global.

My mother and Jean would fight.

"Jean, you've got rice curry all over the front of your shirt," Gran would say.

Jean, leaning into the old lady's face, would say, "Tough shit."

I listened to them playing scrabble one night.

"Asshole is two words," I heard my mother say.

"One word," my sister replied, "because it's one thing — the hole in your ass."

"I'm older than you, Jean," the old lady said. "I've known a lot more assholes than you have. Asshole is one word, goddamit!"

"I've known my share of them, too," Jean replied, then, noting my appearance in the room, "Hey! Here comes one now; let's ask him!"

Gran's short term memory was gone, but she could name names back into the 18th century, and her memory of December 7th, 1941 is as vivid as the day it happened.

"We lived five miles from downtown Honolulu, but we could see the rising sun on the Jap planes as they flew directly over our house.

People were standing in their yards watching them fly over. Your father had taken you and your brother out for a ride, and when you all came back he said, 'Ruth, I think the military has gone too far this time. These maneuvers are just too goddamn realistic. They're dropping fake bombs on Pearl Harbor.' I said to him, 'These aren't maneuvers, you fool, we're being attacked! And then he said, 'By the Germans?'"

Gran resumed her history of the war years.

"We came to San Francisco on a troop ship in May after the attack. It was a ten-day crossing. There were only seven of us women with kids on the boat. The rest were young non-coms sent back to the states for officer training. We had to board ship by climbing nets. Your father stayed in Honolulu where he belonged to the Businessman's Training Corps, a bunch of bumblers like him who were supposed to fight the Japanese if they invaded. I used to tell him he'd probably shoot his foot off before he shot the right people. We left because everyone thought the Japanese would follow up the air attack with a ground invasion. A lot of people who stayed became real estate millionaires — everyone except your father, of course, who managed to become poorer. So many people were leaving that everything was for sale. When we got off the boat in San Francisco the Red Cross asked me where I wanted to stay until we got settled somewhere. We were officially refugees, you see. I said, 'the Fairmont.' I knew it was a nice hotel, and I was surprised when they put us in a cab and up the hill we went."

"From the Fairmont we went to live in an apartment in an old Victorian at 1399 McAllister near Fillmore. It had just been sub-divided into apartments and was stuffed with Okies who peed out in the backyard. The neighborhood was mostly Russians and Jews back then, very few colored people. When your father came over from Honolulu he got a job out at Hunter's Point loading and unloading submarines. That's the way he was; a college graduate doing any old kind of job. He just didn't care."

In fact, they both worked hard all their lives, Mom as a nurse, Pop at a lot of things; he often held down two low-wage jobs at once to partially support his unappreciative wife and his five oblivious children. She always said that if she didn't work "we'd all have to go live in the poor house," which, as a child, I assumed was a literal place in a bad neighborhood.

If he'd been born two generations later, my father would almost certainly have been a hippie. He admired the hippies when they came along in the middle sixties. "They've got the right idea," he'd say. "Have a good time. That's the main thing. Why beat your brains out all your life taking orders from some son of a bitch?" He loved Cheech and Chong movies and Eartha Kitt. The only advice he ever gave me consisted of two instructions: "Learn to drink coffee black because you'll go to a lot of places where they either won't have sugar or they won't have cream, one or the other. If you drink coffee with either cream or sugar in it, you'll go nuts from frustration." And, one day as he watched a fly circle his three-packs-of-Kools-a-day apartment, which we called "The Tray," as in ash tray, "Remember, flies always take off backwards. Aim the fly swatter a little bit behind them and you'll get 'em every time."

Thus armored against whatever life's coffee and flies might throw at me, I went out into the great world, drinking black coffee and always aiming my fly swatter to the rear of flying insects.

As young adults, my brother Rob and I often shared grungy San Francisco apartments with our father, one of which was on Golden Gate Avenue in the same building, and maybe even the same apartment — it looked eerily familiar when it became the most infamous tenement unit in San Francisco of the time — that the SLA had held Patti Hearst in soon after the lunatics kidnapped her. I've re-visited that neighborhood several times, and I'm pretty sure 1827 Golden Gate Avenue was our hearth and home for a brief period in 1961.

My brother and I were deep into radical politics by early 1960 mostly because we were consistently shocked at the country's treatment of black people and, at least partly, because we worked at so many bad jobs as bottom proles we thought the whole works should be destroyed. Pop would say, "You know, you guys are going to get into a lot of trouble reading that crank stuff," a reference to the I.F. Stone Newsletter, The Realist, A Minority of One, and the array of left-wing journalism that supplemented our book reading. He was mystified that we'd joined the Congress On Racial Equality and had participated in every demonstration in the city organized by it. Rob soon went off to federal prison for refusing to register for the draft as an early protest against the Vietnam War, and I went off to an alienated life as a radical of the type who swelled the leftist crowd for the next decades. And my employment history became much like my father's, although unlike him I realized early on I would have to make my own employment because I was unsuited for the 9 to 5.

The house on McAllister where we touched down after coming to San Francisco from Honolulu, is long gone. It's now a big, garish tax-exempt church. A couple of blocks east there are drive-by shootings as the leadership wrings its hands and says, "It's terrible," and then the next day there's another one.

I have hazy 1942 memories of a carriage house out in back of the rambling, sectioned-off McAllister Street Victorian near Fillmore, and a vague overall impression of a spacious, untended flower garden in between that intriguing structure and the main house. I don't remember anyone peeing in the backyard. I remember it as a happy place and the Okies, if that's what they were, as being very kind to the children in the building. I was three, and my first real memories of that time were of my mother saving bacon grease "for government bullets," she explained, and I remember the cacophony of sirens and church bells when the war ended. When I walk that transformed block now I think of an old man I knew in Boonville, an Arky named Jerry Coffman, and how different his experience of World War Two and the boom years that followed it were from my family's experience of those same years.

"I was born in Caddo Gap, Arkansas, on February 7, 1911, ain't a third as big as Philo is now. I was the oldest in a family of eight sisters and a brother, the brother bein' the youngest. My daddy died in 1929, leaving me and my mother to carry on the best we could. Back then there was two sessions of school, one in the winter and one in the summer. They did it that way because the kids had to help out on the farms. I went to around the eighth grade before I went to work. The Depression? Oh, my god! Can't make people now believe what it was like. Couldn't buy a pack of Bull Durham, without takin' it off my food. It was a hard depression; had to do a little of everything to live — saw mills, farmin', row croppin', we called it where we raised all kinds of crops you plant in rows — corn, cotton. And there was a little bit of public work later on with the CCC. We did road work all over Arkansas then we disbanded and they shipped us out to Salinas and Monterey on troop trains. I joined the CCC on the first day of July, 1935. I learned marchin', making up the bunk. All the stuff about the Army I knew before the Army ever got me.

"I was drafted in 1942. They took me in at Camp Robinson, Little Rock, Arkansas. From there we went to Shine, Wyoming, for boot training. Then to Camp Pendleton out here in California for three days. They loaded us on a ship in San Francisco. We didn't know where we was goin', we just rode the waves till we got there. We landed in Brisbane, Australia. From there we went to Sydney, Australia. I was called a Small Boat Operator. I piloted landing craft mostly. They was gettin' us ready to go to New Guinea. A man there in Australia wanted me to stay and work with him in Australia after the war, pilotin' boats up and down the coast but bein' as I'm from over here, I didn't know about that. I liked the people there, they was just fine with me. I knew how to operate those old steam boilers. I guess that's how they got me onto the boats. I liked the job, but I didn't care much for the bombs a-fallin'.

"The Japanese was only in there a couple of days before we got there. There wasn't any hand-to-hand fightin' or anything like that. They bombed us, though, all the time at night. Got blowed right out of one foxhole one time. Another time three of us dove in a hole when the bombin' started while we was tryin' to unload a ship. Three of us in a hole not big enough for one. One guy went to prayin'. The bombs were droppin' all around us. But when you got enough points, you got shipped back to the States. I landed in San Pedro. Went back to Arkansas by troop train where I worked in saw mills. I came back to California in 1952. The first time I ever saw Boonville was then, though I worked in Laytonville for five weeks in 1942 before they drafted me. I got 75 cents an hour on that job.

"There was a whole lot of gamblin' in New Guinea, I can tell you that. There wasn't much else to do. I saw crap games where the money was piled high. Money didn't mean anything because there was no place to spend it.

"The New Guinea people used to bring in whole stalks of bananas they'd sell for a pack of cigarettes. They'd always walk single file. One day they showed up, about 14 of 'em, all with bananas. A guy threw a mosquito bomb at 'em and all we seen were their heels. They thought it was a hand grenade!

"They had a couple of big stockades in the part of New Guinea where I was for Japanese prisoners. Every third week I had to load 1300 of 'em onto ships. Never had a bit of trouble from any of 'em. One man without a gun could guard 'em all. Heck, they used to turn 'em out twice a day to go swimmin'.

"In '52 I worked in Buster Hollifield's mill in Philo. Later on, from about 1964 on, I worked out at Hollow Tree, off the Fish Rock Road. In '64 they was payin' around $1.65 an hour. I did most of the jobs in the mill but mainly I was a oiler. I'd work wherever I could find a shade tree and a coffee pot!"

When I met Jerry Coffman I had just bought a two-bedroom, one bath house on a half-acre a mile northwest of Boonville. It was set to the rear of the lot just off what in 1920, the year it was completed to run out to the ocean at Navarro-by-the-Sea, had been called the McDonald Highway to the Sea. It's now called Anderson Valley Way, conferring on its two-mile length a bland, suburban anonymity which belies its vivid history of Indians, first settlers, Italian immigrants, freed slaves, movie stars, and ballplayers. Among others. The tract-like houses at the Boonville end of the street were called "Millionaire's Row" in the 1950's after the local mill owners who built and lived in them. Those houses looked rich to the loggers and millhands of 1955. Fifty years later there are House Beautiful spreads hidden away off Anderson Valley Way's length, mansions in the hills.

I liked to imagine that I'd been standing out on the road at my mailbox in 1930 when the DiMaggio Brothers passed by for a weekend of baseball games in Fort Bragg where Vince DiMaggio had been hired at the mill so he could manage the town team on weekends, those weekend ballgames being Fort Bragg's primary entertainment through the 1950s. Every little town in the county had a baseball team, but Fort Bragg's town team was consistently the best of them.

In 1973 we'd paid $21,500 for our house on Anderson Valley Way with a thousand dollars down we chiseled from fresh credit cards. Over the next thirty years we covered the half-acre with a ramshackle, non-code collection of structures to house children, dependent relations, hangers-on, and a newspaper; thirty-four years later we sold the house for $350,000, a miracle of capitalism.

Across the road from my house so close you can hear its winter roar is Anderson Creek. It runs down out of the hills separating the Ukiah Valley from the Anderson Valley. Swollen by winter rains by the time it reaches Anderson Valley's flat floor, Anderson Creek is like a mammoth fire hose let loose in a bath tub, ripping down out of the east hills so powerfully that over the years it has gouged out a rainy season bed for itself that's a half-mile wide in some places. One winter, a county road worker and Assembly of God preacher named Ron Penrose, slipped and fell into the upper end of a culvert channeling Anderson Creek beneath the lower Ukiah Road and was shot out the other end, landing heavily downstream some twenty yards from the culvert's mouth. Don't think Preacher Penrose had to think hard about his Sunday sermon about how a divine concrete whale had spared a latter-day Jonah.

Fort Despair, as our place came to be called, rests just east of the stream, and just east of a battered house on stilts. The stilt house is due west of the Boonville Cemetery. For many years now the stilt house's elevation has saved it from being swept away by the creek's rainy season rages. When the house was erected by Judge June in 1945 for an Indian couple named Luff, who'd worked many years on the June Ranch (now owned by Phil Wasson), the creek ran well to the west, behind the house, and even in the high water years the creek stayed to the west. But over the years, Anderson Creek's wild winter flows pounding down out of the hills east of Boonville seem to have become even more thunderous, and more unpredictable in how they course through the valley floor. The Luffs used to walk down off Anderson Valley Way directly to their front door. For some years now, because the stream bed has shifted to the east where it annually gnaws a new streambed between the road and the stilt house, the stilt house can only be reached from Ornbaun

Road, a much less direct route.

Mexican farmworkers who work the nearby vineyards now occupy the stilt house, each man paying an inflated rent for the dubious roof over his head. From my front door, it was a five-minute walk to the Luff's house, not that I did it very often because I never had any business with anybody who lived there, and because Phil Wasson, who succeeded the Junes as the owner of the property, was not kindly disposed to trespassers. With refreshing churlishness in a time "the kids" are totemic beings, Wasson once wrote back to the Elementary School, as it's formally called by generations of unimaginative, a-historical school boards, to deny the school's request that one of its classes be allowed to look at the creek's eroded banks from a vantage point behind the school, which happened to be on Wasson's property. "I'll arrest any and all of you if I catch you one inch on my place," Wasson warned. It is Wasson's Mexicans who are stuffed into the stilt house adjacent to the old man's vineyards. They are called Wasson's Mexicans just as pioneer ranchers and farmers referred to Indians as theirs, and just as some of the first settlers in Mendocino County arrived with their black slaves, and just as contemporary vineyard owners are often heard to say, "Yeah, he's one of my Mexicans."

Every year the rainy season blasts down Anderson Creek to carry off more of Wasson's vineyards. He could get free government money to stabilize the stream banks but he doesn't like the government any more than he likes trespassers. Less maybe. And now it's a race between the creek and what's left of his life to see if the winter's annual Niagaras will finish his vineyard before the old man finishes his days.

Wasson had ample reason to be hostile to me. My fraught household often contained miscellaneously doomed children who, at that time, were sent to us by the cities of the Bay Area without regard to either their respective vulnerabilities or the possible consequences for our neighbors of their various pathologies. A retarded kid with non-existent or incompetent parents — one incompetent parent usually — who'd been caught shoplifting and thus adjudicated delinquent would be sent by San Francisco or Oakland to live in the same rural household as a 16-year-old street thug, a kid long accustomed to using force, or the threat of it, to get what he wanted. The group home thus grouped, it was the full-time job of the adults more or less in charge to keep the internal predators off the internal prey, and to keep them all from disturbing the neighbors.

One of those damned children we called Doc Smock. A diminutive black kid whose jaunty little outline resembled Mr. Peanut, Doctor S. had somehow developed an uncontrollable fetish for certain female garments, particularly smocks and jackets made of specific materials, especially vinyl and imitation leather, with an occasional lunge for a woman's raincoat. But Doc Smock was literally overcome at the mere glimpse of a female K-Mart employee wearing that store's trademark aqua-marine smock. It was easy to keep him out of K-Mart which, after all, was 20 miles away over the long and winding road to Ukiah. We were unaware other materials in other female contexts also ignited uncontrollable passions.

Fetishes, of course, provide endless material for jokes, but Doc Smock's fetish was no joke. Ordinarily an amiable, cooperative little guy, he was fiendishly possessed at the sight of certain fabrics as they graced the female form, and he'd resort to violence to take one off the woman wearing it. In Stockton one day, wielding the open blade of a pocket knife in one hand, he'd grabbed a K-Mart clerk and demanded her smock. The female clerk couldn't make sense of his demand. Doc had never hurt anybody, and he was still standing in the aisle with the terrified clerk demanding her smock when he was gang tackled by male employees. That episode got Doc a therapeutic ticket to Boonville where there were no K-Marts.

I took him to the Ukiah K-Mart, since defunct, to test him, to see if my carefully nuanced strategies to wean him off smocks was working. "Goddamit, Doc, you gotta get off this smock stuff. I'll buy you fifty K-Mart smocks. You can wear them, sleep with them, eat them, whatever you want to do with them. Just stop trying to take them off living people." He'd say, "That's right, boss." He always called me boss, an honorific misunderstood by visiting liberals who looked at as if I were running a 19th century plantation ."I have a problem, boss, and I'm tryin' real hard to stop." I think he was, too, but he just couldn't help himself.

The one time I'd tested him at the Ukiah K-Mart I got a pretty big scare myself because as soon as we'd passed through the front doors Doc was transformed. His eyes went wide as they locked on to a woman wearing that most desired of all objects, an irresistible aqua-marine work smock. Doc began moving towards her in a kind of Frankenstein stiff-walk. "Jesus H!" I gasped as I ran up behind him, wrapped him up and dragged him out of the store, him still struggling to get away from me and back at the smock. A friend told me later he'd seen me wrestling with the kid in the parking lot. "Good thing the libs didn't see that," he said. From then on, which was before I knew it wasn't only K-Mart's uniform that transformed the lad into an uncontrollable, assaultive, roving fabric menace, I simply kept him away from K-Mart. I figured no K-Mart, no problem.

"All right, boss," Doc, with his usual jaunty confidence, had said that morning, "I'm going on out to feed the rabbits now." Our rabbits didn't wear smocks. Doc could take care of the rabbits without, we assumed, straying into the path of temptation.

Mrs. Wasson passed by on foot most mornings with the wife of a retired doctor, Mrs. Banks; both walkers were well into their golden years. Doc, spotting the two women, abandoned the rabbits, dashed out into the street, determined to seize Mrs. Wasson's jacket which, objectively, and given its total presentation as a greenish plastic thing worn by an elderly woman, had to have been the most unlikely object of passion in the whole bloody history of uncontrolled acquisition.

But Doc had to have it and…

The phone rang.

"Hey," an agitated male voice began, "do you have a little ape black kid at your house?"

There are several black youth resident here, sir, what's the problem?

"Well, this little black kid just ran up behind Mrs. Wasson with a rubber knife and shoved it into her back. 'Gimme your coat, bitch,' he told her. Mrs. Wasson gave him her coat and she and her friend ran off and called me. When they looked back this kid was ripping up her coat, and then he jumped up and down on it and ran back into your place."

Ah, I think I may know the responsible party, I said as calmly as I could. Is her jacket kinda greenish, a kinda K-Mart-looking thing?

"What's that have to do with anything?" the voice demanded. "Yeah, as a matter of fact, what's left of it is kinda green. But that little nut can't be doing that no matter what color he, her or the goddamned jacket is."

I agreed.

Mr. Wasson visited that afternoon. He wondered why "these kids have to be here," suggesting that they should be locked up if not somewhere urban, some place far, far from Boonville. I said that the knife was, ha-ha, Phil, only made of rubber, that I'd pay for the coat, that I was sorry, that he and Mrs. Wasson now had an interesting anecdote to accompany them down Memory Lane, that crazy children like crazy adults had a right to live anywhere so long as they didn't harm anyone, that basically I thought the incident, as I euphemized it, should not be unexpected in turbulent times like these.

"Jesus H. Christ on a goddamned crutch if you don't beat all," Wasson said as he got up and walked out the door.

A week later, the Ukiah Chief of Police called.

"We have a kid here who says he lives with you in Boonville."

The chief gave me the magic name.

"We arrested him at Kentucky Fried Chicken. He called 911 and said that he was going to kill the counter girls if we didn't bring him a hundred K-Mart smocks, pronto." The chief chuckled. "He was still talking to the 911 operator when we got there."

Doc Smock was supposed to have been at the movies with an adult supervisor. However, the lurid proximity of K-Mart had apparently pulled the boy from the theater, led him inexorably towards the love that never would have a name, a love so transforming, so fixating that not even the blasts of Ukiah's summer heat could keep him from it. Intense as his desire for the seductive garment was, it was a long walk to K-Mart on a hot afternoon, so Doc sensibly stopped in at the air conditioned KFC franchise down the street from the theater to call 911 to demand that the cops deliver his heart's desire to him.

My tolerance for aberrant behavior may be slightly greater than the next person's, but Doc Smock, the poor, driven, uncomprehending, weepingly bewildered little obsessive who literally couldn't help himself because he had no ability to understand why he did it or how he might stop doing it, well, his smock expeditions were too much to expect the community to suffer. If he'd kept it indoors he'd have been fine, we'd have been fine. We might have eventually gotten him to stop, and Mrs. Wasson and Mrs. Banks could have enjoyed their morning constitutionals without accelerating at our gate. The child was a case for the experts.

Who duly assembled in Ukiah, wafted in to town on clouds of extravagant government per diems and triple consultant fees to group on the boy. The platoon of shrinks asked Doc to please wait in the ante-room while they brushed up on his case particulars. Doc unfailingly met the public with a most helpful, smiling and generally pleasing demeanor. "Yes, sir, I'll be right here," he'd assured the team as they passed on into the conference room. Cute little guy, they probably thought. He can't be that far off. Why, look how appropriate he is to us. Of course if the female shrinks had been wearing K-Mart smocks they would have had to claw their way into the meeting room.

The instant the experts had closed the door and had seated themselves to contemplate the unique compulsions driving their young patient, Doc went furiously to work on their coats and jackets; all those provocations dangling there right in front of his tantalized nose were too much for him. When an earth-toned helping professional opened the door to invite Doc inside so the healers could group on him, she gasped. Doc was urinating on a shredded pile of garments.

The day I met the coyote, I was on my way to Anderson Creek to look for evidence of the Indians who'd lived there. The Indians admired the coyote for its intelligence and humor. I do too. This one was frozen at one end of the culvert that empties an unnamed winter-only stream running down out of the winter hills into Anderson Creek. The coyote stared at me. I stared back. The coyote didn't move, I didn't move. He was maybe twenty yards from me at his end of the culvert, perfectly still, gazing back at me, messing with me, just like the Indians used to say the coyote messed with them.

We looked at each other for long minutes before the coyote won the stare-down, as I'm sure he'd intended when he started it, because I turned away from him and continued down the garbage-strewn path from the end of the culvert to the streambed, the path that the current residents of the stilt house use as a shortcut home from town and atheists of all ethnicities use as garbage dump because only a person utterly without any sense of the world's splendors could so casually defile such a beautiful place. Every year there's more consumer culture detritus for the winter deluges to purge, and every year, after the rains, the volunteer alders and willows struggling up from stream's margins are festooned with everything from disposable diapers to hula hoops.

Twenty-five years after my illuminating encounter with the Boonville coyote, San Francisco is in something of a coyote tiz, especially the San Franciscans who live near the Presidio. It takes a thoroughly urbanized bi-ped to think of the Presidio as a wilderness area, but there are many urbs in my inner-Richmond neighborhood who think the single coyote roaming the thin stands of sea cypress on the city's northwest margin is not only a menace to nearby dogs and cats but has also allegedly been casting yum-yum eyes at toddlers! Barbara Meskunas, an administrative assistant to supervisor McGoldrick, said the other day, "I have two dogs. Since reading and hearing about the coyote incidents, I no longer walk them off leash anywhere in the park at all, and avoid dawn and dusk walks altogether..." Ms. Meskunas was reacting to vague reports by dog owners that their obese Labradors had been faced off by the coyote, who not only seems to be omni-present from Sea Cliff to the Lyon Street stairs, but poised for fanged assaults on warm-blooded mammals in adjoining neighborhoods. It isn't fair to expect one lonely little critter to enforce the city's leash laws all by himself, especially when he is also putting in a lot of o.t. eating the feral cats who in turn have been eating the Presidio's vanishing quail. If a single coyote can do all this good by himself, plus babysit lost children, the city that knows how ought to find a mate for him.

In Boonville, real wilderness can often begin a few feet from the pavement, as it does throughout the Anderson Valley and much of Mendocino County. I would hike due west from my house, down into the summer desert of the streambed, past the stilt house built for the Luffs, Anderson Valley's last Indians, and on into the fertile little draw between the Rancheria and Anderson Creek where a black man named Daniel Jeans established a homestead in the 1870s. Jeans had been a slave. As a boy, the late Richard "Dick" Day remembers Jeans as a large, strong man who would pull up his shirt to show valley youngsters the whip scars from his slave days. Born in 1836, his place of birth not known, Jeans liked to boast that he could out work any two white men, which may have been more than a boast because Jeans' labor was always in demand, and his homestead was a prosperous one that provided much of the Jeans family's sustenance.

The Indians of the stilt house were neighbors of the Jeans whose homestead a mile west of the stilt house became known as Ham Canyon, the name perhaps both a specific site reference to the race of Mr. Jeans and the Old Testament designation of black people as the sons of Ham, the biblical slave. Jeans' apple trees still bear fruit, and you can see from what's left of the Jeans' hillside cabin what a productive and pretty place it must have been, tucked away in that little canyon in the big, wild county of Mendocino.

How Daniel Jeans came to then-remote Anderson Valley is lost to time and another matter for pure surmise, but he probably had some association, perhaps as a slave, with the valley's first settlers, a preponderance of whom were from the slaveholding southern states, especially the state of Missouri. But Jeans and his Indian wife were accepted, if not embraced, by the isolated valley community, which was still difficult to reach up through the 1930s. You could reach Ukiah by train from San Francisco easily enough by 1888, and you could reach Point Arena and Fort Bragg by sea from the time of the first logging of the 1860s, but it wasn't easy to reach Anderson Valley, and there wasn't much reason to go there in 1870 unless you had business there or knew someone there.

Dan Jeans cleared the land for the Philo Methodist Church and the Con Creek School, for years known locally as the Little Red School House where my youngest son attended kindergarten in 1980, the last year the structure was a classroom. Jeans had also worked the convivial hop fields of the valley where old timers remember him joining the evening story telling and singing around the camp fires. Asked once about his religion, Jeans is said to have replied, "Abraham Lincoln is the only God I know."

There were black people in Sacramento soon after the Gold Rush, and black people in San Francisco before the Gold Rush. The Clearlake Indians sheltered several black sailors who, along with their white mates, had fled the excessive brutality of certain Yankee sea captains. General Vallejo's brother, Salvador Vallejo, is assumed to have murdered an awol black ship's cook named Anderson Norris who had successfully sought refuge with Pomo Indians at Clearlake. And there were black people in other parts of Mendocino County, several of both sexes in Covelo alone beginning in the 1860s. There are fleeting references in local histories to Hiram Scott who is described in one of those histories as "a huge, muscular Negro" who lived in Covelo where he worked for white settlers, among them the infamous George S. White, "King of Round Valley," an early cattle baron whose ruthlessness in the Eel River back country made him a national figure of sorts, as well known for murder plots against his wives as he was for so dominating the vast semi-wilderness from Covelo north to Weaverville that for a time White agitated for his own inland county. The "huge, muscular" Scott was one of White's buckeroos, as cowboys were then called, and may have run criminal errands for his boss because thuggery was an important part of the job description for any buckeroo of whatever ethnicity working for White.

The Jeans family stayed on in Anderson Valley until 1946 when Albert Jeans, the last of the family, died at the Mendocino County Hospital in Ukiah at age 66. His brother George died at age 70 in Boonville, in 1940. The Jeans brothers are buried in Boonville's Evergreen Cemetery a mile east of the family homestead in Ham Canyon. The Jeans patriarch, Daniel Jeans, died on May 10th, 1920, in Ukiah where he is buried in the Cypress Lawn Cemetery.

Mrs. Jeans was an Indian. Only Albert and George of her five children survived into adulthood. She and three of her children died of tuberculosis when she and the children were young. Nothing is known about her except that she was an Indian married to a former slave who had two children of five who lived to be adults. The stilt house Indians would have known who she was, but who besides them would have been interested?

One of Jeans' two sons, Albert, appears in an old elementary school class picture from 1910 or so, his alert face dark among his Huck and Betsy classmates. Albert appears to be about ten in the photo. He does not appear in subsequent pictures, but he became locally infamous when, according to the Ukiah Republican of January 6th, 1926:

"Using a shotgun and causing a wound which resulted fatally 48 hours later, Albert Jeans, a colored man who lived on the road between Elk and Philo, shot his neighbor, G. Marcheschi, Sunday afternoon. There were no eyewitnesses to the crime and District Attorney J.C. Hurley is checking up the few facts he has been able to secure."

Within days this initial bulletin was supplemented by a chaste version of Jean's arrest.

"Constable Apprehends Slayer," reads the front page headline. "The murderer was arrested by Constable Buchanan after the slayer had fled the scene. It is understood the victim leaves a widow and three children at Cloverdale. After the shooting Mr. Marcheschi crawled a considerable distance along the road to the Schneider ranch before he was picked up by Ottavio Falleti and rushed to Greenwood where the injured man was treated by Dr. Sweet who advised his removal to the hospital at Fort Bragg. In the meantime, a number of coast citizens, as a result of wild rumors Jeans was on a rampage, and was shooting at everything that got within range, armed and rushed to the scene of the trouble as there were a number of unprotected families in that neighborhood.

"Upon arrival they found the Jeans cabin deserted and a shotgun and two empty shells on the floor. Later they located Mr. Jeans at the Schneider Bros. ranch where he was placed under arrest and brought to Greenwood by Constable Buchanan who lodged him in jail until the following morning when he was sent to Ukiah.

"The stories of the slayer and his victim are decidedly at variance. Mr. Jeans claims the shooting was done in self-defense and asserts his victim had fired one shot at him from a rifle before he opened fire with the shotgun. He states further that, after shooting Mr.

Marcheschi with one barrel of the shotgun the latter again raised his rifle with the intention of firing a second shot when he, Jeans, told him to drop his rifle or he would finish him. Mr. Jeans claims he had no desire to kill Mr. Marcheschi and points to the fact he shot him in the leg whereas it would have been a simple matter to have shot him through the body had he desired to inflict fatal injury.

"As far as can be learned, Mr. Marcheschi's version of the affair is to the effect the night before Mr. Jeans was in a dangerous mood and had done some wild shooting after which Mr. Marcheschi relieved him of his rifle. The following day Mr. Jeans was still in a belligerent state and Mr. Marcheschi went to the former's cabin with the idea of gaining possession of Mr. Jeans' shotgun to prevent him doing any serious damage. When within about 10 feet of Mr. Jeans the latter is said to have exclaimed, 'You fooled me last night and got my rifle but here is where I fool you,' or words to that effect, and fired. The full charge of shot entered Mr. Marcheschi's leg, inflicting a frightful wound."

The shooting occurred on the last day of 1925, New Year's Eve. Marcheschi was a bootlegger up on Greenwood Ridge where quite a number if Italian immigrants had settled. He also maintained a home and family in Cloverdale, much as latter day marijuana growers maintain dual households — one where they produce their illegal substance, the other where they manufacture respectability.

When word got around after the shooting that Albert Jeans, a black man, had shot the bootlegger, a white man, and that Jeans was still on the loose and was a raving maniac besides, lynch mob fever rose on the Mendocino Coast. Jeans was not merely taken into custody. He was hunted down and nearly hanged when he was discovered, trembling and terrified, hiding in a water tower on the Schneider ranch. The press accounts of his arrest make it sound as if the constable simply walked up to Jeans and took him into custody; in fact the constable rescued Jeans from his captors.

A white jury — Indians and other persons of color were prohibited from serving — several of whose members were ranchers from Anderson Valley who knew the Jeans family well, rendered a verdict of manslaughter, much to the disgust of popular opinion, which was then nearly as anti-Italian as it was hostile to the darker races.

"The verdict in the case of the People vs. Albert Jeans, convicted of manslaughter by a jury in the Mendocino County superior court was upheld by the appellate court. The appellate court in its decision held that while there had been misconduct on the part of the district attorney it had been corrected by Judge Preston's instructions to the jury. The appellate court stated also that Jeans was lucky to have escaped with manslaughter as the evidence warranted a conviction of murder."

Albert Jeans went off to San Quentin for ten years just as the Fort Bragg Advocate of Wednesday, July 8th, 1925, was reporting, "A beautiful ceremony and a beautiful setting over which a full moon shone, marked the open air initiation of the Knights of the Ku Klux Klan in Anderson Valley near Boonville last Saturday evening. To the casual onlooker it was solemn and impressive and the white robed clansmen, moving about in the glare of the huge fiery cross lent an air of ghostliness to the affair. Over two hundred autos loaded with those who held invitations were present. Three initiatory ceremonies were enacted on that evening: the first being the Women of the K.K.K. and second the Knights who were then followed by the American Krusaders."

At a time and a place when a black man might well have been hanged for so much as a perceived crime, and Indians could not testify against white people, and there were fewer than twenty black people in Mendocino County, Albert Jeans, a black Indian, received a sentence from a jury of his non-peers which seems to have been proportionate to his crime, an unpremeditated shooting death by a thirsty man.

Albert returned to the Anderson Valley from prison in 1935. He worked at the Clow Mill in Philo and earned a small income from an apple drier he built on the family homestead in Ham Canyon. His obituary appeared in the May 8th, 1946 edition of the Ukiah Republican Press: "Albert Jeans, colored, dead. Anderson Valley Long Time Resident Died Last Week. Graveside services were held Thursday afternoon for Albert Jeans, 67, at the Evergreen Cemetery. Reverend C.L. Goodenough officiated and Eversole Mortuary was in charge of arrangements. Mr. Jeans was a resident of this valley almost his entire life, having been employed in San Francisco for a time when a young man. He was born here December 28, 1878, and attended local schools, and although of the colored race, he numbered many of this valley's residents among his friends."

Reno Bartolomei served as Sheriff of Mendocino County for many years. His terse comment on race and class relations from the late 1920's until the early 1960s included a brief anecdote on another black resident of the county.

"I think the County was fair in the thirties and forties. Them days, people lived on honor. But them days, poor people never did get a fair shake. Colored people didn't have much chance. Joe Perry lived in Fort Bragg, and he had to leave. They accused him of burning something down, so he moved to Ukiah. When I was a deputy sheriff in Ukiah he was still working at the Palace Hotel. He was quite old. He must have left Fort Bragg in the twenties. He made a living being a boot black. Everybody, them days, used to have their shoes shined, even the women. He was the only bootblack in town. He had a girlfriend in Richmond. He went down and visited her. He would give her all this money he made. Then her boyfriend came home and he killed Joe."

And the violence characteristic of Mendocino County from its bloody assaults on Indians did not end when there were no more Indians to kill. Mendocino County has always been a violent place. Two sons of prominent early Anderson Valley families fatally met in the school yard one afternoon at the little red school house that Daniel Jeans had cleared the land for. The graceful little structure is now a museum devoted to celebrating the valley's pioneer families, most of whom do not deserve it. But the little red school house remains a landmark sight on Highway 128 between Boonville and Philo.

The Clows were ranchers, the Irishes ran a saw mill and lived in the fine big house that would later be owned by, among others, John Scharffenberger, who became a well known wine and chocolate entrepreneur. Scharffenberger settled in Anderson Valley in the late 1970s when he was in his late 20's when the valley became rich with wineries and three million dollar men — a mil for the land and the house; a mil for a small vineyard for bottles of wine with Three Mil's name on the label; a mil for Three Mil to live out his life on.

Scharffenberger arrived here with a lot more than three mil, though, and his winery made him millions more when he sold it to a French corporation. The guy was also still one person. When he became a chocolate magnate he became Scharffen-Berger, and has been two persons ever since, I guess.

But on a fatal afternoon in 1877 in the little red school house's boisterous but peaceful playing field, young A.E. Irish and young John Clow were arguing, about what nobody knew. Clow punched Irish, and Irish pulled a knife and slashed at Clow whose brother, Jim, alarmed at the sight of the knife in Irish's hand, ran up shouting, "Boys, he has got a knife!" Irish moved uncertainly backwards but threatened by Clow, cut Clow deeply above the hip. The bleeding couldn't be stanched and Jim Clow died where he'd fallen beneath the big pine that still shades the school room.

One night in the spring of 2000, less than a mile from Dan Jeans' homestead, and only a few hundred yards from the stilt house, a young Mexican named Jamie Vasquez was on his way to the stilt house when he disappeared. Vasquez apparently thought he'd been invited out to the house to see a friend, but as he and his young wife and infant son made their way in their battered Honda through the grapevines towards the stilt house, four armed men had appeared in front of the family's car and told Jamie Vasquez to get out of the car and come along with them. Vasquez was never seen again. The abducted man's wife was able to identify one of her husband's kidnappers. That man was arrested, but the only crime the DA could pin on him was being an illegal in possession of a firearm.

The missing man's best friend, also a vineyard worker, ran off as soon as he heard about his friend's abduction, and he too has never been seen since in the Anderson Valley. The liberals said, "The cops won't even look for Vasquez because he's a Mexican." But the cops had a helicopter with body heat-sensing devices in it flying low back and forth over that stretch of Anderson Creek for two full days, and they had deputies with the search and rescue crew on the ground for several days, walking the creek bed and the surrounding areas meticulously combing the wilderness of river rock and scrub brush, but they never found any sign of the missing man. The rumor went around that Vasquez owed drug dealers forty thousand dollars, but he didn't live like a man who'd ever had forty thousand dollars; he worked in the grapes and went home every night to his young wife and his son.

Where there were once hop fields and the fruit and vegetable gardens tended by the few Indians who'd survived the white onslaught beginning in 1850, and the homestead of a black ex-slave, there is now marijuana and murder. Every fall somewhere in Mendocino County somebody dies a violent death for marijuana, the peace and love drug.

Only a hundred miles north of San Francisco, Boonville's easy proximity to millions of people has led it to its present battered incarnation as a center of industrial-scale wine production and wine-related tourism or, as Gerald Casey has described this odd phenomenon: "Since moving here I've noticed that men and women who are masters of production, finance and opinion have taken an interest in wine. Setting vines in rows as they might have once arranged office cubicles, their genius is now focused on producing the world's best wines, as they know them. The genetic oddity that gives grapes their mystical potential has been isolated and cloned and set out in neat rows of grow tubes. Force-fed and scientifically watered, grafted, canopied and pruned to balance, they'll get suckered and sulfured, their ground covered, leaves pulled, and crop dropped. There's frost to be fought, hand time to hold, the brix to fix, then pick and pack, stem and press, meet the yeast, heat and cool, punch the cap, do the malolactic tactic, filter and fine, blend and barrel. Made in steel, aged in oak behind a chain-link fence, this wine has color and clarity, legs and body, feel and finish, with hints of all the fruits of the cornucopia. A number is assigned that corresponds to price, and the drink that once sent a romantic's senses tumbling back through the centuries now inspires awe among the cognoscenti appreciative of the technical achievements of the people who replaced Bacchus with Bill Gates."

One hundred years after the first description of Covelo as a resort for rogues of all sorts, two idealists whose opinions were widely characterized as criminal in the America of their time, made their last homes in Round Valley. Maybe. One did for a fact. The other, Harrison George, perhaps the outstanding figure in the history of the

Communist Party in California, and a leading figure in the history of Soviet clandestine operations in the United States and Asia, was rumored to have lived in Covelo after being removed from his responsibilities as a member of the Comintern's Pan-Pacific Trade Union Secretariat, i.e., one of the key persons responsible for agitation among Asian labor. Where George died is not known; it isn't known for a dead sure fact that he lived in Covelo, but old rumors wafting over the Mayacamas mountains say that George retreated to Covelo to lick his politcal wounds and maybe even died there.

George had been a Wobbly, or a communist assigned by the CP to sab the Wobs — that argument continues — and, later, an editor of the People's World. He was regarded as an expert on strike strategy, something he had in common with other ex-IWWs in the CP. There is a whole lode of documents in Moscow in which George complained non-stop at the purported errors of Harry Bridges and Bridges' CP allies in directing the 1934 longshore strike in San Francisco. George apparently didn't realize that he was far outranked in the clandestine apparatus by Harry Hynes, the Australian-born underground agent who was Bridges' main adviser. Hynes, who was a top KGB man, was calling the shots. Once the big strike was over George was replaced and, old whispers say, retreated to Covelo from where he vanished into history.

(An aside here to establish the devolution of trade unionism in the United States. Harry Bridges never took a pay check greater than the pay earned by his longshoremen and warehousemen. Leonard Johnson, the father of an old friend of mine, was a warehouseman in San Francisco all his life, a registered Republican, a devoted fan of Stanford football. Leonard was walking home from work one day when a modest Ford pulled up and the man at the wheel offered him a ride. That man was Harry Bridges. Today, the union leader would be in the back seat of a limo and, even if he happened to recognize one of his members waiting for a bus or trudging homeward, it is highly unlikely he'd order his non-union driver to stop for him.)

George must have known Luke Anson "Royal" Hinman, another radical who died in Covelo at age 88. Born in Sheridan, Placer County, Hinman worked as a laborer before he became active in the early 1930s in a branch of the John Reed Club, a communist cultural group. He then became an organizer in a tough campaign to unionize California cannery and agricultural workers, an effort that continues today. In 1937, Hinman went to Spain as a volunteer with the International Brigades, which were recruited to aid the elected left-wing government of the Spanish Republic against a fascist uprising that began in 1936. Hinman served in the Spanish Popular Army until the withdrawal of all foreign fighters in 1938. His combat experience included the brutal battle of Teruel, where many American volunteers were killed. Hinman was cited for bravery and was offered a lieutenant's commission, which he declined, although he was made a sergeant and attached to the battalion staff. His commitment to the forces of anti-fascist resistance remained for him the high point of his life.

Back from Spain, Hinman returned to the fields as an organizer for the old United Cannery, Agricultural, Packing and Allied Workers of America. He was arrested in 1939 for picketing during a tumultuous strike of pear and nectarine pickers against a Marysville subsidiary of the DiGiorgio Corporation. Demonstrations and further picketing led to mass arrests, and the strike became a cause celebre. Hinman was held in jail for a week before he was convicted under the now-defunct anti-picketing law, but was eventually pardoned. He later worked for the federal Farm Security Administration and then joined the International Longshoremen's and Warehousemen's Union as a dockworker. In 1943, he purchased land in Covelo, moved there and went to work at the sawmill that eventually became part of Louisiana-Pacific Corporation. Hinman retired from the mill in 1970. Covelo seemed completely unaware that an anti-fascist hero lived and died there.

There was never much radical activity in Mendocino County until the Earth First! period of 1988-1995. That agitation against the outside timber corporations then dominant in the county was led by Judi Bari, a red diaper baby from Silver Springs, Maryland, and the sister of New York Times' science writer, Gina Kolata. The original Wobblies had agitated some in the woods and the mills of the Northcoast but were never as influential as they were farther north in Oregon and Washington. There was, though, a left radical presence in Eureka and Arcata from early in the century; Mickey Lima, a well-known communist, was born and raised in Arcata.

There have always been radicals stuck away in the great vastness north of the Golden Gate Bridge, real ones, too, many of whom supported the Bari-led Redwood Summer demonstrations against corporate timber in 1990.

By the beginning of the 20th century, there were Red Finns and White Finns in Fort Bragg. Immigrant woodsmen. As they did up and down the Pacific Coast, the two starkly opposed politically-based communities maintained separate social halls and a chill social distance as well, so chill they often suspected each other of not responding to fires and other catastrophes affecting their enemy Finns.

Fort Bragg's left Finns maintained a Comrade's Club (and hall) for years, well into the 1920's, as did the Finns of Astoria, Oregon, home of two competing Finnish language newspapers serving each community — one paper for the left Finns, one for the right Finns. The editors of these publications were brought over from the mother country and could be depended on to fan the flames whose fires had been set in Finland. The competing newspapers were distributed to the Finn communities from San Francisco to Seattle.

One of the saddest pictures one will see is a photo of a group of jubilant 1917 Red Finns departing Noyo Harbor in a small sea-going ship they'd built themselves. They're waving goodbye to capitalism, sailing back to Finland and the Russian Revolution where most of them would disappear into labor camps or be executed simply because they'd lived a few years in America. A few Finns made it back to Astoria after bitter sojourns in Finland and Russia, but none made it back to Fort Bragg.

In 1946, there was a bitter, year-long strike at the Fort Bragg mill. A few communists were active in it, and the owners of the mill, the Johnson family, eventually settled, mostly on the striker's terms.

"We dreamed when we were young. We used to talk about working the woods like a big co-op. No bosses, no owners. We'd cut the trees down and mill them ourselves and sell the lumber to people to build their houses," summed up Oscar Erickson of Fort

Bragg, union organizer, who was acquitted of charges of criminal syndicalism, 1946.

And there was us — the back-to-the-landers, the hippies, the white Indians, the dreamers of rustic peace, the estranged liberals, the defeated radicals.

We were in full flight from the city because the city had become a violent, unhappy place, and when we arrived on the Northcoast, local people tended to be violently unhappy to see us descending upon them with our estranged appearances and practices. They called us all hippies, whether or not we were. I was young and certainly a hippie sympathizer, or hip-symp, because I shared many of the same antipathies — the unending war on Vietnam, the gross materialism of American society, the seething, apparently irremediable racial hatreds, the deteriorating cities of the San Francisco Bay Area, and everything else gone rancid in the land that had caused me and thousands of other young persons to head north for the country. I landed in Boonville, the Anderson Valley, Mendocino County, a three-hour drive from San Francisco.

The history of early Anderson Valley is much like the history of the rest of the Northcoast and, for that matter, America, but beginning in the late 1960s, the 3,539 square miles of Mendocino County became very much unlike any other place in this or any other country. It has since returned to what passes for normal in continuing abnormal times, but for a while there, well, there was no place like it.

I didn't return to the land to learn to live off it, not that I was competent to even try, I came to raise juvenile delinquents as one of a small group of young people who thought that young urban criminals might somehow be less delinquent under the redwoods than they were beneath street lights. A country setting would undo the damage done to them in their formative years, rewind their psychic corkscrews.

All I knew about my new home near Boonville was that the county containing it was larger than several states, and that Slim Pickens, a rodeo caller who went on to fame as a movie actor, had said that 1950 Boonville was the roughest place he'd ever called a rodeo in.

Buck Clark admits to having been an occasional participant in what he called "the fightin' and the fussin'" of the county's logging boom of the 1950s, but it never got in the way of a day's work for him.

"I started workin' when I was a kid near Monroe, Louisiana. I worked the swamps cuttin' down trees for paper mills. I made 50 cents a day. I worked out in the swamp with water moccasins and alligators. Me and my brother fall a tree then we had to float it in and around all the other trees to get it to shore. Later on, we'd make rafts of trees and float 'em down the river in big bunches. Most I ever made was $1.50 a day. Had a little ol' boat that wouldn't do but 5 miles per hour that I used to keep my rafts of logs from runnin' up on the shore.

"1930 was a dry year. The water in the swamp was way down. One day we was workin' fallin' trees when we come up on a alligator. Well, that's a place alligators hibernate and hatch their eggs. There was lots of 'em down in this particular well. We took a can of carbide, put it on the end of a stick and stuck it down in the hole. This gator bit the can of carbide right off the end of the stick and a came up breathin' carbide out of his mouth. I hit 'em one right behind the gill and killed him. That alligator was 9 foot 11 inches. That thing looked like a sea monster a smokin' pourin' out of his mouth. There was days when we would see a hundred alligators while we was workin'. That 9-footer we gave to a family who cut it up and ate it. Taste just like beef steak. If I'd a known it was that good I'd a kept it and ate it myself.

"Times then was tougher than tough! We would do anything just to survive. We'd hunt swamp rabbits, birds — mostly those big breasted robins — and we fished. We'd sell the birds to people for a nickel apiece. Things got so tough we hunted birds with bean flips (sling shots) because we couldn't afford shells for our rifles. I knew everything about that swamp. One time a rich man from somewhere out of state hired me to take him fishing. As we was paddlin' down a little side stream I saw a little 'ol water snake, harmless things, hanging up in a tree. I steered right under it and it fell right on this man. He did a back flip right out of the boat. After that he said he never wanted to see another fish or fishing tackle or fishing pole in his life.

"I was born in Texas, near the Louisiana border. We moved on into Louisiana when I was a year old, a little place called Calhoun, Louisiana, near Monroe. I lived around in there until 1946 with some time out for the war. I cut logs for paper wood, logs for pilings, and floated logs to mills that were 45 miles away from where we cut 'em. Had to learn the river and loggin' both. I got here in '46. Came out here the Brown brothers, Laster, Jay and Highpockets, whose real name was Boyce. We landed in Garberville. I fell my first redwood up there. Twelve foot on the stump. Used a drag saw that weighed about 200 pounds. Took me about six hours workin' by myself.

"I was workin' around and out of Garberville until '49. '49 was the worst year in the woods in California. No jobs anywhere. Finally, I heard of a job in Fort Ross, but after I was workin' in the mill there for six weeks it burned down. A guy in Fort Ross told me there were 21 mills in Boonville. So me and my partner drove up Highway One, come over the road from Manchester. The road at that time was real bad. Pot holes took up most of some parts. I never seen so many people in such a little place as there was in Boonville then. People everywhere. At night in the bars crew bosses was buyin' drinks and tryin' to steal men for their crews, one another's crews. People at the bars was six deep sometimes, had to pass the drinks back. You could wear corks right in the bars. Man up near Garberville was stomped to death one night with corks so you couldn't wear 'em in bars anymore.

"In Boonville, I worked peelin' logs. I set chokers. Worked up off the Manchester Road on what is now Mannix Road. Went to work for Hollow Tree in Ukiah before it was Masonite. Worked in mills. Quit the mills because I wanted to fall. My first day fallin' I made $300 and they fired me. I got enough money to get my first chainsaw — a Mercury. That thing weighed about 200 pounds without the bar and the bar was seven feet long. Worked on the Masonite Road out of Ukiah then I went back to Boonville fallin' for Blackie Lattin at Indian Creek Mill. I fell enough timber by myself to keep that mill goin' steady for five years.

"My biggest day was 71,000 feet. The biggest tree I ever fell had

50,500 foot of lumber. I made $3,100 once for two weeks fallin'. They wanted me to scale back. At the time I was workin' for Twink Charles. Twink told me, 'You're makin' more money than me and I own the mill!'

"That big tree I was tellin' you about was cut up off the Greenwood Road. Darndest tree I ever saw. It was bigger at the top than at the foot and it had huckleberry bushes growing out of it at the top. Never seen anything like it. Buster Farrer's brother, George, was the scaler then. The logging boom was over by '55. Work got a little thinner each year after that.

"I've never missed a day of work in my life due to accidents or injuries. Got hit one time not too long ago by a big ol' branch that knocked me out for a minute or so. I was smokin' then and when I come to the ash was close to the mouth end of the cigarette. That's about how long I was out. I seen lots of accidents in the woods. When all the mills was goin' they was losin' one or two men a week. I was workin' the day Danny Huey got hit by a widow maker and fell on top of his chainsaw. He was real lucky he wasn't killed that day.

"When I first got to Garberville you could buy redwood land for $4 a thousand foot. I worked for a while up in the Sierras, too. We had an old G.I. truck we could drive from job to job. Had everything in it. Freezer, too. Worked up around Chester and Quincy. Had a fight with the boss up there who just got out of the Army, and he bossed everyone like he was still in the Army. He come up on me one day and said, 'Your log is too long.' I never heard of a log bein' too long. Me and him tangled up and fell to fightin' in some blackberry bushes. The briars hurt worse that the fight! He came up the next day with a fifth of whiskey and tried to get me to stay workin' with him.

"There was something like probably 2000 fallers because they wouldn't let you single jack. Had to have two guys. Worked up around Piercy, out on the Elkhorn Road, everywhere around here. Never used a plumb bob, never will. Don't need to. I just look at 'em. Never been fooled yet. The only way you can get fooled by a tree is if the wind comes up on you.

"I started makin' split stuff when I was a kid in Louisiana. I made railway ties. When I come out here I learned to make fencing, grape stakes, beams — all kind of split stuff up in Garberville. I used to get 3 and a half cents a grape stake, $37.50 a thousand. I made 1,100 7-foot stakes once in nine hours. I've sold split stuff to people as far away as Los Angeles. Now I get $4.50 a post for seven footers for fencing. I've made bean poles for the Gowans, redwood shakes for lots of houses around here. Most all the fencing you see at Navarro Vineyards I did. In the old days people wouldn't take a sawed stake. The young guys don't do much split stuff. Too much work for 'em.

Buck points to a rusting vehicle that looks like an ancient oversized tow truck.

"This here machine will do darn near anything you ask it to do. It'll buck logs, skin 'em, skid 'em, lift'em, winch 'em, drag 'em, loosen 'em — all of it, whatever you do in the woods. I thought Ford Motor Company had stopped making them in 1938, but I was out on the beach at Navarro where I saw one working there that was built in '53. I bought this one from a midget. He's about that high. He used to log out at Hollow Tree. The midget had blocks wired onto the pedals way out so he could drive it. Me and Kay Hiatt went over to the midget's place in Ukiah and brought it back over here on the lowbed. That little sonofagun backed right on there. All it needs now to run is a new carburetor. I'm thinking about putting it into the parade this year. Mainly, they skidded logs with it. Out at Hollow Tree they skidded logs seven miles with it. They loaded shingle bolts with it, too. Its got 400 feet of cable on it. Me and Rex made 1500 posts one winter with it. We hauled the post logs right out of Bear Wallow Creek with this thing. It'll pull a big log. It's geared real low, maybe it'll go 12 miles per hour. Tops. One winter right up the road here in the park [Faulkner Park] they had some blow-overs right over the camp part. We slid them sonofaguns right out of there. They'd gone over right into the camp ground. I hauled one of the blow-overs to the Philo Saw Works. He sawed it right up for me. If I'm not mistaken, Steve Holmes drove this sonofagun over at Big River skidding logs. Put right on here and skid 'em right out of the bush! Regular old Ford motor, four cylinders runnin' since 1938. Its got no generator on it. You got to use two batteries to start her up. Heck, I need on battery to start myself up in the morning!

12 volts to start it up. The 6 keeps it going. This here windshield looks like it come off a car. She's something else, little bits of her from all over the place. Right now there might be some water in the dad-gummed gas tank. It'll run a little bit then go dead. I'm going to get underneath there and get it fixed up one day soon. I loaded a 28-foot log on my old green pick-up one time. Bob Mathias has a picture of it down in his office. That thing there will pick up a helluva load. Bob Trotter had her going one day. I looked around and this old sonofagun was standing nearly straight up! It'll work! It'll go right up anybody's hill. You could use it as a tow truck if you wanted to. See that swivel up there? It'll go thataway, thataway, thataway, thataway. I got chains for it. They fit right over both sets of back tires. You can work this thing in all kinda mud. I'm fixin' to crank it up. I could use it this place I'm working. You can take this machine, put you a block on a tree that gives you lots more power. I broke about ten feet of line off that cable one time hauling a log out with this thing. I like to skid up hill. Down hill is no good. Logs get hung up too easy. It's a good machine. Built to last."

The Boonville I found in 1970 was a somnolent, dusty, run-down, one bar, one store blip beside the road, a place sped through without so much as a glance at it by tourists on their way to the Mendocino Coast, and there weren't many of them, either. The town was dying but not quite dead. The logging boom that had made it the thrilling place Slim Pickens and Buck Clark remembered had come and gone, and had taken lots of people with it. When the mills closed, the timber people moved on. The high school had been built to accommodate 500 scholars; by 1970 there were less than a hundred students, and a hundred twenty more, maybe, in the elementary and junior high combined.

Four decades later, Boonville and the Anderson Valley have been revived, transformed not by the bar fighting rural proles who'd made it so vivid, but by the very rich who have converted it to one more stop on the gastro-booze trail, all of it made possible by immigrant Mexicans who live as they can on the valley floor while the rich, including ridgetop neighbors writer Alice Walker and second home revolutionary, professor Angela Davis, rusticate in lush, urbanized estanzas in the hills above, safe from America, safe, safe, safe from everything behind solar powered electronic gates.

The very rich include the owners of the Ornbaun Valley, the Mailliard family, whose matriarch, Charlotte, is prominent in San Francisco social circles. She's now married to the former Secretary of State, George Schultz. The Mailliards own 14 miles west from Highway 128 half-way to Anchor Bay on the Pacific. The Ornbaun Valley once supported a large population of Indians, now it supports gentleman farmer Mailliard and his weekend relatives.

Chocolate magnate John Scharffenberger lives near downtown Philo on a spread often featured in newspaper inserts celebrating gracious living. And there are computer fortunes in abundance, one of which bought a large property on the Navarro River whose acres segue into an old trail to Hendy Woods, a state park dedicated to preserving a rare stand of old growth redwood. A few years ago you could cross the Navarro on a swinging rope bridge and walk, unimpeded, unmolested, down two shady miles along the river and into the big trees at Hendy Woods, a state park.

But the present owner of the ranch, who made a fortune in electronic gadgetry, makes access to the old trail to Hendy Woods nearly impossible. He's erected an impenetrable gate at the public end of his three million dollar, all-weather vehicle bridge, a structure as carefully engineered as the Golden Gate with one pillar resting on the site of an ancient Indian village. The handful of local hikers, reinforced by white Indians upset about the sacrilegious placement of the bridge, circulate the gate combination as fast as Gadget Man can change it. Gadget Man is sabbed from within his streamside fastness.

One afternoon, having let myself in by the combination lock as if I owned the place, I was mid-bridge with my dog, Perro; we were on our way to the trail to walk to Hendy Woods. A big black Buick pulled up alongside me, its window rolled magically down and a female face with a plump 70 or so years on it appeared where the tinted glass had been. I supposed the face belonged to Gadget Man's mother. Or grandmother. Or CEO in charge of ancient affairs. Who could know?

"Get off this bridge right now!" emphatically ordered the old lady.

"I'll jump, ma'am if you'll take care of my dog."

The window instantly purred up, and the big black car drove on.

The Anderson Valley is now filled with people to whom big black cars are second homes, the pod people, the magic money people, the Gatsbys, a whole new layers of ad-sals for Taikomol to purge before the Indians can come back.

The city I'd fled in 1970 had finally caught up with me in what I thought would be the permanent sanctuary of the Anderson Valley. But I was too close to the city. The land was too cheap, the weather too good. The valley had been tardily "discovered" by the wrong people, but it went bad fast.

I thought about the rapid changes which had overtaken both Frisco and Boonville when I read a story in the Santa Rosa Press Democrat called, "San Francisco Fights Over Its Character." This from the newspaper of record in a town — "the city made for living," as the paper deludes itself, that paper which has done much to make its town one that's made for leaving, a town whose character vanished when Santa Rosa and CalTrans, at about the same time estranged San Franciscans were sniping cab lights, drilled a freeway right through the middle of The Rose City straight on through to newly built Coddingtown at the north end of town. Lately, the paper's editorials fret about gridlocked streets and wonder why remedial readers are gunning each other down in its downtown parking lots and its second mega-mall. According to the paper, San Francisco's "character" is expressed in the 2008 condition of Haight Street.

There have been obnoxious young slobs strewn up and down Haight Street for forty years because the left-lib bloc that controls the vote in San Francisco says that public intoxication and living on the streets and in the parks are guaranteed by the Bill of Rights. Which is a lot easier than taxing the comfortable to build cheap shelter and to revive the state hospital system for the armies of drunks and the drug addicted stumbling along the main drag of a major tourist destination as if they had destinations other than self-induced oblivion.

These days, the city that knows how simply confines the walking wounded to certain areas — Haight Street with its open air drug bazaar at its Stanyan end, an open air thieves market on the north side of Market at 7th; to the Tenderloin where many of the thieves live; to a few blocks in the Mission; and to the distant bantustans of Hunter's Point and Visitacion Valley, two neighborhoods far from the shopping areas of downtown where most of the shootings in San Francisco occur because the city that knows how is also the city that still doesn't care.

In the areas of contemporary San Francisco where aberrant behavior is more or less tolerated, or simply prevails through sheer numbers of aberrants, areas like Haight Street and the Tenderloin, the crime rates are surprisingly low because, it seems, every third person is an undercover cop. It's fun to watch the cops work the weekend crowds, cutting the dope dealers and the worst of the street crooks out of the herd as neatly as cowboys culling a herd of yearlings. But a lot of police effort goes into keeping street crime at a minimum in places like the Haight and the Tenderloin because both areas draw so many tourists and shoppers, and that effort, it seems to me, explains why there's no police time left over to at least try to stem the epidemic of car break-ins and other relatively minor crimes, all of it expressions of the class war gathering steam here and everywhere else in the land. When the 35-year-old single mother of a 19-year-old boy arrested for a gun murder said, "My son breaks into cars, he doesn't shoot people," she neatly summed up the state of the city's underclass, 2008.

Back in the day, I'd made minor contributions to the 1960s chaos myself, pretending to myself that my participation was more political than the pure anarchic joy that political demonstrations were for most of us.

It was a short walk to the riot sites from my grungy tenement apartment at 925 Sacramento Street. I could walk two blocks up the hill to the Fairmont and the Mark Hopkins, two preferred stops for the enemies of the people, or two blocks through the Stockton Tunnel to the Union Square hotels, where enemies of the people were also certain to be spending the night.

One night at the Fairmont may have given the feminist movement major forward momentum when the "chicks up front" seated on the curb across the street from the Fairmont took the first blows from the Tac Squad's fungo bat-length batons when the sadists in blue jumpsuits suddenly charged across the street at us dissidents massed between the Fairmont and the Pacific Union Club. The Tac Squad was selected for their size; they were all big, agile bastards who enjoyed beating people up, especially longhaired, loud-mouthed, highly irritating people like us.

We were hollering up at the impervious hotel facade for Field Marshall Ky, one of LBJ's interim Vietnamese stooges, to go home. Ky was home, as it soon turned out, melting into Los Angeles to run a restaurant rather than the second hand country he'd been looting for LBJ's blundering imperialists. That night, however, he was at the Fairmont.

Someone, probably an undercover cop grandly rechristened as provocateur by us lefties who were on perpetual alert for infiltrators, sabs, and miscellaneous running dogs although we couldn't have been better than we were at sabbing ourselves, threw a sandwich bag or a balloon full of red paint up against the implacable gray wall of the grand old hotel, monarch of San Francisco's inns.

No sooner was the paint running bright red down the hotel's great gray edifice than the Tac Squad sprinted across the street and commenced clubbing their pre-selected demonstrator of choice. The chicks up front got the worst of it because they were no sooner on their feet to flee when the clubs fell on them.

My brother and I jumped the stone wall into the Pacific Union Club. Sprinting for the relative safety of Huntington Park, we were running through the backyard of the No Jews and Certainly Not No People of Color Club when a man in the black and white checked pants and cook's hat of the kitchen worker, a bona fide member of the proletariat whose interests my comrades and I were theoretically committed to advancing, yelled, "You can't come through here!" The guy behind us straight-armed the kitchen man, sending him clattering among empty garbage cans and soon we were beyond the Tac Squad's clubs. Behind us we could hear the screams and curses of the targets of opportunity, and then things deteriorated into the usual ritual stampedes up and down the flat Nob Hill block of California Street between Mason and Taylor. They'd chase us, we'd re-group to get close enough to throw stuff at them and call them pigs, then they'd chase us again. On it would go back and forth for several hours, romanticized later in song and selective memory as Street Fighting Man. It was more like the running of the bulls, with one or two cops scattering, then pursuing a thousand middle-class book readers, most of whom had never been in so much as a fistfight.

We certainly weren't the longshoremen of 1934 in support of whom San Francisco was completely shut down. The old working class stood and fought. The 1967 working class was with the cops all the way. We represented no one but ourselves, although public opinion was beginning to oppose the war even while enjoying the weekly spectacle of us getting whacked around by the Tac Squad and their East Bay counterparts.

That night the cops batted us with their three-foot lengths of hard wood, their long fly ball bats, and we ran up and down Nob Hill streets, and very soon the worst of us, the fanatics, the true nut cases, the stone killers, the dwarf Lenins collected themselves into faux revolutionary cults like the one at Stanford run by the English professor, Bruce Franklin, Melville man and Mickey Maoist. Franklin got some of his mesmerized students killed or locked up for long periods of time while he went off to the Rutgers faculty lounge where he rests today among the scholars and the teacups. I wonder when one of these fine fat tenured radicals will finally write a true memoir of what really happened, including those murders in Santa Cruz, the one of the young escort cop outside Bakersfield, and the one of poor old Betty, the Panther bookkeeper, pulled shot to death out of San Francisco Bay.

I was a delegate representing the Noe Valley to the 1968 founding of the Peace and Freedom Party at the Richmond Auditorium; for the three days that strange assembly gathered to organize opposition from the left to the liberal's war on Vietnam, I commuted from the city to the convention with a black maniac named George, no last name. We'd pick him up on Broadway and we'd drop him off on Broadway. George was very pleasant, funny even, on the trips back and forth over the Bay Bridge. But one day, as a kind of warm-up act for Bobby Seale, George was transformed. Literally spitting into the mike, my fellow commuter said he hoped to see "every single one of you white motherfuckers strangled in your motherfucking sleep." Then he said he wanted to cut our motherfucking throats and thin-slice our mothers, fathers, grandparents, and children unto the tenth generation. As an organizing tool, a rallying cry, George's position would be a tough sell, but George received a standing ovation from the people he'd just said he hoped to murder.

I was so dumb I hadn't even realized the guy was black. I'd thought he was one of those guilt-ridden white guys who'd spent a lot of time organizing his hair into an afro in solidarity with the black struggle. On the ride back to the city that night I made sure I was the first guy into the back seat. No way George was getting the drop on me.

I still wonder if George told us his name was George to test us, to see if any of his fellow commuters, all of us white, knew that "George" was the old time racist shorthand for black men working as porters on trains. If that's what George was doing, we flunked the test, not that he was likely to have spared any of us even if we'd passed.

I never saw George after the convention, but I thought about him a few years later when the Zebra killers began snatching random white people off Frisco's streets and murdering them to qualify as Killer Angels for the Black Muslims. The Zodiac killer was also doing his part to keep up the body count, and Big Z, ironically, said he too was racking up white slaves for the next life.

It was an unhappy time, kids, and don't you think it wasn't just because the music was cool and your grandfather still smokes the bazooka.

Back at the Richmond Auditorium and the Peace and Freedom Party, Seale, the star attraction that day, announced for openers that he hated us all "as the white liberal racist dog-pigs" that we obviously were. He went on to say that although we were racist dog-pigs and a hopeless bunch of crackers, we must, nevertheless, "free Huey by any means necessary." Seale then asked, "What's wrong with picking up the gun?"

Well, for one motherfucking thing the white racist dog-pigs on the motherfucking government side have a lot more motherfucking guns, big ones, too, and they outnumber lunatics like us about

500,000 to motherfucking one. Seale closed by assuring us that he had "hate in his heart." He, too, received a standing ovation from the suicidal throng.

Eldridge Cleaver was next. The Black Panther "Minister of Information" also wanted Huey freed by any means necessary. "You're either for us or against us," Cleaver said, adding, "And we don't care if you're with us or not."

The Roberts Rules of Order Boys — and wouldn't you know we all had laminated name tags? — representing various com-cults, quickly introduced a couple of clarifying resolutions. One was simply to free Huey, the other was to free Huey by any means necessary.

Mario Savio got up to point out that "by any means necessary" could be interpreted as burning down Oakland to free one man. A couple of hundred maniacs leaped to their feet to cheer that reading of the resolution.

Robert Avakian, aka Chairman Bob, of the Revolutionary Communist Party, said Huey had to be freed, and whatever it took was fine with him. Chairman Bob compared Huey to a man being held by a lynch mob, and you wouldn't stop at killing a lynch mob to free an innocent man, would you?

Yes, as it turned out.

The by any means necessary resolution lost 227-223, but when it was amended to read, "Free Huey Newton by any means necessary which would further the black liberation movement," it passed by a 3-1 margin. The motherfucking white liberal dog-pigs had prevailed!

I was still pondering what I could do to free Huey which would also advance the black liberation movement when Huey was freed to await a new trial on cop-hunting charges. The liberals the Panthers said they wanted to garrote had put up the $50,000 bond to get Huey out of jail. Then I read that Huey was living in neo-socialist luxury overlooking Lake Merritt, had hired a bodyguard, had beaten up his elderly tailor. The great revolutionary went on to murder a black prostitute and, strung out on crack, was finally shot to death by a drug dealer. The whole pathetic show, romanticized to this day by the amnesiacs at places like KPFA, was added confirmation that the decision of thousands of disillusioned radlib hippies to move to the country was the right one.

By 1970, the hardcore nuts were rolling, many of them commuting back and forth between their city bomb factories and sympathetic communal hideouts in Mendocino, Humboldt, Trinity, and Siskiyou counties. There were 56 bombings in the Greater Bay Area in 68; 236 in 69; 546 in 1970 before the revolution ended in 1975 when the Vietnamese, all by themselves, won the war.

There are lots of people in Northern California who've put their felonious revolutionary selves in brand new packaging as Democrats. They're everywhere, these little red book cadres of 1970, running schools, practicing law, sitting as judges, one even serving as spokesperson for Jerry Brown when Brown was governor. 2008's murderous concoction of imperialism and prisons has no more loyal servants than the revolutionaries of 1968.

An anonymous poet called Ares posted a summarizing ode in the Bay Area neighborhoods where it had all gone the wrongest:

> ruling guru greybeard bards
> having new fun in yr. rolling rock renaissance
> have you passed thru the Haight
> have you seen yr. turned-on kids?
> u promised them Visions & Love & Sharing
> clap, hepatitis, fleas, begging and the gang bang
> sure, you didn't want to see the scene go that way
> but that's how the shit went down
> & i do not hear yr howl
> i do not hear exorcising demons
> u told the congress that yr. acid
> had taught us how to love
> even that blood-soaked thieving swine of a cowboy
> The Others call their president.
> is there nothing left over for the kids
> sleeping on the sidewalks
> waiting to be carried off by the bikers
> of yr. children's crusade?
> yr. disciples are dying in the streets, gurus,

u have been among the philistines too long
u have become their Spectacle.
heal the sores upon thine own bodies, prophets
yr. word has brought them as far as the Haight
can you not carry them to the seashore?
 or is it your power and not theirs which has failed?
can it be we warrior poets were right all along?
can it be all the buddhas r hollow & like the Dalai Lama
u have been sipping butter tea upon a peacock throne
as Tibetans perished in the snow?
is it not time to admit that hate as well as love redeems the
world?
there is no outside w/out inside
no revolution w/out blood

John Ross, well-known left journalist, was prominent at the
convention as the main man for Progressive Labor, a Maoist
grouplet. He was badly beaten by the Panthers for, I think, arguing
tactics with them. John was also regularly worked over by the San
Francisco Police Department who, for a time, viewed him then as
the city's Public Enemy Number One.

You'll never read this in the Santa Rosa Press Democrat, but the
famous cartoonist of the Rose City, Charles Schultz, supported the
Peace and Freedom Party's '72 presidential candidate, Doctor Ben
Spock.

It was quite a time, wasn't it?

When the hippies cleaned up and stopped being hippies in the
late 1970s, public policy in Mendocino County grew crueler in
direct proportion to the number of the formerly estranged at the
power levers. For $30,000 a year, a re-tooled flower child would
put the programmatic boots to anybody a rung down the social
ladder. Pay an old hippie with a law degree a $150,000 a year with
a package full of fringes for him and his, and he'll kill, which is
what Mendocino County's seven "liberal" judges, most of them Up
From Hippie, do five days a week every week in the Mendocino
County Courthouse and in superior courts up and down the state.
"Life without, punk, but I sure feel your pain."

Congressman Mike Thompson picked up a Purple Heart in Vietnam. He has said that when he got home a hippie spit on him. The hippies of the Northcoast, two decades removed from long hair and tie dye, voted Thompson into office and have kept him there although Thompson has been a reliable vote for war and an even more reliable vote against the environment Northcoast liberals claims to be "dedicated" to protecting. Incidentally, not a single vet was spat upon; I refer you to the definitive book on that bogus subject by Jerry Lembcke, "The Spitting Image: Myth, Memory and the Legacy of Vietnam."

Thompson is the wine industry's main man in Washington. He was instrumental in getting the ban on ozone-destroying methyl bromide delayed for five more years because the wine industry wanted to continue to use the stuff. Pumped down into the earth to depths of twelve feet, methyl bromide sterilizes the earth in site-prep for plantings of new vines. Immigrant Mexicans, upon whom the industry rests, apply not only this particular poison to the earth, but a variety of year-round poisons that kill all weeds and insects. The poisons then run off into what were once productive fish streams.

Michele Salgues, a PhD in chemistry, and the former boss at the huge, French-owned Roederer Winery in Philo, was quite candid about the realities of wine making in Mendocino County.

"Why do you think we're here? We can do things here we cannot do in France because the wine industry in France, right down to labor practices, is heavily regulated."

One bright spring morning back in the early 1970s, as clusters of hippie kids waited on Greenwood Road for the big yellow buses to carry them to classrooms as dull as the ones their alienated parents had fled for California's backwoods, a Louisiana-Pacific helicopter, spraying the freshly logged hills with herbicides to prevent non-commercial re-vegetation, accidentally doused the little Rainbows and Karmas as they stood at their bus stops beside the road adjacent to the logging site. Outraged hill hippies quickly passed a county-wide ban on the aerial application of herbicides. But within months, state Democrats, including the Northcoast's lock-step contingent, and led by mega-Democrat Willie Brown, their pockets stuffed with corporate ag cash, passed legislation which prohibited individual counties from regulating herbicides and pesticides; henceforth only the state could decide who could poison the kids and who couldn't.

Law-degreed hippies, circa 1970, were quick to note that Mendocino County's far-flung communities were served by one-day-a-week justice courts whose judges were "lay persons," i.e., non-lawyers. People living in the county's outback were happy with their non-lawyer judges because the judges lived in the community, knew the community, and were trusted to do justice by the community. Nobody in Mendocino County was unhappy with the lay judges in any organized sense of unhappiness, but the hippie lawyers, their eyesight undimmed by drugs when they realized that big, guaranteed pay days were theirs for the taking. They began to say, "The quality of justice is likely to be inferior if the person dispensing it isn't properly trained. We really should have lawyers sitting as judges in these justice courts." The law was duly changed by the preponderance of lawyers sitting in the state legislature, and the lay judges, who had sat in judgment of their friends and neighbors for a hundred years without complaint and at little public expense, were gone. In their place was a very expensive person who'd spent his youth flaunting the drug laws.

There has indeed been a dramatic change in the quality of justice in Mendocino County; it's worse, a lot worse. Not only are many more people going to jail for longer periods of time, and. where the "lay" judges cost taxpayers $300 a month for a court that convened one day a week, thus sparing outback plaintiffs and defendants alike the long trip to Ukiah or Willits, the law-degreed justice court judges cost us upwards of $140,000 a year plus fringes for them and their families, a rate of pay and a benefits package few defendants or, for that matter, citizens, enjoy. And instead of going before the law in, say, Covelo before a lay judge, you now must travel many miles round trip to either Willits or Ukiah for your day in court. Or to serve on a jury. The courts operate for the comfort and convenience of the judges and their supporting apparatuses. All of us must come to the seven of them, not the seven of them to us.

The hippie takeover of local government, and all of Mendocino County's public bureaucracies, was still a decade away in 1970 when my peculiar collective of estranged adults with our 6-pack of delinquents arrived at our leased ranch six miles south of Boonville. We thought that away from the adrenal provocations of the city our six court-certified underage criminals would somehow be restored to their pre-juvenile hall innocence, insofar as innocence can be said to exist in a country as crazed as this one; we thought we could the remake these damaged and doomed little sociopaths into more or less productive citizens, people like ourselves — book readers, organic gardeners, social philosophers, and earnest liberals. We were already fools, as the delinquents knew almost immediately, but our idiocy hadn't occurred to us until we moved in with them.

As newcomers, we had no way of knowing that we were no odder and, as it turned out, a lot less lethal than several of our neighbors, who would come to include Tree Frog Johnson, Charles Manson, Kenneth Parnell, Jim Jones, Leonard Lake and Charles Ng, and the Moonies, the last having since become so respectable that they are no longer called Moonies, publishing a daily newspaper whose flexible journalists regularly appear on Sunday morning's political talk shows. Nobody has dared called the Moonies a cult in a long time. If Manson could have hung on long enough to smooth out his ideological rough edges he might today be sitting in the state assembly as wine country's elected rep instead of a prison cell. There have been Love Generation transformations nearly as improbable.

But in 1970, the Moonies, formally known as the Unification Church, were still considered a roving menace to America's unmoored youth. Moonie proselytizers would haunt the bus stations and airports of Oakland and San Francisco where they'd pitch the wandering backpack kids, "Come with us for a free weekend at our beautiful New Ideal City in Boonville where we live a life of love and good works."

From where we were established six miles south of the New Ideal City with our "troubled youth" — pick your euphemism — troubled youth; juvenile delinquents; junior psychos; hopeless cases — the Moonies' hypnotic chanting reached us in eerie waves, like a late night car radio whose signal fades in and out.

The New Ideal City was a collection of sheep sheds, leaky barns and old chicken coops strewn over a hundred acres of hillside just south of Boonville into which literally hundreds of duped recruits were stuffed, scrupulously separated by gender, while their zealous minders herded them, sleepless, from one group activity to another, love bombing the susceptible into lives of volunteer work for a Korean electrical engineer who said he was God. The Moonies' Boonville zombo-izing mission was finally shut down by the county because, even by Mendocino County's then mostly non-existent standards, so many people in one place without adequate water or a functioning sewage disposal system represented a health hazard.

Reverend Moon was compelled to move his NorCal recruiting operations south to a Sonoma County site, this one complete with modern facilities. The Moonies converted their Boonville ranch to a chinchilla farm run by a naturalized German married to a naturalized Italian in one of Moon's famous mass weddings, bride and groom being selected seemingly at random. Local teenagers who worked with the little beasts often spirited them out of their temperature-controlled stalags, brought them home, and gave them away to their friends. (If you've never seen one, a chinchilla is a better-looking but bad tempered version of a guinea pig.) The Moonies sold their pelts to haute designers for women's coats.

Mendocino County was the last county in the state to file a general plan. Much as they hated hippies, there was nothing the supervisors could do about all those undesirables up in the hills building their dream houses their own way outside what the Board of Realtors considered appropriate shelter for a modern American. When conservative supervisors railed about hippies all they could do was rail because there was no legal framework, in the sense of an enforceable building code, to order the hippie shacks knocked down and their owners chased back to wherever they came from. Supervisor Cimolino (Fort Bragg) would say, "I think it's about time we sent some bulldozers up those back roads." Those back roads were cul de sacs and housing associations in another twenty years, but Cimolino, like so many "straights" of the time, took the hippies personally. He wanted them out the day before they got here.

The Manson Family lit down near Navarro where they rented a house from an old timer with a strong aversion to hippies but a much greater love of pornography and young women. Manson traded his girls for rent while word went round the valley's more adventurous youth that they could buy marijuana from the hippies on Gschwend Road. A few years later, marijuana was Mendocino County's number one export crop; the county's commissioner of Agriculture, Ted Erickson, was fired for not only saying so but saying so in print in his annual ag report to the supervisors.

Manson himself was arrested and booked into the Mendocino County Jail where he was held while the sheriff's department investigated a puzzling murder south of Ukiah in which a mother and her teenage daughter were hacked to death one afternoon. They had no enemies. It was your generic senseless crime. The cops couldn't link Manson to the killings, so he was released to go on to grander slaughters in Los Angeles.

Alvie Price was a woodsman whose long working life began when big trees were still being cut down by two men on each side of a big hand saw to, well, the Manson Family settling in just down the road. Alvie spent most of his life in Navarro maybe a hundred yards from the roadside grove of redwoods locally known as the "drunk tree" after the convivial group of old loggers who'd gather there every day for lubricated discussions of current events and local personalities.

During a mad period of my life when I got swept up in the running craze, I'd jog from Boonville to Navarro to get in shape for marathons. One morning, in a heavy spring tule fog, I appeared in an exhausted sweat at the drunk tree where I was greeted by Rob Bloyd, a gruff old-school woodsman, "What the hell are you doin'?" the old man demanded. "You look like a goddam Stanley Steamer comin' up out of the fog on me like that." I said I'd just run down from Boonville. "Buuuullllshit! That's humanly impossible. Well, what the hell. You got me feelin' like some exercise. I think I'll jog on over to the store and get me some wine."

Navarro has always been a thirsty place. On April 3, 1880, an hospitable man named Hammerland killed his wife and a man named Frank Olson less than two hundred yards from the drunk tree. Hammerland, his wife and their two small children lived in a very small shanty consisting of one room and a shed kitchen. They were poor people, kept poor by their fondness for drink.

The entire family occupied one bed. About a year before

Hammerland killed him, Olson was taken into the family whose overcrowded bed he climbed into every night along with the four Hammerlands. On the night of the killing the three adults ran out of beer before their thirst was quenched. Mr. Hammerland volunteered to walk over to the hotel bar for a fresh bucket of suds. If the kids hadn't already been fast asleep, the beer run would have been their task. Hammerland set off, but he lingered at the bar, enjoying a few glasses before heading home. When he got back he found that his year-long house guest, Mr. Olson and Mrs. Hammerland with him, had retired, and were now sound asleep in the communal bed, the children with them, the four of them snoozing away.

Mr. Hammerland never was able to say what set him off. It may have been the suspicion that Olson had come to believe that Hammerland's hospitality included access to Mrs. Hammerland. Or maybe Hammerland was upset that his boarder and his wife had rudely drifted off into dreamland rather than wait up for him. Whatever set him off, Hammerland ran for his logger's ax with which he quickly reduced his wife and his lodger to kindling as his two children ran screaming into the night. On July 12th, a little more than four months later, Hammerland was sentenced to eleven years at San Quentin. It is not known what became of him and the two Hammerland children.

Navarro has seen many incarnations, most of them benign, and Alvie Price saw many of them.

"The old school was too small so just before the war, around 1912-13, the new one was built on Wendling Street. There were 91 kids here in Navarro. I was two years old at the time of the quake. My mother and father told me it knocked everything clean off the walls, including a big clock of ours that took a long time to get fixed. My dad had just got out of bed when it hit. (Maurice Tindall, 16 at the time of the big one, was on a hunting expedition high up on Vinegar Ridge above Philo. 'I was already awake to get an early start on the deer. When it all started to rumble and move, I looked out over the valley and all the trees were swaying like they were in an underwater sea.') The water from the old soda springs was wonderful. It had so much carbonation in it that you could put vinegar or wine in it and the water would bubble right up over the

rim of your glass. The spring was covered up when they changed
the creek bed behind today's post office, in 1937. The first mill was
a shingle mill right on the same site where the old Navarro mill was
for years, just west of town here. Most of the shingles went out to
the coast then on to ships for San Francisco. In 1937 was when logs
were first hauled out of here by truck. Before that logs were hauled
by horse teams, mostly 4-horse teams, some 5-horse and rail. Walter
Gschwend had a 6-horse team to pull his 16-foot bed wagon. His
was the biggest team I remember. The horse teams would haul the
logs out to Albion and the logs would be sent down the coast by
boat.

"I went to work in the woods when I was 14. I started right out
fallin'. In those days you worked the woods year round, stayed out
in camps. We'd only stop working when the wind came up. I was
lucky, never had an accident in 50 years. The work slowed way
down during The Depression, especially from '29 to '31 when the
woods were closed down. The best a man could do then was a dollar
a day. There wasn't any welfare. Once a month the County would
send over a wagon with 50-pound bags of wheat. Unemployed
people would get one bag of whole wheat for a month. That's all.
Lots of people hunted and fished to get by.

"The mill was going strong, top wage was 37 cents an hour in
1924, 25, 26, along in there. There must have been about 300 people
living here then. Everywhere there was a house, you had a bar. You
could get a half gallon of wine for fifty cents and a fifth of whiskey
for 75 cents. No one had the real stuff, though, made their own. All
bootleg. The Italians would get grapes out of Sonoma County and
bring 'em up here to make wine out of. Around 1920 we had seven
whores right here. They'd come in and leave, come in and leave. Go
on up to Fort Bragg after bein' here.

"There was a landing at Christine, a little place just the other
side of where Bobby Glover's place is now. There was as many as
125,000 railroad ties there at one time before they were shipped by
boat down south. They used to call Navarro Dago Town because
there were so many Italians living here then. My old friend Joe
Pardini worked the mills, didn't know a word of English when he
got here. They built the Navarro Hotel in 1907. You bet you could

get good food there. It burned down in 1944, I think it was. There were seven hotels here at one time, the biggest one had two stories. And we had 27 saloons. You could get a half-gallon of beer for 5 cents, if it didn't blow up on you. That first home beer was wilder than hell!

"My house was built in 1907. We bought it and the acre it sits on in 1924 for $1,000. That was a lot of money then. The oldest buildings in Navarro are about from that time, 1907 or thereabouts. The big old house on Wendling was built by the company superintendent of the Albion Lumber Company, man by the name of Ed Dusenberry. He lived in that big old house by himself and his Chinese cook. Herman Schmidt built the store in 1924 but the company had a store and ran him out of business. If you bought from Schmidt, and the company found out about it, they'd cut off your credit. I believe Schmidt wound up over in Lake County where he did pretty well."

Alvie Price also remembers a little mill town just down the road which, like many once thriving little towns in the county, has disappeared almost without a physical trace, and when the last children of the last people who lived there are gone, Hop Flat won't even be a memory.

It was west of Navarro, near the 1964 high water mark, a bustling community complete with post office, a school and even its own telephone exchange even though telephones were still new to America. Hop Flat was a kind of suburb of Navarro when Navarro itself was large enough to support three hotels and a round-the-clock brothel.

Hop Flatters are remembered as hard working people "who danced every night 'til midnight and then fought each other until the sun came up and it was time to go to work." The town boomed when the big mill at Navarro boomed and died when the big mill died with the end of World War Two.

Situated in a leisurely bend of the Navarro river, and almost hidden by that perpendicular point of upthrust rock which still rises 200 feet above the river bed, Hop Flat was spread out along the slopes above the Navarro less than a stone's throw from the white stenciled high water memorial the traveler marvels at on that pinnacle today. "The Navarro River got all the way up there? That high?" In Humboldt County the big rains of '64 killed whole towns bigger than Hop Flat.

When winter floods forced the Hop Flatters who lived right on the Navarro out of their homes, they moved in with their neighbors higher up the hillside. When the river dropped and the sun came out, the Hop Flatters scrubbed their floors free of silt, lit a big, drying wood fire in the stove, and moved back in.

The banks of the Navarro River, which overflows almost every winter, especially at its narrow juncture where Hop Flat was unaccountably situated, would seem an unlikely place to build a town, but Hop Flat was up and humming in the flood plain by 1880. The village, like a rainy day mushroom, simply seemed to appear, established by tough, resilient, resourceful families who worked the woods for the Navarro Lumber Mill and its adjacent railroad that ran up through Hop Flat to Comptche, and then on to its terminus at Albion where the mill's lumber, and usually a few passengers, were loaded onto schooners bound for San Francisco.

The town got its name from the many weekend dances, or "hops" held there by the exuberant loggers and mill workers and their lively families. The 200-foot cliff where the Navarro River crested in the famous downpour of December 22, 1964, looked directly out at these spirited gatherings and the town hosting them. As late as 1970, there was a white post with "Hop Flat" lettered in black on it, and a small sign, also of wood, that said "Ray Gulch R" which marked the site of the railroad that ran up the canyon, but they're gone, and even if they survived who would believe that that narrow bend of the Navarro once rang with happy laughter and the merry sounds of fiddles?

Wholly a creature of the early timber industry, Hop Flat was reached by the also long-gone train that ran from Christine, on the Boonville side of Navarro, up through Comptche and on out to Albion where passengers and lumber would make sea connections for points north and south. If you were a passenger on the old railroad, you rounded the high water bend on what is now Highway 128 and burst into the throng and hustle of a tiny town, and just as quickly Hop Flat was lost to view when the railroad took another turn, meandered through Ray Gulch and on up to Comptche.

If the train lingered at Hop Flat, the most imposing building a passenger would see was the tannery, then the surprisingly large, pleasingly ornate hotel, and next door to the hotel a post office and a small structure housing a telephone office and a laundry. And there was the one-room school house in which all the town's hopes were invested, as they were then invested in every hamlet of the Northcoast. The rest of the village was comprised of neat little dwellings surrounded by carefully tended gardens.

When they couldn't find any other housing, single mill workers stayed at the Hop Flat Hotel not far from the barn that sheltered the bull teams that hauled the logs from the woods to the railroad. There were several cookhouses, each of them presided over by a Chinese cook.

The famous dance hall was unromantically, and odiferously, located in a large room over the tannery vats. These much anticipated events temporarily helped the revelers forget how hard and for how little they worked, and when the work ended, the Hop Flatters and their music moved on to new stands of timber, and there hasn't been a song sung in the high water place since, but the descendants of two generations of Witherells, Mains, Grants, McCartys, Hargraves, Quinns, Andreanis, Devers, Kings, Freemans, Whiteds, Simpsons, Stumps, Linscots, Rileys, Shirles, Bradburys, Franklins, and Dyers, if they pause on a still night at that unlikely bend in the road where the river one December night 1964 ran higher than it ever had, they might hear laughter, and fiddles playing the old songs fast in time with dancing feet.

From the establishment of the first lumber mill at Mendocino in 1853, fires periodically destroyed much of San Francisco which, tragic as they were for San Francisco, provided a large impetus for Mendocino County's fledgling timber industry, hence the mills of Anderson Valley as the loggers worked their way inland from the coast, hand mowing the giant redwoods as they went. Sailing ships called dog schooners, many of them built at Fairhaven, a small town near Eureka, carried lumber to the large ports from tiny landings on the Mendocino coast called "dog holes" because they were so small the sailors said that a dog could hardly turn around in them.

The Wawona, a Yosemite Indian word for Spotted Owl, was a

lumber schooner built in Fairhaven in the late 1800's. The Indians believed the Spotted Owl was the guardian of the forests. Indians, however, were unlikely to appreciate the irony of a lumber schooner being called after their sacred bird, but they might be somewhat mollified when Spotty was revived as a talisman wielded by environmentalists, many of whom regard themselves as white Indians. The white Indians say if an area of forest is home to the owl, it is relatively healthy. No Spotty, no health.

Beginning in 1880, ship builders installed boilers on the old schooners, which meant that the new hybrid sail and steam vessels could now get up and down the California coast faster and mostly on time. Prior to the installation of the boilers, a sailing schooner, if the winds were right, could get from Fort Bragg to San Francisco in 15 hours. If there were no winds, the voyage might take a month.

The schooners were retired by the time of The Great Depression and they, along with the many dog hole ports and the little Hop Flat towns that went with them in all those numerously improbable inlets from Bolinas to Crescent City, were gone.

The late Joe Scaramella remembered the schooners and how vital they were to Point Arena.

"Lumber schooners made Point Arena a regular point of call. One came on Wednesday and the other came on Friday or Saturday. There were two per week. That was also the way for passengers to go San Francisco. If you went by stage it would cost you $6.00 as compared to $5.00 on the schooner; that dollar meant something in those days. And the stage was one of those one-horse stages. You were on the road all day and part of the night. It took you a long time to get all the way down to the city. You had baggage and so forth so most people would go by boat unless they got so deathly sea sick that they couldn't possibly stand the boat.

"Just like the airplanes of today, once in a while a ship would go down, but they were pretty reliable. It was a little dangerous to go bouncing around out there, of course. You could get on the schooner here in late afternoon or early evening and the next morning you'd be in San Francisco. You got a berth and meals. The meal you ate provided you weren't too sick to eat. People blamed that Australian activist, Harry Bridges and the San Francisco longshoremen, for stopping it by their strikes for higher pay. But, hell, the thing was declining. It's like today, timber is declining, the logs are gone. You can't keep blaming individual people for big changes like this.

"Business was highly competitive in those days. People who had business rivalries got quite intense. There was a hotel here in Point Arena that has since burned down run by a man by the name of Gaines. Then there was the old Point Arena Hotel run by a man named Davison. They both had teams of horse-drawn wagons, and they knew when the schooner was scheduled to arrive. So whenever a load of passengers and the whistle blew they took off in their teams to see who could get to the wharf first to get those passengers. That was the rivalry, to see who could get there first."

In 1911 the Skunk rail line running between Willits and Fort Bragg linked the Mendocino Coast to the north-south rail line running between San Francisco and Eureka. By 1935, lumber was moving from Northcoast mills mostly by train, with a few trucks toting an increasing share of the load. Then the trucks replaced the trains and logs, lumber and the rest of us have been on the road ever since.

Time was accelerating, and vast Mendocino County was less and less the isolated, anarchic place it had been since 1850. But anarchy, this time with a laff track, re-established itself with the arrival of the back-to-the-landers beginning in 1968.

As the hippies established themselves in the empty, logged-over hills of the Northcoast, and began cultivating annual cash crops of marijuana to pay their mortgages, the annual fall pot robberies, many of them deadly, also began.

Robert Salisbury, aka, Rainbow, 33, was held up in his Manchester Road home one morning about eight by armed intruders. Rainbow told Mendocino County Sheriff's deputy Keith Squires that he had answered an early knock at his door to find a young, attractive blonde woman asking for assistance with her pick-up truck, which she said had run out of water. Rainbow gave the young woman an empty container and suggested that she help herself to the water in Rancheria creek just below his home. The woman soon returned with the water, whereupon Rainbow accompanied her to the truck, which was parked at the entrance to his driveway with its hood raised. Rainbow described the vehicle as an older model white Chevrolet pick-up. As Rainbow and the young woman approached the vehicle, two men emerged from behind it, one holding a pistol, the other a rifle. These men were described as "biker types" in their mid-to-late twenties.

The two men and the woman marched Rainbow back into his house where they tied him to a chair with Rainbow's psychedelic neckties. One of the men told Rainbow, "You know what we want!" Rainbow, at first recalcitrant, was jabbed in the leg with a knife and one of his ear lobes sliced to draw blood. The two men, apparently inspired by the popular movie, Chinatown, also flicked Rainbow's nose with the knife point and threatened to "cut off your hippie-ass toes and fingers" if Rainbow didn't produce the cash and marijuana they were looking for.

Rainbow produced $40,000 in cash and several pounds of processed weed. The bandits also helped themselves to a wood stove, a stereo, carpenter tools, and a chainsaw. Rainbow said the intruders were in his home from 20 to 30 minutes. When the robbers went briefly outside, Rainbow was able to free one of his arms from his prisoner's chair, but no sooner had he done that than his tormentors reappeared, this time to tie Rainbow even more securely to his chair before sending it and its pinioned occupant flying backwards with a crash. The invaders were chuckling as they left Rainbow's house for the last time, pleased at the spectacle of their upended victim. On their way out to the Manchester Road from Rainbow's cabin, the thieves slashed all the tires on Rainbow's two vehicles.

A white, older-model Chevrolet and a smaller, perhaps foreign-made car were subsequently seen hurtling east toward Boonville at what the police said were "excessive speeds."

Rainbow soon freed himself and made his way to a neighbor's house to call the Sheriff's Department. Although they were not disguised, Rainbow said he did not recognize any of his assailants, whom he described as a white male adult, 6'1" with short red hair and beard; an Asian male, 5'10" with black hair worn in a long queue running down his back, and a white female adult 5'9" and 140 pounds. All the suspects, he said, were in their mid to late 20's.

Several people living in Rainbow's Manchester Road neighborhood moved into town for a while.

Marijuana-related robberies would become commonplace everywhere on the Northcoast, as would pot-related murders. Every fall someone dies in a pot field or during a pot-related robbery. Every fall at harvest time there's a palpable tension in the little cabins in the hippie hollows of the Northcoast. By 1975, with so many people dependent on the drug culture for annual cash, and with the wholesale price of Mendo Mellow ranging from $5,000 to $7,500 a pound, an outlaw culture, begun by the original back-to-the-land-non-criminal hippies, came to prevail.

Did the rednecks of 1970s Mendocino County present an ongoing menace to people unlike themselves as the hippies said they did? No. The redneck's erotic imaginations were stimulated by the perceived sexual availability of hippie chicks, and the hippie drug of choice — marijuana — caught on fast among all sectors of the indigenous population, especially the working class and the young. The 'necks did woof occasional insults, though, like the time I was walking by the Boonville Lodge with a black kid who was nearly 7 feet tall, a majestic visual anywhere and certainly one in Boonville. A scraggly character was exiting the Boonville Lodge just as we passed.

"Goddam!" he yelled, rubbing his eyes in mock disbelief. "Either I'm drunk or I'm looking at a 7-foot nigger!" He laughed and disappeared back into the black hole of the bar.

The Lodge was a fighting bar then, an unwelcoming brick bunker fronting the highway. It seemed to radiate hostility even before one entered the stark murk of its interior where the hostility, to outsiders especially, instantly became real. For us newcomers, getting accepted among the younger locals to the point where we could come and go unmolested at the Lodge was a kind of rite of passage.

The first time I'd visited the Lodge I was unaware that Boonville was an identifiable community, let alone one with a high school, a secret lingo called Boontling, and a long history of interesting people and events, many of them violent or bizarre. On my very first recreational outing to the Boonville Lodge a voice belonging to someone I couldn't quite make out in the cave-like dark of the place had yelled out, "What are you looking at, four eyes?" I bought a six-pack to go and got out.

Another night a burly young man who'd overheard me say something he didn't like said, "You talk like the man with the paper asshole." That was another golden oldie. Hadn't heard it in years, maybe since the early 1950s. Boonville 1971 seemed lost in one of time's more obscure hidey holes. That particular night had passed in an alcoholic blur of astonishing events: the female bartender had plopped her large breasts on the bar and had demanded, "Which one's bigger?" There were several head butting contests and a young man had emerged from the men's room brandishing a urinal cake and had then taken a large bite out of it as he shouted, "Try this, you bastards!"

I was on my way to the Lodge one Saturday morning to pick up a six-pack for later that night when the bar's door suddenly banged open and a small, wiry young man came flying out, running for his life down the middle of 128, hellbent south for Cloverdale, or whatever sanctuary came first. Right behind him came a very large, muscular, shirtless man with a broken off pool cue stuck so deeply into his back it vibrated without coming loose, as a thin stream of deep red blood ran down into the big man's Levi's. No way the bull could catch his matador, and back into the Lodge the wounded beast went, the pool cue still quivering in his back like a picador's lance.

In the summer of 1984, there occurred a pivotal Lodge event with both real and symbolic implications for the greater community. It was a soft summer Saturday morning, but Mexicans were already being recreationally heaved through the Lodge door out into the street. The door would bang open and here came an airborne Mexican. The tough guys were Mexican-tossing. When a Mexican entered the bar, a few seconds later he came flying back out. Three or four Mexicans kept walking back in. These same determined individuals had already been heaved through the door several times; the raucous laughter from inside the bar could be heard across the street at the post office.

The Mexicans were supposed to drink down the street at a place called Mary Jane's or The Mexican Bar. Mary Jane was a formidable Spanish-speaking woman sympathetic to the area's first immigrant laborers who suffered from extra-low wages, marginal housing, insults, and random humiliations including the Mex-Toss as it was being played out this day. Mary Jane had opened her business because she knew Mexicans weren't safe at The Lodge. And she was married to a Mexican. Her roots went deep in the Anderson Valley, maybe as deep as the Feliz land grant ranchero at Hopland because Mary Jane was part Indian and her family went way back. She knew what it was like to be on persecution's receiving end.

She was a tough one, too. One night at her Boonville home a few steps from her bar, Mary Jane shot her estranged husband to death, hitting him with one perfect round right between the eyes after he'd snuck into Mary Jane's bedroom and she'd awakened, she said, to find him arrayed in the rafters above her bed, about to drop on her as she slept. Mary Jane told Deputy Squires that she'd "heard something moving around above her," grabbed her bedside pistol and plugged her ex, making him a double ex with an exclamation point right there in the middle of his forehead. Down he'd come in a dead heap.

The Lodge could be unsafe for Mexicans, but Mary Jane's "Mexican Bar" wasn't always safe for Anglos either.

Arturo Flores might be Boonville's least known serial killer. In 1987, Flores would tell his friends that "all anglos should be exterminated." Then he exterminated one. Maybe he'd exterminated others, too, but we knew from the cold, dead fact of Gregory Evans, a 27-year-old softball player from Rohnert Park, that Flores exterminated Evans because two men saw Flores do it. That was twenty years ago, and Flores got away with it. He got away, too.

You'd see Flores around Boonville at all hours of the day and night. Couldn't miss him. He was tall for a Mexican, lean, knotty lean, hard lean, and he stared a big-eyed stare right at you, unblinking, not hostile exactly but homicidally indifferent, a vacant-eyed psycho-stare, a pitiless panopticon. Vehicles, people, dogs, insects disappeared into those eyes. You got the feeling that Flores wanted to kill it all.

Some people thought Flores was crazy. Others were merely unnerved by him. "That Mexican creeps me out big time," someone would say. "Does he sleep standing up? He's always here," another person would say. There he was, a constant staring public presence, a brooding human surveillance camera, leaned up against the wall of the Lodge or Tom Cronquist's cyclone fence downtown or the Anderson Valley Market, never saying a word to any anglo body, not much to his countrymen, always staring that blank stare that somehow seemed to go blanker at the gringo visuals.

Of course it is better than likely that Señor Flores had had unhappy encounters with gringos some of whom, as described, amused themselves by heaving Mexicans out the door of the Boonville Lodge like so many bags of pinto beans. Mexican-tossing finally ended the memorable afternoon the Mexicans counter-attacked, beating down the locked door of the bar with half a telephone pole; the Mexican tossers had barricaded themselves inside the bar when fed up Mexicans suddenly appeared outside the bar in seriously angry numbers.

When a contingent of riot-geared deputies arrived from Ukiah, the Mexican assault force was inside the bar where a replay of the Alamo was underway. A small group of Mexican-tossers was backed up in a corner where they were beating back their attackers with pool cues and bar stools. Another gringo — a fat, strong one — was all-fours on the floor with a determined a Mexican riding El Porko's bucking back, sawing away at the big man's enlarded throat with a knife not quite sharp enough to penetrate the suet. "His fat and his arm strength saved him," a deputy commented later. "The Mexican couldn't cut all the way through the neck because the guy was able to scrunch up tight enough to keep the knife from penetrating. He was starting to fade, though. Another minute or so and the Mex would have had him sliced and diced."

Boonville was a hard place for Mexicans in the late 1970s. Arturo Flores didn't bother making distinctions between gringos. He hated them all.

The night Flores launched his gringo eradication program, assuming he hadn't already notched one or two before he touched down in the "bucolic Anderson Valley," as it's inevitably described in the wine and food pages of contemporary newspapers and magazines, Anastacio Yanez and Luis Orozco had met Greg Evans in the Boonville Mexican bar. Yanez and Orozco had watched

Evans drive in the winning run in a Boonville slo-pitch softball tournament across the street at the Mendocino County Fairgrounds. It was the first tournament of the year, and the weather was in and out; it rained a little, the sun came out, it rained a little more, the sun came out. That night it rained steady and hard.

Yanez and Orozco said Evans was drinking a lot of beer before he left the Cantina. They said they next saw him outside the bar trying to flag down cars for a ride somewhere. When Evans saw Yanez and Orozco walk out of the Cantina he asked them for a ride to Ukiah. Evans said he'd pay them for the ride. Yanez said he was going to Ukiah anyway so Evans didn't have to pay him.

Yanez said later that "Evans was a very good person."

Yanez invited Orozco and Flores to drive with him to Ukiah in his Ford Pinto. Yanez said he was headed to Ukiah for a dance. Flores and Orozco climbed in the back. Yanez got behind the wheel, Greg Evans rode in the passenger seat, which Flores may have seen as an undeserved concession to the gringo or, worse perhaps to Flores, gringo-hood's assumed front seat privilege.

Yanez said Evans was "friendly" during the trip over the hill. He said that he and Evans hit it off so well that Evans offered to introduce Yanez to some bimbitos in Ukiah. (Bimbito, n. 1. Spanish for bimbo. 2. Loose woman short in stature. 3. Bi-lingual welcome wagon specializing in intimate trans-national relations.)

Yanez said that Evans gave him a card with Evans' name and address and telephone number on it. Evans and Yanez chatted as best they could in mutually unintelligible languages all the way up and over the Ukiah hill until the carload of merrymakers was about five miles from Highway 101 and Ukiah's whoop de doo night life, which is widely assumed by the young to be more exciting than Boonville's merely whoop de.

Gregory Evans suddenly threw up his hands and exclaimed, "I'm sorry, I'm sorry!" Whatever Evans thought he'd done to be sorry about, it was neither audible nor visible to either Yanez or Orozco. Flores, seated directly behind Evans had suddenly reached over the seat and driven a knife blade deep into Evans' heart. Evans said he was sorry and then he was gone.

Orozco asked Flores why he'd done it. "This is nothing," Flores said. "These guys we have to exterminate."

Yanez and Orozco couldn't have been too upset about the murder of the Rohnert Park softball player because the three amigos dumped Evans' body about a foot off the pavement of Stipp Lane, then drove the short distance to a Mexican bar on North State Street to recommence their Saturday night festivities. In the men's room of the bar on North State, Yanez said he saw Flores wash the blood off the folding knife he'd murdered Evans with.

Evans' body was discovered by a passing motorist at about 11 p.m. only a few hours after his final apology. Evans hadn't even been dragged into the bushes, just let's get outta here dumped on the side of the road.

Flores, Yanez and Orozco saw the cluster of police and police vehicles as they drove back to Boonville.

Yanez and Orozco said their fear of Flores prevented them from voluntarily turning themselves into police. They didn't say that Flores had threatened them; he didn't have to. After all, Yanez and Orozco were fresh off a first-hand demonstration of Señor Flores' apparent lack of impulse control.

There being few secrets in the Anderson Valley, and the few secrets that aren't in general circulation being fully known by Deputy Squires, the three Mexicans were arrested three days after Gregory Evans said he was sorry. Orozco and Yanez quickly agreed to tell all in exchange for immunity from prosecution. Their stories matched, and Yanez and Orozco were released from custody. Flores was arrested and more or less confined to the County Jail to await trial.

The Mendocino County Jail was rather loosely administered in the middle 1980's. An inmate was caught boffing a female jailer in a broom closet, and tennis balls stuffed with marijuana frequently sailed into the prisoner's outdoor commons by dope missionaries passing by on Low Gap Road. The day before he was scheduled to be arraigned for exterminating Gregory Evans, perhaps while inmates scrambled for a pot ball, Flores vaulted the jail fence out onto Low Gap and hasn't been seen since.

The old timers called all us new arrivals of the early 1970s "hippies" regardless of our relative commitments to drugs, promiscuous sex, bad housekeeping, and George McGovern, the whole package being Boonville code for "menace." The first time the hippies, as an organized force, fought the old timers occurred when the hippies combined to oppose an upscale, over-sized, time-share housing project proposed for Navarro by a San Diego investment group. Us hippies having just arrived, we wanted to keep the valley as we'd found it — condo-free.

It was a clear split. The old timers were mostly for the development, the hippies against. Of course many of the old timers were for the development simply because the hippies were opposed to it, and lots of hippies were opposed to it simply because the old timers, or rednecks, were for it.

The old timers also had the attitude that community seniority gave them exclusive rights over what did or did not happen in the Anderson Valley. They were citizens, we weren't. To the old timers, these long-haired libertines suddenly among them, or whatever they were, represented walking insults to all right thinking persons, and who the hell did these freaks think they were, coming in here and complaining about everything? The old timers had been in the valley all their lives, and by god they weren't going to be pushed around by a bunch of unwashed communists who just got into town yesterday.

The high school gym was packed for a meeting called by the would-be developers who anticipated the event as a show of relative strength. The developers had apparently been assured that the only opponents to their faux-Aztec piles of sterile boxes at the northwest end of the valley were a few stoned malcontents who would realize how isolated they were when the true community assembled in one place.

But the hippies turned out in such numbers that they took up one whole side of the gym while the old timers, glowering on the other, seemed surprised that there were now enough hippies in the Anderson Valley to oppose bad ideas, and this thing proposed for Navarro by the San Diego condo gang was a very bad idea for many reasons beginning with its overwhelming size and the impact the monstrosity would have on the battered, overdrawn Navarro river.

The old timers cheered the developer's rep, a glib young man who emphasized what an economic boon the condo plan would be to an area perennially short of jobs. The arguments went back and forth, as did groans from the opposing sides at the more provocative statements by each.

But then there was a dramatic and major defection from what the old timers saw as their side, the right side, in the form of an old, old timer named Cecil Gowan who tottered up to the mike and, looking directly at the old timer's side of the gym said, "As a lot of you people know, the Navarro dries up most summers. There's not near enough water for a development as big as this one. I'm against it."

Doubling his apostasy, the old man slowly made his way to the hippie side of the gym and sat down among The Enemy. The hippies cheered and beat their feet on the wooden bleachers.

The old timers were silent, many of them undoubtedly thinking, "Doesn't the old fool know this isn't about water? It's about Us against Them!"

No sooner had Gowan been embraced by the hippies than Myrtis Schoenahl, a formidably large woman unaccustomed to defeat, walked briskly to the microphone. Mrs. Schoenahl glared at the hippie side of the gym before she yelled into the mike, "Can you hear me?"

A few people on the hippie side of the gym cringed in mock terror at the aural assault. A long hair shouted, "No! Louder!" The hippies laughed. Even a few old timers couldn't help chuckling.

Mrs. Schoenahl got right to the point.

"This is really very simple," she said. "What do we want in Anderson Valley? Nice houses for nice people or teepees for more hippies?"

The gym exploded into competing cries.

"Teepees! More hippies!" the hippies shouted.

"Nice people! Nice houses!" the old timers yelled back.

The issue wasn't decided that night, but the hippies went on to a resounding victory. They collected money for a lawyer, accumulated negative environmental testimony, got ready to haul the condo brains into court. The old timers didn't do anything but complain about "hippies taking over," as if the capture of the dusty, semi-abandoned hamlets of Yorkville, Boonville, Philo, and Navarro was a great coup.

Great or not the San Diego-based developers soon gave up. The hippies won that one. They'd achieved political parity with the old timers, and would soon elect a very silly man as their very own supervisor whose supporters, ironically, lied Mr. Silly into office by spreading the utterly false claim that the incumbent supervisor, Ted Galletti of Point Arena, was behind another huge condo project allegedly proposed for Cameron Road near Elk.

But the old timers went down hard, and continued to fight the hippies whenever they saw the hippies moving to consolidate power. The old timers kept control of the Boonville school board for another few years, they held on to the Community Services board for a while, and to this day they have the Boonville-based Mendocino County Fair Board in a seemingly unbreakable headlock.

One big victory over the hippies, as the old timers saw it, was the prevention of a community swimming pool.

The State Fire Marshal's office had decreed that a sprinkler system be installed in the Fairgrounds' several exhibition halls. Technically a state, i.e., public facility, the Fairgrounds sit on twenty or so under-used, fenced-off acres in the center of Boonville. From the outside, the place looks like a medium security prison. Inside, it is one. Or at least its heavy institutional vibes are not what you would call liberating. Trespassers, known in the outside world as taxpayers, can expect an immediate heave-ho if they happen to walk on in and spread out a picnic on a Fairgrounds lawn.

Onerous insurance and rent rates, arbitrarily imposed by the local board of directors, discourage use of the facilities between annual fairs, although over the recent past commercially driven music, wine and beer events have drawn thousands of people to Boonville for weekend debauches on the facility's grudging premises. These events, of course, can pay the big fees.

But through the 1970s and well into the 1980s, the Fairgrounds several acres of grass and trees were open to the public only for the five annual days of the September fair while the high school football team was gang tackled in sheep shit left on the rodeo infield by a fair board insider whose animals grazed free "to keep the grass down."

To be effective, sprinkler systems need a lot of water in a big hurry. To get a lot of water in a big hurry you need a standing pool of the stuff. Hey! I've got it! A swimming pool! Why, the kids will have a healthy place to spend those long summer afternoons and the Fairgrounds will have plenty of water for its sprinklers. Cloverdale, which also has a fairgrounds in the middle of town, installed the required sprinkler system with a community swimming pool as the system's water supply. Sensible people naturally assumed Boonville would follow Cloverdale's one-stone, two-bird lead and do the same.

But an unusually hysterical — even by their seething standards — segment of the old timers besieged their hippie-fightin' pals sitting as trustees on the fair board, begging their buddies not to build a community pool for water storage because You Know Who would swim in it. Not only would You Know Who swim in it, You Know Who would swim in it nekkid! Buck nekkid! And disease? Why bless me, Janese, it's a known fact that hippies are walking pustules of fatal pox, plus a few new ones they've probably developed right here in the hills of Boonville! If there was a community pool at the Fairgrounds every kid in the valley would soon be a walking contagion of communicable cooties.

The option to a combined water storage and community swimming pool was a storage tank, and the damn hippies and their feral, lice-bearing children could hardly swim in that, could they? Hell, they'd have to climb up the thing and pry its top off to get in, har de har.

To ensure that Boonville opted for the storage tank, the old timers, perhaps having learned an activist lesson from the hippies who'd defeated them over the proposed Navarro condo development, began circulating petitions against a community swimming pool. A handful of perpetually angry women — rednecks seem partial to the "chicks up front" approach to public controversies — stationed themselves at the valley's four post offices, petitions in their determined hands. Any person who in the slightest resembled a hippie, any person who looked like he might be susceptible to hip-think the petitioners spun out taxpayer arguments, primarily that a public swimming pool would cost too much to build and maintain.

But to people they recognized, people the hysterics knew held the correct retro opinions, the gargoyles would come right out with their true objection to the pool. "Do you want your kids swimming in the same water as hippies? Do you want your children to get sick?"

The specter of hippie-itis trumped community benefit. The battle axes presented their petitions to their allies on the Fair Board and, to this day, at the south end of the Fairgrounds grandstand sits a huge, metal water tank with a cartoon bronco buster a'bustin' his bronc painted on it. That eyesore could have been, should have been, a community swimming pool if it weren't for the pure terror inspired in primitive minds by the vision of verminous hippie dippers enjoying a swim alongside antiseptic little Republicans.

But only a few years later, the sons and daughters of hippies and rednecks were not only swimming together up at Maple Basin, they were marrying each other, and soon a whole new plague-proof beast, the hipneck, was born, and Anderson Valley was at last one.

Yeah, yeah, I got into scuffles once in a while but nothing serious, and not nearly as serious as many of the fights in the Lodge back then, and not nearly as serious to me as the rifle round whistled over my head as I walked past a Boonville cowboy's front yard rodeo pen, prompting me ever afterwards to carry an unregistered handgun with me when I hiked in the lonelier venues of the valley, hoping to catch the gunman alone somewhere so I could whistle a retaliatory bullet past his pointy little red head to even things up. Mendocino County has always been a force-and-violence place, and you have to be prepared to use it yourself against the people who operate, with impunity, outside the law.

One night I was waylaid by a soft man whose condition was unequal to his desire to do me harm. Flab man popped me feebly on the side of my head as I walked out of a Boonville school board meeting where I'd said something he apparently didn't like. I hit him straight on the point of his surprised jaw and down he went; I was sitting on top of him trying to make up my mind whether or not to hit him again when Deputy Simon drove up. "Why don't you guys grow up?" And that was that one.

What I'd said at the school board meeting was, "You can't cut my kid's hair." The kid was a future enforcer for the Black Guerrilla

Family named Randy Alana. At the time, Randy was 12 and wore his hair in a big Afro, as was the black style. I was his legal guardian.

The hair issue had already been to the Supreme Court and all the way back to where it even applied to Boonville. But the Boonville School Board and its demented superintendent thought long hair on any non-female person was the first sign of disorder that might, if not forcibly checked, engulf all of Mendocino County, all of America, the world.

"If you touch the kid I'll have you arrested for assault. I'll sue you individually and I'll sue your school district and you'll lose," I'd rattled righteously on, reading off legal decisions a lawyer friend had prepared for me; I even delivered a brief history of long hair in America back to the Founding Fathers, throwing in some asides about how silly it was to be having this discussion in 1971. As I was speaking, there were mutters behind me to "sit down and shut up."

In reply, the superintendent, a fellow called Mel "Boom Boom" Baker, reminded his school board of five glaring ranchers, four of whom had no hair at all, "I've seen people hide knives and razors in those things," Baker's apparent reference to the Afro as both hairstyle and weapons cache. "Our high school looks pretty good with the all the boys' hair cut and our school dress code, and I hope we keep it that way."

Traditional Boonville was violently opposed to hippies although quite a few locals were making money off the hippies who'd bought logged over land in the hills and the hippies were bringing new businesses into Boonville, and into all the dying little towns everywhere on the Northcoast.

The vote was 5-0 to enforce the school's hair code, but they never enforced it on my guy, and I knew then that the only kids they dared push around were those kids who didn't have anybody looking out for them. That was the night I was popped on the side of the head by the "old timer" as I left the room, and with my answering thunder punch solidified my dubious reputation as point man for hippies of the fighting type.

Doubting the depth of Boom Boom's black experience, I went to the school one day to talk to him privately about the hair issue; to repeat my promise of big trouble for him and his school if he tried to cut my guy's hair. But I didn't want to be at permanent war with the valley's primary institution either. I thought maybe I could cool Boom Boom out a little. Talk him down. Take a little percussion out of his drums. The school secretary, the usual ultra-capable woman who runs most schools for 25% of the money the man gets who's theoretically in charge, this one named Frances Lytle, told me, "Mr. Baker is out back behind the gym, probably," her voice suggesting that Mr. Barker spent a lot of time out in back of the gym because he didn't have much else to do other than fulminate about long hair.

I walked on out behind the gym, a structure larger than all the school's classrooms put together, and found a man in brown janitor khakis throwing rocks at the barn swallow nests nestled in the gym's eaves some fifty feet up. The superintendent heaved a couple more futile stones skyward before turning to me. "Oh, it's you," he said, immediately segueing into a monologue of his serially improbable life experience, including one seemingly improvised for the liberal he perceived me to be which informed me that the unprepossessing man standing before me had been Satchel Page's catcher and had been a personal friend of Dwight D. Eisenhower. Now pitching for the US of A, Satchel Page, behind the plate Dwight D. Eisenhower.

"Mr. Baker," I said, "you can't cut the kid's hair."

Baker repeated his claim that he'd seen "razor blades up there."

And on he went with more chapters of his life's book, none of them related to hair, occasionally pausing to heave a futile rock at a swallow's nest. I knew he wouldn't try to cut the kid's hair, and he never did.

The kid with the troubling Afro grew up to be a guy who would have hidden a bazooka in his hair if he thought there was tactical advantage to be gained, but in his Boonville incarnation the only thing up there was a hair pick.

Years later I picked up a Bay Area newspaper and read, "A man described by prosecutors as an enforcer for the Black Guerrilla prison gang strangled a trustee to death in the Oakland City Jail yesterday. Randy Allana, 6'7 and 270 pounds, reached through the bars of his cell and, before guards could break his grip on the trustee's throat, strangled the man to death. Allana is awaiting trial for a murder he allegedly committed in federal prison."

Randy had certainly been irritable as a child, but we couldn't have expected such eminence as this from him. A killer among killers? Yes, he enjoyed hurting animals and the other boys, but so did his similarly doomed peers. Add chronic fire setting and bed wetting and most of our boys met the serial killer's early child psychological profile. They all bore watching, and that's what we were paid to do, that and containment.

In his youth, The Enforcer was fascinated by any loco-moted object, anything propelled by an engine, but by the time we'd resolved the hair question with Boonville's school authorities in a way that was consistent with the law of the land, The Enforcer had been sent home to Oakland to live with his drunken father and dad's beaten down Brunhilde of a German wife, The Enforcer's mother. "Family reunification" was the social work fantasy of the time, the assumption being that there was a family to be reunified with, not the incubators of dangerous youths these fragged families obviously were. If The Enforcer had been allowed to stay in one place long enough to consummate his fascination with automobile engines he might have grown up to become a talented, functioning psycho of a mechanic.

"Reunification is in the best interest of this child," the court order said, standing all semblance of objective reality on its head. Dad was mumbling drunk every time I saw him and, drunk or sober, he beat on mom so often she seemed brain damaged, punch drunk as it used to be called. I arrived one afternoon to find mom, a forlorn figure in a ratty house dress, defrosting the ice compartment of her refrigerator with a blow drier, not necessarily proof of brain damage but an indicator. "Damn ting too iced up," she explained.

The Enforcer, more dangerous by the day, was soon stuck away in the California Youth Authority. At age 18 he passed on into the adult penal system, bigger and stronger, so strong that by the age of 30 he could reach through the bars of a prison cell and strangle a man to death.

But hair continued to obsess the more conventional sectors of Mendocino society.

Boonville's first wave hippies called a meeting one Sunday

afternoon to discuss what to do about a loose knit, perhaps mythical, Boonville association calling itself Cold Steel, whose stated purpose, the hippies said, was to cut hippie hair, beat hippies up, burn hippie shacks, and generally purge the valley of hippies, hip-symps, latent hippies, closet hippies, and all carriers of the hippie virus as determined by Cold Steel. With these long-haired men and the neo-floozie women back in Berkeley and San Francisco, the valley's decent people could return to their pre-hippie peace of serial adultery, wife beating, alcoholism, and bar fighting.

What to do about Cold Steel?

We gathered in a ridgetop owner-built hippie house to talk mutual protection. There were so many hippies stuffed into the three-story shack for the meeting, and so many women in granny dresses, I half-expected the old woman who lived in a shoe to appear to with a tray of lemonade and cookies.

We were directed by our host and his "old lady," a young woman who looked like she was about 16, to array ourselves in a circle which, the very young old lady explained, "will discourage hierarchical thinking and facilitate communication and community."

The meeting flier had been illustrated by a male cartoon figure smoking pot. It had said the gathering would be potluck. Potluck, get it? We were supposed to bring something to eat that was "healthy, preferably organic," and right there you knew why so many Americans wanted to force feed hippies cold steel and deep fried jelly donuts. And since the occasion was an afternoon affair, why would we have to bring anything to eat since the meeting time was after the lunch hour and would be ended before dinner? Come to find out, as a redneck narrative would put it, there was a minority of hippies who seemed to live for these things; they stuffed themselves on cadged meals in between which they lived on giant blocks of government commodity cheese.

I brought a big bowl of potato salad that the hippies, without asking if the dish had been prepared according to hippie halal, was nearly consumed before I could find a hole in the circle big enough for me to sit down in. Mine was the only real food anybody brought, and I never did get my bowl back. From that day forward, whenever I went to any kind of liberal potluck, and liberal politics inevitably meant circles and dope, I brought stuff straight from Safeway's sale table and no eating implements. The negative food value items disappeared just as fast as the organic whatever.

That day's banquet also included some scraggly strands of unappetizing blackish-green vegetable matter that a man told me was rendered seaweed; there were a couple of hunks of homemade bread with the appearance and texture of cannonballs; and a big vat of watery slop billed as soup. And, of course, there was marijuana, the sacred herb around whose consumption so many stoned lives then revolved.

At a Green Party meeting several years later, the circle meeting format had been expanded to include a tiny, Peter Pan-ish man who said his name was Morning Light. Morning Light held up a battered asparagus fern. "Only persons in possession of this fern are empowered to speak," he said, "and I will start the discussion by passing it to the person to my right." I wondered who had empowered him. Had the gnomish little fascist simply taken advantage of stoner inattentiveness to seize power?

Morning Light said he would also function as "vibe watcher," explaining that if the discussion became too heated, he'd play a tune on his flute until proper rhetorical order was restored. Morning Light added that instead of clapping and cheering when we heard something we approved of, we should "twinkle" or raise our hands over our heads and silently wiggle our fingers. "It's so much less disruptive than clapping and cheering," he explained.

These protocols kicked in the early 1980s. At that Cold Steel meeting we were merely arrayed in circles.

A big bush hippie was one of the few sensible persons attending the what-to-do-about-vigilantes meeting. He was only a year from the fighting in Vietnam, a fierce looking man with long, unattended black hair and a big black beard and wild eyes to go with it; he'd mustered out of the Army with enough money and VA benefits to buy 40 acres somewhere up around Spy Rock, north of Laytonville. He told me that he was visiting a friend "near Boonville" when he saw the flier. The bush hippie was about sixty miles south of his Spy Rock neighborhood, which had already established itself as, ah, self-governing. He didn't introduce himself and no one seemed

An Informal History of Mendocino County

inclined to pry.

"Why don't we just grab some of these Cold Steel assholes and shove some cold steel up their ass?"

A perpetually smiling, curly-headed man hurriedly began to speak, rushing his words as if to cancel out the tactical suggestion of the alienated man fresh off his jungle adventure.

"I really love living in Anderson Valley, and love the people, plants, animals, streams and rivers, the whole place and everybody and everything in it. By 'love' I mean I sense the ultimate oneness of all, and the love force which is the most powerful force in creation. Also I am a person of strong political opinions — opinions which change with the help of my friends; opinions which sometime differ from those of my friends and neighbors. I love and respect my neighbors, even though their politics may differ from mine. We are all coming from different life experiences, and are viewing these different experiences from different perspectives. I relish political debate, but only if the participants love and respect each other in the process. I especially love the notorious characters of Anderson Valley, whose comic and or tragic flaws, are as apparent to me as my flaws, entirely invisible to me of course but are seen clearly by my Anderson Valley neighbors. I am a 'radical' in that I love to get to the root of things. Now our country has become so dominated by men of fear, greed, and the desire to exploit and dominate, that it is rapidly destroying itself. This means that every year I, as a landless family man and worker-entrepreneur in Anderson Valley, become more dependent on my friends and neighbors for all I need to survive and live happily. Indeed, we in Anderson Valley need each other more every day, in so many ways. Let's get together in love, relishing our diversity."

Translation: I'm a deadbeat and a leech, and if the purpose of the meeting is to stop rednecks from ambushing hippies the rednecks have already won.

The bush hippie, a big smile on his hairy face, answered, "Me too. I love the valley. The robins here are much better than the ones around Laytonville. Down here they're so nice and fat and all fluffed out they're easy to pick off with a bb gun."

A wiry little fellow announced solemnly, "Politics is the art of

165

the possible," and the meeting plunged irrelevantly on until one of the stoners finally asked, "So, who are these Cold Steel people anyway?"

No one knew, but everyone seemed to have a preferred villain. Names tumbled into consideration, but not one could be confirmed as Cold Steel.

"Maybe there isn't a Cold Steel," a woman suggested. "Maybe there's just kind of these freelance rednecks who beat up hippies whenever they get a chance."

"Well, my friend from Albion," began a long hair, "said he went into the Boonville Lodge last Saturday night to buy a six-pack, and while he was inside some rednecks hooked up his VW bus to the tow bar on their pick-up. truck. My friend came outside just as they got his bus connected to their tow bar. He told them to leave him alone and un-hook him. They just stood there laughing at him. Finally, one of them pretended to un-hook him and told him he could go. But my friend was still hooked up. The rednecks got into their truck and towed my friend all around Boonville for about half an hour, like it was all a big joke."

The bush hippie laughed.

I laughed.

"Sounds like an initiation ceremony to me," I said.

A large woman with a small, downturned, perpetually unhappy mouth had been grazing the potluck table ever since she'd arrived; she suddenly shouted out, "We must remain non-violent!"

Volcanically angry herself, as I came to know from seeing her in action at succeeding hip-lib events, the unhappy woman, whom another bush vet hippie called a "power cow," was always pretending to be shocked, gasping so loud at public meetings whenever something was said or done that violated hippiedom's stated ideal of collective peace and love, the people in the gasped room would have to take a timeout, like a flock of birds sent suddenly airborne from a telephone wire, until the traumatized flower child stopped hyper-ventilating. A discussion would be stumbling along when suddenly there'd be a kind of coyote-like yelp that segued into great gulping, alarmingly audible, inhalations on the frontier of hyper-ventilation until these eruptions finally de-escalated into sighs and, we all hoped, peace. These explosions were a staple of hippie gatherings, as predictable as pot and patchouli.

Deep in the Cold Steel meeting, a terrible scream erupted from the righteous one. It was so loud, so piercing that for all anybody knew she'd just taken a machete stroke to her back. I wasn't the only one who was startled.

"I'm in your drift! Your drift! Aiiiiieeeeeee!"

We stared at her, shocked. What the hell had happened? Nothing, as it turned out. A man had fired up a non-marijuana cigarette a good forty feet from where earth mother, wrapped in layers of shawls and a mammoth earth-toned muumuu, had spread herself out like a graffiteed freeway pillar. The cigarette smoke had somehow penetrated the marijuana haze that hung over the room to make its evil way to earth mother's nostrils, her sacred space, her drift. The woman had been violated! Raped!

The drift interlude took up about half an hour because it had given birth to a prolonged argument about the relative lethality of cigarette smoke versus marijuana smoke.

Just before the meeting broke up with no resolution of the Cold Steel problem other than the bush hippie's stated intention to meet violence with ultra-violence — "if any of those assholes fuck with me…" — earth mom announced that she would appreciate donations so she could continue "doing important political work."

And that was the end of Cold Steel.

Among the county's hippies Boonville did indeed have the reputation as a place to avoid, but there was never any evidence of organized hippie-bashers.

The do your own thing ethic of the counter-culture opened the door to some very bad people getting over in the hippie psycho-social context of Mendocino County, 1968-1978, but the baddest of them all, Reverend Jim Jones, was a pure creation of the established order.

The amphetamine-driven Jones, who fastened vampire-like on the idealism of the time to shove himself forward as a new model, race-blind white man, rode his mostly black congregation from Ukiah to the most important political offices in San Francisco's city hall, and then he rode them to their deaths deep in a far off jungle.

Every step of his depraved way, the reverend got big boosts from people who should have known better.

We would learn that Jones solidified his murderous hold on his church by keeping them in a perpetual state of fear of the world outside. If it wasn't nukes, it was racists. If it wasn't racists it was the government. If it wasn't the government it was the media. All the while, the great apostle of tolerance farmed his mostly black parishioners as efficiently as they'd been farmed on Southern plantations a hundred and fifty years earlier.

Lena and George McCowan had dropped out of the odd Redwood Valley church when they discovered the secret of Jones's long-haul rhetoric.

"Jim was always popping pills," Lena remembered, "mostly uppers. Between the wine and the pills, naturally, you know, that would start it off, I mean he would almost go to the ceiling."

Sailing on speed, Jones's dramatic sermons went on for hours. He'd throw the Bible on the floor and point at it and say, "See! The goddamned thing's full of lies. Every time it's rewritten, the Catholics fill it full of lies."

Parishioners remembered a favorite theme of the pastor's as amended from Isaiah 7:20: "I come shaved with a razor! I come with the black hair of a raven! I come as God Socialist!"

A fellow named Tim Carter was once pulled aside by Jones who told him, "Any time you want me to fuck you in the ass, I'm here for you." Another man wrote, "Your fucking me in the ass was, as I see it now, necessary to get me to deal with my deep-seated repression against my homosexuality. I have felt resentment at being fucked even though I knew your motives were utterly pure."

Jones, the Leninist butt-fucker of the pulpit, explained his anatomical left-deviationism: "If it would save you, or promote a revolutionary cause or this movement, you should give your vagina, your penis, your asshole, if it's called for, and if you can't then you're not a dedicated Communist."

The rednecks, so called, could have cared less about Jones' church; they never said boo about Jones when Bible Bob, the Boonville school superintendent, was rumored to have traded Jones a teaching job for the dozen or so People's Temple students Jones brought to Boonville every day to boost Boonville's depleted student body. The logging boom — more than twenty mills in the Anderson Valley in 1950 — had ended and many of the logging families had moved on. The valley's schools, designed for 500 students, were dying from a lack of children.

Another theory of Jones's Boonville employment is that the reverend had been so broke when he arrived from Indianapolis he needed to work, at least until he and his church were fully established. So, this line goes, Jones and the Boonville school superintendent, both being former Hoosiers, and both being servants of the Lord, worked out a deal that gave Jones Boonville's 6th and 7th grade classes in exchange for the twenty or so young people Jones promised to bus over from his fledgling church in Redwood Valley, the then-thinly populated suburb of Ukiah. Every school day Jones and his average daily attendance chits would make the nearly two hour roundtrip commute to Boonville, back and forth over the hill between the Ukiah Valley and the Anderson Valley.

"I was a student of Jim's in 1966-67," Wayne Pinoli recalls, "when he taught full-time at the Anderson Valley Elementary School. He was a guest at my parents' home, and my mother and I visited him and his wife and attended church services a few times in Redwood Valley. Through some administrative quirk, my best friend and I were the only fast track seventh graders in his class of 6th and 7th grade pupils, and we got a substantial portion of his time directed towards us. I think I may have spent more time communicating directly with him than almost anyone else in Anderson Valley. I'm pretty sure that Jones did not furnish students to the high school in return for a full-time teaching job; he just wanted something to do during the day. He first taught full-time in 1966-67. I know, I was one of his students. He didn't start importing students to the high school until 1967-68.

"I attended his church several times between 1967 and 1974. There were no guards until the early 1970s. There were certainly none in 1967. The 'healings' I think started sometime after the guards went up. In my attendances, I never witnessed him defacing a bible or claiming to be God, but I can easily believe that he went on to do so. On my last visit it took us about half an hour to get past the guards so we could listen to him rant for a couple of hours about how many forces were out to get the temple; then he cured a few people and that was the service. At that stage of my youth and ignorance, I left without any clear concept of what was really happening. I was, however, sure that the man I had just seen was not the same brilliant, charismatic teacher that had so strongly influenced me in Boonville.

"My own opinion is that Jones was more sane than not until about 1968. Then, through drugs or whatever, he started to lose it. By 1974, he was full tilt off-the-rocker. What I still don't understand is why we go through this macabre ritual of periodically dredging the story up and re-telling it with so many of those involved trying to aggrandize or color their roles in whichever direction or shade that suits them. It might be very interesting to research old stories in the local papers to see how some people's quotes have changed in the years since Guyana.

"I recall reading that Jones had a large sign somewhere with the quote, 'Those who do not learn from history are doomed to repeat it.' If accounts of other historical events are as altered by time as this one, I find it difficult to believe any of it... I may be going out on a limb, but I think the high school's first hippie was a guy named Camozzi who lived in a group home in Philo. I will lay claim to being the first native one by virtue of having been kicked out of school by Boom Boom Baker (whom I would like to spend 15 minutes with in a locked room) for such transgressions as having my hair too long, having a beard, not shaving, wearing dark glasses on campus, and not parking my car between the lines in the school parking lot."

Homer Mannix, publisher of the Anderson Valley Advertiser, sat on the school board. A handsome, easy going, hippie-tolerant man in his fifties when the first counter-cultural scouts began to appear in the valley, Mannix was also judge of the local justice court, which he housed in his eponymous headquarters in downtown Boonville. Additionally, Mannix was the go-to guy at the Community Services District whose primary function was to preside over the volunteer firefighters, of which Mannix was one. And Mannix was associated with the Anderson Valley Ambulance, a decrepit station wagon outfitted as an emergency response vehicle. The local joke was that if you weren't dead when you heard the ambulance's siren coming towards you, you soon would be. This, ah, informal service would be professionalized in 1980 when the volunteers turned out drunk to retrieve a car full of people from the same wedding party who'd driven off the Ukiah road and tumbled several hundred feet down the hillside. Several of the volunteers were so drunk they'd also tumbled over the side of the hill and had had to be rescued by sober passersby.

In a famous edition of his newspaper, Mannix, feeling the pressure of skeptical parents coming at him from one side and People's Temple propagandists and parishioners on the other, adopted an equivocally neutral editorial stance on the controversial Jones.

"There have been several letters to the Advertiser recently that have been highly complimentary of James W. Jones, Anderson Valley sixth grade teacher who was hired on a provisional credential, on a one year contract, last year. Because Mr. Jones resides in Redwood Valley and commuted daily very few people in Anderson Valley have ever met him. Some, however, have been critical of his teaching ideas — which has brought about letters of support from those in Ukiah, Redwood Valley and Willits who know the man."

Jones, of course, was a great one for soliciting testimonials from persons who knew him only through his self-advertised good works; Mannix duly printed several of these when Jones's lax teaching methods began to be criticized by some of the parents of his students.

One letter, dated March 1968, came from "William M. Vest, M.D., 415 Standley Street Ukiah: "James W. Jones is a teacher and ordained Minister of unusually high caliber. He is a public servant of unbounded energy. Those who know him best respect him most as a tireless leader for the betterment of mankind. He is at present a teacher, and as I am told of his standards, a pastor of a flock numbering almost 300 church members of a devotion sought for in other congregations. He is serving the public also as foreman of the County Grand Jury, as vice president of the Legal Aid Foundation, and is serving with honor to himself and benefit to us all in many other ways, all without at all accepting his salary as a teacher. Students he brings to Anderson Valley from his congregation of families bring with them tuitional income to that school district more, much more I believe, than he is receiving as salary. He loves children and indeed I feel that his dealings with all people are as with deep concern for them. He has had a prominent part in the formation and operation of a very large orphanage and with no income to himself. I personally consider any child fortunate to come into the tutelage of James W. Jones."

Mrs. W.C. Cartmell wrote to the Boonville paper to praise Mannix and her spiritual leader.

"Our pastor, Jim W. Jones, has spoken so highly of you, and the Anderson Valley Advertiser. He mentioned particularly your dedication and tremendous service to the community and praised you publicly in our large congregation. I was deeply touched by the things he said, and I want to subscribe to the Advertiser. Words are so faulty and often fail to express fully one's true feeling, however I want to say Thank You for your conscientious concerns. Jim Jones has always taught us, and based his entire life on, one precept that 'the highest service to God is service to our fellow man.' If ever we can help or be of service in any way, please feel free to call."

The promise of a subscription probably swung Mannix's newspaper to a discreet support for the embattled teacher. Cold cash can work miracles of editorial perception as marvelous as any cancer cure wrought by a crooked preacher.

Jim Jones had arrived in Mendocino County virtually without resources other than the fairly large contingent of human capital he'd brought with him from Indiana. There were some 150 of them, a few with dependable social security incomes, and as a group probably containing more than enough cash flow to spare the reverend himself the rigors of the workaday world. It's also fair to say that the reverend also brought with him a truly admirable history as the man who had organized the first truly integrated church in the history of Indiana. Mendocino County's history of race relations was sorry indeed put alongside Jones's pre-Mendo civil rights record.

The reverend was alright until he got into speed.

After temporarily settling his flock at the site of the Golden Rule

Church on the Willits Grade north of Ukiah, Jones began commuting to Boonville to work as a school teacher. Parents soon became suspicious of Jones' teaching techniques, which seemed to mostly consist of games, entertainments, cookies and kool aid. Jones kept the kids mesmerized with demonstrations of what he told them were his magical powers. He once told his sixth graders that he could cause a fly to light on the end of his finger, which one immediately did. The kids thought their teacher was swell, but their parents knew that cookies and bug tricks wasn't reading, writing and arithmetic.

Norman Clow has vivid memories of Jones.

"On the second day of classes in the fall of 1967, Jim Jones integrated Anderson Valley High School. Walking down the hall to our first period senior government class, a group of us were startled to see a black girl, Ava Cobb, talking to a teacher in Room One. Imagine our surprise when we got to Room Five and found another, Anita Ljames, sitting quietly at a desk waiting for class to begin. Forced to put our money where our mouths were, those of us who professed a lofty world brotherhood color-blindness in racial matters was a big challenge. Those who professed one degree of bigotry or another had a bigger one.

"Jones had been around the local schools for about three years when he brought Anderson Valley into the melting pot mainstream. He had worked part-time at the Elementary School and subbed at the high school. As I recall, we had him fairly often one year in Spanish class. It took a while for us to realize he couldn't speak Spanish — Portuguese was his foreign language — but that class was our first real exposure to his charismatic personality. I remember quite vividly one girl who came from a family of meager means being just enthralled when he told the class that he had a 'ranch' in Redwood Valley. Of course, we didn't know at the time that his crop was old people's Social Security checks and property deeds. This girl just sat there practically swooning at the suave and handsome Reverend Jones who owned a ranch in Redwood Valley. Anybody who knew the harsh truths of trying to scratch a living REALLY ranching in Mendocino County in the 60s (the advent of the pot plantations) had a slightly different reaction. When he subbed at the high school, it was always, 'Oh, we're having Jim Jones today

— you know, Jim Jones.' (Or maybe, that nut.) His reputation and persona magnified daily, but not all of us were favorably impressed. The unsubstantiated story has always been that Jones provided a dozen students from the Temple, and the average daily attendance money they brought with them, in exchange for a full-time teaching position at the Elementary School.

"That second day of class in 1967 was the beginning of a strange experience at Anderson Valley High School. All of a sudden local students were confronted with a dozen or so 'different' kids, some with a skin color we had all heard about and seen in pictures but never actually rubbed up against, from some off-beat church called 'People's Temple.' We'd heard of it, but knew very little about it. Supposedly, it was some sort of Protestant sect, but those of us with strong Protestant faiths were a little skeptical when we talked to them and heard some of their beliefs and found out that admission to their church service was by invitation only and protected by armed guards. None of it sounded very Biblical to us — and we got the distinct idea they were actually worshipping Jim Jones, not the Lord. Indeed, as the year wore on, I became increasingly convinced, and correctly so as history says, that all of Jones' parson's garb and Bible-pounding was just a prop, a hook to snare weak-willed believers. (That was also confirmed in the Spring of 1968 in an incident witnessed by one of our local classmates which I will describe later.)

"The kids themselves were an interesting bunch — polite, short hair, clean-cut and, for the most part, studious. They weren't standoff-ish but there was definitely a 'difference.' Later, we found out they were sort of 'outcasts' at Ukiah, perhaps another motivation for Jones to produce them one morning in Boonville. Socially reserved, the ones in my classes were outspoken and took an active part in class discussions, whether it was science, English or, particularly, government or history. They would never salute the flag. Even then the People's Temple seemed to have a fascination with the Soviet Union, and a couple of fellows would go on and on about what a paradise Brezhnev's repressive regime was. Some of us would ride them mercilessly about their obvious folly and they had very little to say when the Soviet tanks rolled into Czechoslovakia to crush out the last little tiny bit of freedom that flickered in that occupied country.

"We tried hard to make them feel welcome, and they appreciated it. While it seemed in a way that the kids wanted to really be part of the gang, there was this apparent if invisible wall between them and us. It was also interesting to watch the changing attitudes of some of the local kids, going from writing papers advocating the shipping back of all blacks to Africa 'where they belonged' to actually accepting people of another race as equals. I became very close friends with Ava Cobb and with Jones' adopted Korean daughter, Sue. But only at school. There was nothing socially at all — the wall was up. Anita Ljames, black, whose father served as one of the Temple's assistant pastors, had a singing voice that would just knock your socks off. I played guitar along with David Knight in a half-baked rock band, but when Anita showed up with her Motown vocal chords, the band quickly became a rhythm and blues act — a lot of Wilson Pickett, Otis Redding, Aretha, the Supremes, that sort of thing, and her performance of 'Midnight Hour' in one of the school variety shows brought down the house. She and I spent hours working out arrangements on the piano and talking about this and that, but there was always this wall. My conservatism always kind of confounded her.

"Others experienced the same thing. Except for the two variety shows that they organized, Jones' students took part in practically no extracurricular activities. At 3:30 they were gone, headed back over the hill to the sanctuary of 'Father' in one of the cars provided by the school. About the only other exception was when we elected Faith Worely, who later defected from the movement, homecoming queen. I think it was Tom Rawles who planted a big smooch on her at the halftime ceremonies and Jones was furious. Afterwards, Jones denounced her in front of the congregation for her 'loose morals and disgraceful public display.' A year or so later, he had forced her to be his mistress, apparently less concerned for 'morals' than he had been at Homecoming.

"Jones' kids seemed to be struggling with their relationship with him. There was an obvious but unstated adoration of 'Father' but at the same time there was a subtle fear that they displayed and a distaste for the circumstances. Dale Parks, who would later watch his mother get murdered at the airstrip in Guyana when they tried to escape with Leo Ryan, would sometimes just sort of sigh when the topic would come up (always indirectly — it was never discussed in the open.) It was almost like he knew what he was going home to every evening and dreaded it. Other times they would be fiercely defensive of Jones and the church, expressing great admiration and loyalty for the man who was revolutionizing social action in Mendocino County. If we had a class report to do in government, you could count on Judy Stahl to make a presentation on the social welfare system in this country and Anita to expound on racism and how the Temple was working to eliminate all class barriers. Judy and I each took a turn at interpreting Alice In Wonderland, of all things, and James Joyce in English literature and the differences in our analysis were startling, to say the least.

"I often hear people remark that they can't understand how so many people would fall for Jones' line, how they would just turn over everything they had to him and literally follow him to their deaths. I can. I don't understand all of it, but I was around him enough to recognize the terrific, terrible charisma he possessed. He was cool and calm and handsome and polite and could pull you right into the palm of his hand. In class he had a magnetic presence that came close to snaring a few local students. At a Thanksgiving assembly one year he gave the main inspirational message, and Jim Bakker or some other charlatan could have taken lessons from him. I can remember vividly sitting there listening to him speak and thinking, 'This guy is amazing — and scary.' His message was obviously a fake, but the power was certainly there. Nobody should ever fool themselves into thinking, 'It could never happen to me. I'm too smart for that.' A lot of the 912 people at Jonestown were 'smart,' too, and I doubt that any of them ever had any idea what they were getting themselves into.

"In the spring, one of our classmates visited the Temple. He and Judy Stahl had been a steady item at school, but Jones had forced her to break it off. Dan went to Redwood Valley to try to negotiate some sort of arrangement with Jones, and left after being scared nearly out of his wits. Jones confronted him with a gun outside the Temple, ordered him off the grounds and to never associate with Judy again. Dan hung around, sneaked back in and observed an evening church service through the window. What he saw included a fake cancer healing, a beating and Jones throwing his Bible to the floor and stomping it to pieces, screaming 'I am your God' over and over at the top of his lungs while the congregation roared its approval. The next day, school authorities just pooh-poohed the story, telling Dan that he had an over-active imagination and to please not slander the good Reverend Jones anymore. Right. Of course, none of us could have predicted the carnage that was to follow, and nobody's boasting, but some of us, including a number of parents whose children were in Jones' classes, had that guy figured out well in advance, but a fat lot of good it did anybody.

"And so it went. Mike Bloomfield put a wrap on 'Super Session,' Anita sang 'Up, Up and Away' at our senior graduation, Robert Kennedy was tragically shot a couple of hours later and we all went off to somewhere else. Jones pulled up stakes in Anderson Valley and his brood went back to Ukiah, the great average daily attendance experiment over. A couple of us would see Anita or Judy or Faith or Jim Cobb on the campus at Santa Rosa JC once in a while, but they were clearly in a different world. We might bump into them in a hallway or on the lawn, but there was never any going over to anybody's apartment or anything, just hello, how are you, as we passed one another. And no, none of them showed up at our ten-year class reunion just five months before the slaughter.

"Jonestown and People's Temple had been in the papers a little bit more and more by then, and I kept looking for names. I started seeing them and it wasn't until then that we realized the depth of what was happening. We'd had no idea what our old friends had been into. It was amazing stuff, almost out of a movie, not real life. The last time I saw Ava Cobb, one of the best friends I had in school for the year she and I were classmates, was in a parking lot in front of the Ukiah Purity store that summer after graduation. She didn't look too happy. She shouldn't have been. She was going to spend the next ten years, along with her brother Jim and her sister Theresa trying to get the rest of her family — parents, brothers, sisters — out of the Temple and out of Jonestown. They didn't make it, and the next time I saw her it was on television being interviewed the day after the massacre. They had started a sort of halfway house rescue program that had been one impetus for Congressman Ryan's fatal trip to Guyana. Judy and Anita and a whole bunch more of our classmates were dead. There wasn't much to say at that point except Holy Toledo or I told you so, and there is no solace in that. We mostly just sat shaking our heads.

"A few months later Dale Parks walked over to my desk at Crocker Bank and was amazed that I remembered him 'from school.' Like a dummy, I asked him how he was doing, and he said fine. I had no way to respond to someone who could say 'fine' after what he had been through, and so for once I just shut up.

"To this day, particularly after having lost a son of our own, whenever I think about this devil, this madman, this murderer, I want to either hold my own two boys as close as I can or go get the sledgehammer out of the shed and go smash Jones' coffin to smithereens. The only satisfaction I get, and it's meager, is listening to Willie Brown or some other fool fumble around trying to explain their former undying support for that lunatic, but it's tempered by the fact that so many people tried for so long to get the government or the media to help them rescue their families from the horror of People's Temple and got nothing but a deaf ear and a pile of corpses. It's a little late. People's Temple indeed.

"Jim Jones integrated Anderson Valley High School. Eleven years later he proved to be the ultimate 'integrator,' leading hundreds of people of all races to their deaths. Death discriminates against no one, and Jim Jones was Death."

The Reverend Jim Jones got his cash flow flowing at Redwood Valley where, along with his People's Temple church, he opened group homes for the elderly; group homes for dependent but non-delinquent youth; group homes for delinquent youth; group homes for the mentally ill then being cut loose by the hundreds from the state hospitals, including the state hospital that employed Mrs. Jones at Talmage, a mile east of Ukiah; and Jones started up group homes for the elderly, mostly black, who'd already turned over their property and possessions to him. Every group home resident made money for the People's Temple, and Jones had soon amassed a tax-derived fortune that may have convinced him that he could do what he was doing in Mendocino County on a much larger scale in San Francisco.

Thanks to his parishioner-funding units, and the lax oversight characteristic of Mendocino County government, Sharon Linda Amos, sometimes called Linda Amos, sometimes Sharon Amos, and a half-dozen or so of her co-parishioners had gotten jobs at the Mendocino County Welfare Department where they steered additional public benefits to the Temple. Jones picked up such a big head of fiscal steam in Mendocino County, and such a burgeoning reputation as a fighter for civil rights, that he picked on up and moved down to the big circus of San Francisco where Willie Brown would soon describe Jones as "the greatest human being who ever lived," and the Reverend was pictured shaking hands with Mayor Moscone and pioneering gay supervisor Harvey Milk in mutually admiring photographs in the San Francisco Chronicle.

The indigenous population of Mendocino County would be slow to accept, then assimilate, the influx of hippies who began arriving in force at the time of Peoples Temple's ascendancy in the county, but Jones who looked like what he billed himself as — a short-haired man of God — had no trouble placing himself as the county's leading liberal. He may have been a liberal but he was no hippie, and thus acceptable to the diffuse but dominant county powers. The charismatic Indiana preacher repaid local hospitality by claiming that violent rednecks were trying to run him out of town.

From my experience in the county with my own multi-racial flock, I thought the reverend's fears, while perhaps minimally plausible in the sense of the prevalent private disapproval of the county's influx of new people of all kinds, it was obvious that the 'necks, outside of barrooms, were only passively, if grudgingly, disapproving. They weren't any more Klan-oriented than any other segment of the white community, including hippies who, in 1970, were still calling black people, including little old ladies, "spades."

Reverend Jones, though, got a lot of mileage out of pretending to be fending off racists. He made it sound like his People's Temple was besieged. He played the race card as craftily as Al Sharpton would ever play it, and was soon presiding over big, guilt-ridden ecumenical community meetings which included everyone from Ukiah's leading liberals to the chapter head of the local John Birch Society, Walter Heady, the whole bunch of them emerging to swear their commitment to multi-culturalism. Then Jones would go back out to his church and tell his parishioners that the people he'd just had lunch with wanted to kill them.

Jones used Mendocino County as a fiscal launching pad for his eventual re-location to San Francisco and, then, his apocalypse in Guyana. But before he departed from Redwood Valley hundreds of Mendocino County residents had had some association with him. My link was Sharon Amos, the social worker with the Mendocino County Department of Social Services.

Mrs. Amos was short and sad and gray, even when she was dressed in vivid reds and yellows. She seemed to suck the life out of everything around her. If birds fell dead out of the sky, flowers suddenly wilted, small children broke inexplicably into tears, to me it would come to mean she was up and on the move, heading for Boonville.

The day I met her for the first time, one kid ran for a tree when he spotted her green county car coming up the road to the main house, while the other one bounded off over the side of a hill, poised to run farther from her if she came closer.

I didn't have the flight option because I was in nominal charge of the operation, a group home six miles south of Boonville.

She'd seen both boys sprint off, and now she could see one of them, Merrill, resting as near to the top of an old oak as he could get without breaking off a limb too small to support him. Merrill looked down at us like a buzzard contemplating fresh kill. All that could be seen of the other boy, Domingo, was the long, wild strands of black hair framing his wary brown face.

"They're acting out," the social worker observed in a monotone, adding, "They're very difficult, these two."

The social worker's remarks sounded like audible reminders to herself that there was a difference between these guys and normal kids. I thought she probably went around all day murmuring mental reality post-its to herself.

The times were odd, of course. Millions of people were "acting out," and most of them were adults. A social worker colleague of Mrs. Amos's had just made the local newspapers when she was stopped for speeding on Highway 101 near Ukiah with her nude self encased in Saran wrap, a helping professional in need of help.

And here was this People's Temple sad sack standing in the blast of the summer sun in matching gray skirt and sweater, her white blouse secured at the neck with a large black ribbon. City social workers turned up in Boonville in modified cowgirl outfits, country social workers togged themselves out in the conservative urban power garb of 1970, blacks and greys and sensible shoes. Quite a few of the local social workers were weekend hippies, or real (sic) hippies who'd taken "straight" jobs to support their "old man."

I tried to divert the social worker from whatever embarrassment she might be feeling at her unhappy reception. When you're here to help and the helpees run at the sight of you, well, people have been known to make career changes for lesser reasons.

"I saw your name in the Ukiah paper the other day," I said. "What's the People's Temple?"

"It's the only real church in this country," Sharon Amos replied, emotionless even for such a big claim.

"Jim Jones has brought people of all races together in Redwood Valley where we practice a true social gospel. It's exciting and it's beautiful." The social worker said she would put my name down "on our guest list if you would like to attend services."

I was getting a definite cult vibe from Mrs. Amos. Numberless hours on hard benches with a congregation of joyless, zombo-ized social workers listening to the rantings of an outback Gantry? The social worker was not an effective proselytizer.

She seemed too tired to notice summer from winter, too exhausted to care that the two boys she had come to see had run away from her because, to them, Sharon Amos, Christian multi-culturalist, was just one more in a series of people who did things to them they didn't like — teachers, psychologists, doctors, judges, social workers and, of course, cops. The two boys saw Mrs. Amos as one more cop, a different kind of cop, but a cop. They saw me as their live-in cop, more or less benign, but still an agent of the state, an enemy in a world of them.

The judge had sent the two boys to Boonville because they'd been arrested. When the cops tried to locate their parents, it was discovered that they didn't have parents, although a chronological adult may have answered the door.

Merrill the tree climber had a Tourette's-like habit of shouting out profanity in school and in other contexts where you get a mental health jacket the second time you do it. He'd been caught shoplifting food several times because he was hungry. Domingo was in Boonville for assaulting other children and adults at the slightest, and sometimes no provocation. I saw my job as getting Merrill to curse where it might do some good and to teach Domingo to attack only people who have it coming. I did not share these rehab strategies with the authorities.

It was Sharon Amos's job to check to see if the two victims of a crumbling society were being properly fed and housed. She may even have expected them to be better behaved than they had been, but only a social worker could think they were redeemable in any conventional sense. If they somehow learned to cope before they were permanently put away in prison they'd do it on their own; there was no help available; the damage had been done. If government had been there when they popped from the womb and had taken them off to those first crucial years of regular meals and sane adults they might have had a chance. As they were — crazy as hell and getting crazier — the best we could do was provide a pleasant rural interregnum before they met their inevitable doom.

"I spend all my off time working with the church," the social worker continued. "Reverend Jones is doing something very special. His sermons are amazing, and he lives what he preaches.

These superlatives were also delivered in the voice of a person reading off a bus schedule.

The newspaper story I'd read said that the Reverend Jones not only tended to an ever-larger, multi-racial flock, he had just been appointed foreman of the Mendocino County Grand Jury. Mentioned among his parishioners was Mrs. Amos and Tim Stoen, the latter a Stanford graduate who functioned as both Mendocino County Counsel and as Jones's legal blocking back. Since she was mentioned by name in the story, it was clear that Mrs. Amos was a church bigwig.

Jones was quoted as saying that local "racists" were hostile to his church because it contained a large number of black people. This hostility, Jones said, had prompted him to erect the sporadically manned, forty-foot gun tower that loomed up over his Redwood Valley church. There were usually a couple of men with rifles in the tower for Sunday services, as if the racists might try to bull rush the congregation while they were all in one place.

The reverend told the Ukiah paper that he'd headed west from Indiana after reading an article in Esquire magazine that said the winds off the Northcoast would puff nuclear fallout right on past Mendocino County but Indianapolis, presumably, right down to its famous race car track, would be destroyed.

When the gun tower went up on the church grounds, Jones seemed to be conceding that he'd traded one terror for another — incineration for incipient, race-based, rural assault troops. Of course the tower aggrandized the People's Temple as an oasis of tolerance in a sea of hostility, and Jones as a kind of multi-cultural Captain Courageous. The reverend would protect his flock whatever it took, and his flock would believe they were besieged.

Sharon Amos bought everything the Reverend Jones did and said, bought it all unto death, as things turned out. And here she was, a flat-affect, monotonal social worker, the saddest sack in all of Mendocino County, wrapped in gray wool six miles south of Boonville on a hot August day, droning joylessly on about the great hope she'd found with Reverend Jones. She may have been doing spiritual handstands in her head but her droning voice gave up not a hint of enthusiasm. For anything.

Jonestown was still seven years away.

Having half-heartedly invited me into the Temple's embrace that morning as we stood beside her green county car, the social worker asked, "Do you think you can get Merrill to come down from there? I want to talk to him about a home visit. He can't go, and that's going to make him very unhappy."

I couldn't imagine how much more unhappiness Merrill could express; he'd already run for the treetops when he saw her coming. Besides, the kid knew in his bones he'd never hear any good news from his social worker. Or any other representative of the state.

Merrill was his last name. It seemed somehow easier to apply his surname to him than Shane, his given name. A pie-faced little boy with a perpetually worried expression on his broad features, Merrill looked more forlorn than he was. He had his coping strategies, which tended to work to his disadvantage, but they seemed to console him, and he did deserve consolation. He was half-crazy from a life that was whole-crazy, and he was only eleven.

Some people thought Merrill had Tourettes. Applied to him, we called it "voice-activated Tourettes." At the sound of a conversation that didn't include him — especially didn't include him — he'd run up and blurt out obscenities which, of course, coming from a child had the emotional effect of verbal hand grenades. A group of teachers would be talking among themselves and here comes Merrill, walking confidently on up as if someone had called him over for his opinion. "Sounds like a great big bowl of dicks to me," he'd say, and walk off chuckling to himself. Then, when some inevitable someone told him to watch his mouth, Merrill would come back with, "Twat's that? I cunt hear you." He said his father had taught him these conversational ice breakers "so I could fit in better."

Our task, besides trying to keep a straight face when Merrill went off, and he went off many times a day in howling, obscenity-laden rages, was to tutor the lad in the wisdom of time and place. But he never was able to make the distinction because what he was really doing was getting back something, getting a little revenge in his demented way for all the bad things done to him. When he was able to shock a group of adults he was briefly in control of them. It was him making people hop up and down and sputter indignantly instead of them doing it to him.

Merrill had been referred to the child welfare office because he'd been arrested for shoplifting and because the school people wanted to know if the boy's home life was all that it should be given his distressingly foul mouth. Merrill's father, who was drawing government nut money as a disabled person, freely admitted to the responding social worker that he'd taught his son "how to swear like the rest of the kids." Merrill loved his father, and his father was all he had in the way of role models, to borrow a tired descriptive from social work school.

"Come on down here, Merrill," I yelled up the tree at him. "Mrs. Amos wants to talk to you."

Merrill, silent, stared down as if he hadn't heard.

"He's not going to cooperate," I said, revealing my powerlessness to this odd representative of local government, the blessed congregant of "the most amazing church ever."

Mrs. Amos turned her gaze landward.

"That's Domingo over there, isn't it?"

"That's the top of his head," I said.

We walked over to the side of the hill for a full body shot.

"You can suck my…" Domingo began, instantly animated when he saw us coming toward him.

I tried to obliterate the looming, referent body part with a loud, gargling sigh as Domingo, now hopping up and down like he was gearing up to actualize a psycho-sexual attack, concluded, "to the root!"

"Are you going to let him do that?" Mrs. Amos asked in her usual monotone, so flat the question mark was inaudible. She might as well have just stated the fact: "You're going to let him do that."

Yes, of course I was going to let him do that. It was a hundred degree day and Domingo was a good thirty yards away down a hillside. I suppose I could have hurled myself at the little bastard and chased him into the goddam hills, but let's be realistic here, I thought, knowing that this lady and I shared no reality other than citizenship.

I made a little joke, hoping to make it clear to Sharon Amos, MSW, that there was nothing I could do. Why did she think the state and federal governments were paying me to confine these little nutballs to a remote rural ranch if their behavior was anywhere near manageable? Did she have any idea who she was dealing with? This is what these kids did. This is what life on the lowest rungs of capitalism had done to them. They had no control over themselves. They were all impulse like the rest of America is all acquisition and envy. They were only a more extreme expression of the national, I dunno, gestalt? I had no idea how to get them to stop acting crazy because they were crazy and the country was crazy and I was feeling a little unhinged myself.

"Strictly speaking," I began, hoping against hope that a little irony might mollify the social worker, "the lad hasn't done anything except threaten us with sexual assault. I'm pretty sure I can repel him if he tries anything."

I imagined a tiny brown boner charging up the hill at us like a dwarf rhino.

Mrs. Amos stared at me, then looked back at Domingo.

"Suck it baby," Domingo screamed. "Yeah you, bitch."

"Come on, Domingo, knock it off. This isn't right," I pleaded, trying not to whine.

"Fuck you too, fat boy, and the horse you rode in on."

Tired of hearing midgets telling me to go fuck myself all day every day, I'd taught them some new insults. I'd taught them the horse comeback and I'd thrown in a few more hoary witticisms like, "Fuck me? You'll have to get in line." These not so bon mots broke the rhetorical monotony for a while, but now they, too, were played back at me all day every day. Which is what I got for not keeping "professional distance," as the therapists might call my "coping strategies."

I apologized to Mrs. Amos for the verbal mayhem.

"I've never seen him this bad, Mrs. Amos. He's outdone himself today."

He was this bad every day, all day long and into the night. He was often worse, much worse. Any more or less sane adult can deal with bad language, even from a kid, but try living with a kid who sniffs glue, paint, and gasoline whenever he can, a kid who assaults whomever pops up into his addled viewmaster, child or adult. I spent a lot of time every day simply restraining the little psycho.

Mrs. Amos stared at the kid. I hoped Domingo's obscene exertions in the summer heat were wearing him down, but he showed no signs of fatigue. Every time we looked his way he got off another obscene blast. But I still felt a need to reassure the social worker that I wasn't as impotent as I appeared. She seemed completely out of it, but I didn't know her very well so I couldn't be sure she was as zoned as I suspected she was.

So I said that I thought it was a shame a 12-year-old boy was shouting obscenities at us, that it was subversive of good order, not to mention a violation of even the loosest known adult traditions of child rearing.

A normal person would have told me to spare her the bullshit, but this lady had no irony, no emotional roll bar. It wasn't that her bullshit detector needed new batteries, she didn't have the thing to begin with.

"America does this to people," Mrs. Amos said. "I know that."

Domingo fired again.

"Come down here, bitch, so I can bone you up…"

Mrs. Amos responded to the boy's abrupt switch from oral to anal intercourse by saying, "I think he should be tested for Simian Crease Syndrome."

"Pardon me?"

"I attended a conference last week on it," Mrs. Amos continued. "Some hyper-masculine males have an extra crease on the palms of their hands. There's a strong correlation between these creases and an extra male chromosome, which causes an excess of testosterone and increases the likelihood of violent criminal behavior."

"That's very interesting," I said, trying not to laugh, and beating back an impulse to check my own palms. "It sure would explain today's outburst," I added, lathering her up a little more, wondering how much insincerity this woebegone creature could take before she woke up and denounced me as "an enabler," as another social worker had done when I laughed as I described a routine episode of aberrant behavior to him. Lots of these helping pros didn't seem to know that there was a difference between laughing at unacceptable behavior and sanctioning it. And the people who didn't know the diff seemed to be running Mendocino County and, for that matter, the country.

The social worker took a last look at Domingo, who now was chanting, "Suck it baby, suck it," cupping his crotch and thrusting it forward to an imagined disco beat. I had to admire the boy's commitment to outrage.

Without further comment on either the boy's verbal aggression or his possible links to the higher primates, Mrs. Amos turned her back on Domingo and we walked over to the tree for a second round of negotiations with Merrill. I wondered if Merrill had a simian crease. He sure got up that tree fast.

Merrill looked down, expressionless, unmoving.

"Coming down, Merrill? Or do we have to talk from here?," I shouted up the tree.

Silence from the treetop.

"Shane? I went to see your father in Laytonville," Mrs. Amos said in her depressed, unamplified voice, too soft for Merrill to possibly hear.

"What did she say?" Merrill yelled, presumably at me.

"Mrs. Amos said she went to see your father in Laytonville," I shouted back like a cop trying to work out a hostage release.

"I'm not going to relay everything like this," I yelled, tardily realizing the absurdity of my role as relay man. "You want to hear what Mrs. Amos says, you come down here and talk with her like a gentleman."

"Your mother's a gentleman," Domingo yelled from over the side of the hill.

"Yes, I went to see Mr. Merrill," Mrs. Amos continued, speaking directly to me, perhaps realizing on her own that both the substance of what she had to tell me about the boy's father and my bellowed relays of her words to the boy in the tree were not an effective way to communicate.

"He lives in Laytonville in this run down old motel. It was about eleven in the morning when I got there. I knocked on the door and Mr. Merrill told me to come on in. The room was so dark I could barely see him at first. There was no light on and the shades were drawn, and Mr. Merrill was still in bed." She paused. "And he was in bed with one of those blow-up sex dolls."

Mrs. Amos seemed to shudder at the recollection.

I laughed.

"I thought it was totally inappropriate of him."

I laughed again. I knew by then she was nuts and that it didn't matter what I said or did, short of ripping her clothes off and throwing her over the hill to Domingo.

"Well, heck, I dunno," I said. "Maybe after his rough experience with Mrs. Merrill the poor guy thought he needed a less demanding relationship."

Mrs. Amos looked hard at me. I'd finally gone too far.

"It's not funny," she said, reflexively, without heat. "Mr. Merrill has real problems."

I snapped myself back into a state-sanctioned posture of Appropriate Male.

"Yes, you're right. That's terrible," I said. "What did he think he was doing?"

"Mr. Merrill is not my problem," she said. "I have to do what's best for Shane, and it's clear that Shane cannot see his father at this time. Mr. Merrill's home environment is not suitable for a young boy. It's totally inappropriate even for a visit."

It was suddenly raining inappropriates. Mrs. Amos was way ahead of the appropriateness curve. Today, that bland judgment is applied to everything from mass murder to body shirts at funerals.

Seven years later I was driving back to Mendocino County from Sacramento. It was late in the afternoon and raining, a November day just before Thanksgiving, 1978. Out of the car radio came a series of announcements, all beginning with "What appears to be a mass suicide in Jonestown, Guyana…"

The announcer went on to say that a woman identified as Sharon Linda Amos had been found dead in a house called Lamaha Gardens in Georgetown, Guyana, which served as a sort of reception center and clearinghouse for Reverend Jones' new society deep in the jungle. Mrs. Amos's job was to screen visitors. With Jones gone deep into pharmaceutical speed and paranoia, the social worker was one of the few persons he trusted among his all-white inner circle.

Sharon Amos had received the news that "revolutionary suicide" had kicked off out at Jonestown. It was over. Jones was killing his church, and it was time for her to go, too.

Amos radioed the mother church on Geary back in San Francisco. "Do what you can to even the score." The score was already something like 700 to nothing because out in the jungle almost everyone had downed the cyanide-laced koolaid, or had had it forced down their throats.

San Francisco would have to get busy. They were supposed to dispatch teams of "avenging angels" to kill the Temple's critics and defectors, and then themselves.

The San Francisco temple ignored the instruction.

Described as hysterical by the 75 or so Temple people at Lamaha Gardens, Amos told them it was time for them to transition themselves into the next life. Amos said that this was it, the last order from J.J. himself. Kill yourself for the revolution. The Temple people stared at Amos. She had no authority with them. They considered her a snitch for Jones and, well, even by their questionable standards, a nut.

Amos turned her back on the backsliders and, summoning her three children to follow her, Amos ordered Charles Beikman, a forty-three-year-old ex-Marine, and the only Temple member on the premises likely to do what Amos told him to do, to come upstairs with her.

Amos's overweight and under-brained adult daughter, Lianne, carried a butcher knife into the upstairs bathroom with which Amos promptly slit her 11-year-old daughter's throat; then she cut her 5-year-old son's throat. Amos ordered the cretinous Beikman to hold Lianne while Amos sawed Lianne's jugular. Having dispatched her three children, Amos didn't have enough left to finish herself off. She couldn't get the butcher knife deep enough into her throat. Semper Fi Beikman closed the social worker's file for her.

Out in the jungle, the official body count was 883, of whom 660 could be identified. The rest of the corpses were those of children who had been born in Jonestown. Nobody was sure who they belonged to, the devil it seems.

Back in Mendocino County everyone who had helped Jones along, wittingly or not, ran for cover.

The history of Mendocino County before and after Jim Jones goes like this:

> Indians for 12,000 years.
>
> **1800** — Spanish soldiers begin to raid southern Mendocino County to kidnap Indians for the missions at San Rafael and Sonoma.
>
> **1820** — Mexican slavers raid southern Mendocino County for sale to the great rancheros and the not so great ranches.

Indian women are in great demand as sex slaves.

1850 — Gold prospectors, followed by outlaws and settlers, the two often indistinguishable, descend upon all areas of Mendocino County with small herds of cattle and horses, immediately disrupting the Indian's food ecology. Indians begin to die in large numbers from disease, starvation, murder.

1851-52 — Lumber mills established in and around Mendocino.

1859 — Fort Bragg reservation is established. Some 3,000 county Indians were first forced to live there, then herded to the reservation at Covelo on the old trail linking Covelo and the Mendocino Coast. It ran along what is now the Branscomb Road, past the ancient Indian settlements of Sherwood and Cahto, through Long Valley and on into Round Valley.

1860 — Mendocino Indians in the eastern parts of the county are murdered in even greater numbers by state-paid gangs of resident bounty hunters.

1870 — Most of the county's Indians are dead or on the reservation at Covelo. A surviving few have managed to return to their home areas in places like Point Arena, a few in Fort Bragg, Stewart's Point, Anderson Valley, the Ukiah Valley, Sherwood (east of Willits), Hopland. Enough Indians have survived the onslaught to establish themselves in rancherias at Point Arena, Ukiah, Sherwood, Hopland, Laytonville. The Anderson Valley Indians are gone except for several families in Yorkville.

1875 — The county remains isolated from the outside world except for schooners that supply the booming coastal logging and farm communities. Inland ranches supply coast mills with beef.

1889 — The railroad reaches Ukiah via which the county's cattle, sheep, hogs, and farm products are shipped south. The line is extended to Willits in 1912 where it connects to the logging rail out of Fort Bragg; Eureka-Trinidad are connected to the line by 1915. It is now possible to get from

San Francisco to Eureka on an overnight train.

1945 — The post war logging boom begins with large numbers of rural white Southerners coming to Mendocino County to work in the mills and to start their own small-scale gyppo logging operations.

1960 — Logging slows, the county's far-flung communities lose populations.

1970 — Hippie influx of the back-to-the-landers throughout the county, buying logged-over land at low prices, re-populating and reviving the county's limping economy.

1975 — Marijuana, perfected by hippie botanists to today's intoxicating strength, becomes the county's number one export crop, which it remains; by the middle 1980's the large-scale growers are mostly Mexican immigrants organized into criminal syndicates.

1980 — Wealthy people begin buying property on the Mendocino Coast and in the more attractive areas not far inland. Land prices soar. Comptche, the Anderson Valley, and the South Coast from Point Arena to Gualala and Sea Ranch are particularly attractive to retirees, Silicon Valley entrepreneurs, Gatsby-like young people with millions in mystery money. The highly industrial, chemically dependent wine industry begins to proliferate with a simultaneously large influx of rural Mexicans who provide the industry's non-union labor.

1984 — Methamphetamine becomes widespread and, by 1990, is manufactured and distributed by criminal gangs, increasingly Mexican, but the crippling drug is consumed mostly by white addicts. Fort Bragg feminists tried to get the Gloriana Opera Company to tone down the witch in the Wizard of Oz.

1990 — Timber Wars. Hippies and environmentalists unsuccessfully fight the outside timber corporations who are clearcutting the Northcoast in an orgy of short-term profit-taking.

2000 — Hippies and former hippies have re-entered mainstream society with a vengeance. Ex-flower children occupy the top slots in all the county's public bureaucracies; hippies also dominate public agencies which, unlike the county's private sector, pay well and offer a range of fringe benefits generally not enjoyed by private sector employees. Public policy is carried out by the Love Generation, now Public Radio liberals, who delude themselves that public policy is not increasingly cruel.

2007 — The affection claimed by the Northcoast's liberals for Indians and Mexicans is historically consistent with the affection for Indians claimed by the founding Franciscans.

All manner of solipsistic activity occupies the counter-culture and its descendants.

The harmonic convergence body/psyche/earth attunement day. Beginning at dawn everywhere on earth on Sunday, August 16, 1987, at least 144,000 humans will be meditating and celebrating a unique phase shift in the process of global civilization. This workshop is an opportunity to prepare yourself and optimize your psychic participation in the new cycle. Opportunities available will be: psychic readings and healings; clearing trust; massage; biofeedback for stress reduction; being with your body; dance and drumming for strength and visioning; meditation and clearing the relationship with the earth and the convergence; healing the astral body; find out about spirit guides; children's hour — stories, dance, healings. CosmoGenesis program.

The harmonic convergence be-in that year was hyped as the long awaited "Dawn of the New Age," but was actually just a coming out party for people with befuddled minds. According to several recent scholarly publications, an inaccurate translation of ancient Mayan glyphs resulted in a "one cycle" error in determining the precise harmonic scale calibration points for the important "galactic window of opportunity" which ushers in the New Age. In other words, the recent Harmonic Convergence fiesta was one click off the mark — 52 years too late.

The new scholarly information also reveals that it's possible to determine the year for Harmonic Convergence, but not the exact date. In this case, the actual year for "Resonant Re-Entry" should have been 1935 — a year in which we actually witnessed the long anticipated return of the Aztec god-hero Quetzalcoatl, the Plumed Serpent. Elvis Presley, the god-hero Plumed Serpent of Rock and Roll slithered through a crack in the galactic window of opportunity in 1935 and twenty years later ushered in the "New Age" of Rock and Roll.

It's too bad, but due to a simple glyph glitch we missed the opportunity to tune in to the real Resonant Re-Entry which happened over fifty years ago. In fact, since August 16, 2007 was the thirtieth anniversary of the death of Elvis, Plumed Serpent Presley, we can assume that this is the dusk, not the dawn, of the New Age. We lived through the New Age and didn't even know it. We could have avoided World War II, Korea, Vietnam, etc., but we blew it. It must be embarrassing for the New Age gurus to be over fifty years out of sync, but, what the hell, everybody makes mistakes. The toga manufacturers made a few bucks, and people had a good time, so all is not lost.

Sad as it may seem, though, Harmonic Convergence is just a comforting myth, while Catatonic Divergence is the harsh reality. Demonic Emergence is at hand. Mayhem's coming! But don't tell the "foodists" frantically sniffing and sniveling near a big white building identified by a strange sign as the New Boonville Hotel. Apparently, these sheep are firm believers in another comforting myth: "You are what you eat." The harsh reality, though, is that: "You are what you don't poop."

I converged my harmonicas years ago so I didn't feel any pressing need to update. I converge my lips on several bottles of Bud a week after which I generally feel completely harmonious with all living things plus a few dead ones, and sometimes I'm pretty sure I feel the earth move.

Olompali, translated from the Miwok as "southern people" or "southern village," lies just north of Novato, directly off Highway 101. It's a state park these days but goes way back as the site of a large Miwok village, the only California land grant made to a Native American that withstood legal challenge, then came to belong to a pioneer family named Burdell whose magnificent old house became a hippie commune then burned down. A low-down retaliatory murder was committed near Olompali at the direction of John Fremont, primary among California's founding fathers. Olompali, in 1846, when Fremont was in the neighborhood, was the property of Camilo Ynitia, a Miwok educated at Mission San Rafael. Ynitia obtained a land grant from the Mexicans for several thousand acres at Olompali where he successfully grew wheat and raised horses.

Think about this next time you cruise by Olompali on 101.

General Vallejo said that Bernardino Four-Fingered Jack Garcia "was the wickedest man that California had produced up to that time." Which was 1846 when Garcia, a nominal citizen of Mexico, murdered four of freebooting John Fremont's men whose "bodies presented a most shocking spectacle, bearing the marks of horrible mutilation, their throats cut, and their bowels ripped open; and other indignities perpetrated of a nature too disgusting and obscene to relate." This happened out around what is now Sebastopol.

Fremont and Kit Carson were nearby, just down from Oregon, and now working to grab California from Mexico. When they got to Somoma a bunch of drunks and miscellaneous free booters had already made a flag with a rough depiction of a pig on it they said looked like a grizzly bear and declared California independent of Mexico. This was the Bear Flag Revolt. The rebels placed Vallejo under house arrest and drank up his wine cellar.

Carson was Fremont's premier hitman and aide de camp, and a very tough guy who once walked barefoot through hostile territory from Salinas to LA. Fremont and Carson were fresh off retaliatory murders of an unknown number of Klamath Indians several of whom had attacked them one night while Fremont and Company slept near present-day Klamath Falls. Kit Carson would write that the Klamath tribes were the bravest, fiercest Indians he killed anywhere in the country, and he'd fought Indians all over the West, including the Apaches of New Mexico where Carson made his home near Taos.

When Fremont got word that Four Fingered Jack and a small Californio army — native Californians loyal to Mexico — of maybe 50 soldiers was at Olompali on the edge of the bay which, at that time, came up to where the railroad tracks are now, Fremont made the short ride down from Sonoma hoping to avenge Four-

Finger's murders of his four men who'd had their private parts cut off and stuffed into their mouths, a desecration that was to re-occur in the American Civil War, World War Two, and by both sides in Vietnam.

Carson and two other Fremonters, on Fremont's orders, shot and killed the twin 20-year-old De Haro brothers and their uncle, Jose de los Reyes Berreyesa, memorialized today by De Haro Street on Potrero Hill in San Francisco and a Napa County lake. The three had rowed over from San Francisco, still called Yerba Buena, to see what was up at Olompali, scouting the scene for the main body of Californio troops at San Francisco under a combat-averse Californio general named Castro. Castro had sent the three to negotiate with Fremont. Fremont saw the trio of would-be negotiators rowing toward Point San Pablo more or less out where the Marin County Dump is now, and dispatched Carson, Granville Swift and Sam Neal to ride out and confront the would-be negotiators when they got ashore.

The two boys and their uncle were gunned down by Carson and the two thugs as they stepped out of their row boat. Fremont blamed Indians for the killings, blamed his own body guard of East Coast Delawares because, Fremont said, the Delawares were "excited by the death of comrades." The great historian of early California, Bancroft, called the killings of the De Haros and Berryessa "cowardly vengeance."

Soon after commenced the Battle of Olompali June 24th 1846 the only fight of the Bear Flag Rebellion, a running gun battle with Fremont's ragtag army in pursuit of Castro's ragtag army. One Mexican, Manuel Cantua was killed.

In 1853 Ynitia deeded a portion of Olompali to his adopted daughter and her husband John Pinkston, a freed black man, one of nine Marin County men licensed to sell liquor.

My faithful correspondent, Wanda Tinasky, a literary bag lady who lived on the Mendocino Coast, turned out to be an old San Francisco beatnik named Tom Hawkins. One couldn't have known from Hawkins' Wanda's always funny, always optimistic letters that Hawkins would murder his wife, torch his Fort Bragg house and drive himself over the bluffs into the sea. Some people still think the letters were the work of Thomas Pynchon, the famously reclusive author.

"Dear Mr. Anderson: As we approach the synchronic festivities of The Great Pumpkin and the Big Horse's Ass, people keep throwing sample ballots under the bridge & I finally looked. Who is this Bob Richards who is the American Independent candidate for President? Is he the guy who ate all the Wheaties? I really don't know, and don't know if it's obscure or if I'm just out of touch too much. Would I know these things if I still read the San Francisco Chronicle? I used to read the Chronicle in the Fort Bragg public library, but I quit going there a couple of years ago because I got tired of Don Rickles in drag. Is Herb Caen still alive? How about Don Sherwood? I suppose I have a sort of limited perspective, just reading the AVA and the Mendocino Commentary.

Incidentally, Mr. Anderson, the Commentary seems to be publishing rather irregularly lately. What's the matter with them? Are they sick? Did they all get three-piece jobs in Sacramento like their pal Luke Breit? Why is it that everything that I love dies? Why can't I love President Reagan?

Well, I don't expect you to know the answers to all these questions, Mr. Anderson... if you were smart, you'd be rich... and I'm not going to vote for any Bob Richards, even if he has a pole and Wheaties bowl. I'm going to vote for a winner: Emily Wong. Her relatives and I will elect her. A couple of years ago, when I was still reading the Chronicle, the Wong family held a reunion in San Francisco, and the Chronicle said that there are fifty million people in the world named Wong, and I feel sure that there are plenty of them to elect Emmy, although I can't believe that there are really fifty million of them, because fifty million Chinamen can't be Wong.

Actually I did see another newspaper the other day... I remember it was the Fort Bragg Advocate-News. I remember that it had a picture of a poster some local had made, with Ms. Ferraro as Miss Liberty and Mr. Mondale as Honest Abe, and I thought it was very nice but it would have been better if each of them had had one tit hanging out.

P.S. Is the Mendocino Commentary going broke? Could we help

them by holding a benefit? I would be willing to present my epic poem, "Shit Fight At The OK Corral," with Wyatt Earp and the Clayton brothers having it out with horse turds.

Dear Mr. Anderson: A few hitches hitching back from the circuses in SF & LA, or Sodom and Gomorrah West, as the folks from Rapid City say, and although I enjoyed my outing in the wonderful world of the Billygoats Gruff it's great to be back under the bridge. Don't let them kid you, Mr. Anderson, there are definite drawbacks to sleeping in a Port-a-Potty.

Of course it's no bed of roses either being the only shopping bag lady on the Mendocino coast who carries a typewriter (and I wish someone would give me a portable; after all, you gave Antonia an electric, didn't you?) and I'm not going to eat at Rhonda's any more because $23 a month really isn't enough to feed six people, and winter is icumen in, lewd sing goddam, but wotthehell, Mr. Anderson, wotthehell, the word is toujours gai.

I cried all the way to the bank of Jughandle Creek; it was the longest trail of tears since the Cherokee pogrom, but I cry at everything: card tricks, politicians' lies, human courage and decency, happy movie endings... life isn't like that, so I'm in no position to criticize Mary Decker Eddy and the rest of those girls for blubbering, and anyway you spend your youth taking those pills to retard menstruation and doing flipflops or playing volleyball eight hours every day and you don't even get a tacky gold medal; it's enough to make anybody cry.

What really touched me in L.A. was Joan Benoit and Bowdoin banner; I thought Benoit of Bowdoin was great (Benoit of Beloit would have been too much) and I was glad to find out that Joanie did it all on pineapple juice, although I am not totally naive about commercial endorsements, in fact it wouldn't surprise me if 7-Up got Mary Decker Eddy and Zola Budd to plug Coke and Pepsi. You could tell there was big money involved in the doings in L.A. because Howard Cosell had a new wig. A new, old wig. I think Mr. Cosell could learn a lot about aging his wig gracefully from Cary Grant (perhaps you saw me on TV sitting by Cary at the Coliseum) but of course Cary's face lift is inimitable, as they were able to lift not just his face but his whole body by hooking the hole in his chin onto his belly-button. (N.B.: That last part is not true, Mr. Anderson. I just made that up. I thought you might like a laugh.) The only one of that golden gang I really envy is the West German girl gymnast who was lucky enough to break her back on world T.V. ("She's alright, folks!") She's making millions doing commercials for an iron lung. That's my idea of having it made.

I decided against trying to make the Republican convention in Dallas... or any part of it... a girl's got to draw the line somewhere... but I know without looking how L. Ron Reagan will counter Geraldine's candidacy if she stays out of jail: "O.K., George... you like Georgia or Georgina? I'll see you get the purple heart..."

What started me off on my crying jag was the outburst of delight of recognition from the fags at the SF Demo convention when Geraldine got that one off about a cynic being someone who knows the price of everything and the value of nothing... or maybe they thought she made that up herself, but anyway you got the feeling that not since the halcyon days of JFK have we heard the Middle School Debate Team eloquence of Geraldine Ferraro (I can survive anything but a misprint.) and although I seem to recall having voted for a lady of African ancestry the first time that Ron ran for President (vowing to reduce federal spending and the national debt... "Excuse me while I laugh meself black in the face..." Mr. Dooley) and I don't recall that we have yet conceded the honesty of the returns in that election, I think it would be cute to have a President with a lady vice-president, even if she can't sing Tangerine (from the motion picture, 'Double Indemnity,' starring Fred MacMurray and Barbara Stanwyck, from the novel of the same name by James M. Cain. There was a period when a number of film dramatizations were made from the novels of James M. Cain, beginning with 'The Postman Always Rings Twice,' of course... 'Mildred Pierce,' for which Joan Crawford received an Academy Award, and a comedy called 'Career In High C.' The last and worst by far was 'Serenade,' which ended the careers on the screen of Mario Lanza and Joan Fontaine, and high time. 'Serenade' would make a terrific movie now, but they couldn't do it right in 1951 because it was the story of an operatic singer whose voice went weird on him when he started making it with a queer impresario. They changed the queer to a plutocratic patroness of the arts (Joan Fontaine), and that messed the whole thing up. Of course, Lanza wasn't exactly empathetic, either. Today, Robert Redford would be dynamite, lip synching to Pavarotti, and for the old queen, George Plimpton, or almost anybody.)

Besides people taking my name in vain in the local prints, I was really shocked on my return to Mendocino to learn that the county supervisors decided to continue selling dogs and cats to vivisectionists, Mendocino being one of only ten counties in California that do it. What was that smozzle about stopping it for? To jack up the price? As I understand it, the only justification for doing it is to raise money, and the supervisors could save more money than they get for the dogs and cats by cutting our Poets in the Schools, or some other useless crap.

Still, it's great to be back among real folks, Mr. Anderson, and I'm looking forward to seeing all those millionaire political and spiritual leaders of the land on the free and the home of the slave selling tortillas, but only on TV, because, as everybody knows, some of them don't wash their hands after they scratch their ass. (Wanda Tinasky) P.S. If Geraldine can't sing 'Tangerine,' could she sing 'Eggplant?' P.P.S. If you won't consider changing the name of The Anderson Valley Advertiser to the Boonville Bugle or the Philo Vance, how about 'The Bowdoin Banner'?"

Bret Harte departed Arcata in a big hurry in 1860 when, filling in as editor for the Humboldt Times, he wrote critically of the slaughter of peaceful Wiyots then living in Humboldt Bay on Gunther Island, later called Indian Island, a short distance from the town of Eureka. Early the morning of February 26th, 1860, a small number of white men believed to number no more than six, snuck up on the sleeping Indians to attack them with hatchets, knives and pistols. The white boys knew that most of the Indian men were not present and that there could not be much resistance from the sixty women and children they hacked to death in their beds or shot as they tried to flee. On the same morning another gang of white killers raided two other nearby rancherias where they slaughtered large numbers of women and children. They were unresisted, apparently, because the Indians, exhausted from three-day religious ceremonies, were unprotected by their men who, also apparently, were separated from their families in observation of religious requirements. Newspapers as far away as New York reported the atrocity. As for Harte, aside from his editorial expression of outrage at these unprovoked attacks on peaceful people, he was mostly silent about his stay on the Northcoast. He wrote an account of sailing up the coast to Eureka from San Francisco, a poem about the Mad River and his impressions of Humboldt Bay.

Ulysses S. Grant served as a lieutenant at Fort Humboldt, but the weather and the isolation seemed to have conspired to send him to the bottle for consolation. Grant left in 1854, going on to better things. Grant said even less than Harte about his Fort Humboldt days in his memoirs, but he does say that he always wanted to return to California, which he never did.

Tuesday was July 22, my birthday. Like every Tuesday it was a work day. As always I rose at five, put the coffee on, tottered out to get the morning paper which, in Boonville, is the Santa Rosa Press Democrat with whom I have been at war for years, a war I've steadily lost because they're a big paper, I have a little one.

As I take my first sip of coffee, I scan the empire, as in Redwood Empire, section of the paper where I can't help but see a story about my attempt to stop the county from paying public money to a private lawyer to defend a lunatic the county hired. A photo of a man identified as me but who isn't me sits in the middle of the story. The photo is of one of a Santa Rosa pedophile priest the paper is always writing about. I'm not a priest, and I'm not a pedophile.

I've been awake for ten minutes and I've already been defamed. It's as if the newspaper knew it was my birthday. We're off to a bad start, birthday boy.

The mail arrives. I receive a single birthday card. It's a computer-generated congratulation from my insurance agent, a person I've never met and, for all I know, doesn't exist.

The day grows warm, then hot. The work day grows long, then longer. But Tuesdays are always long. So are Mondays and Sundays and most other days in this business. Outback newspaper publishing is a fool's game, and I'm right where I should be — old and broke in Boonville. But it's my birthday and, at a minimum, I anticipate a slab of Safeway birthday cake on which I'd planned to erect a single candle and sing happy birthday to myself, with my wife perhaps even joining the brief festivities.

But when it's time for the merriment she's watching the Fox Network News and says she can hear me from where she is in the other room if I feel like singing happy birthday. Which seems to mean I'll be solo.

I look for the cake. It's not where a cake should be. It's outside on the porch where it was 105 two hours ago. The cake is a pile of Safeway grease. My colleague, The Major, "forgot" to bring it inside and stick it in the refrigerator. He says later that since it was Tuesday he was so overwhelmed with last minute production tasks he couldn't afford the 13 seconds it would have taken to open two doors, the front door and the refrigerator door twenty feet from each other.

To redeem what's left of the day, and just as Bill O'Reilly begins barking at my wife in the next room, I decide to take my dog Perro up into the hills for a quick, restorative, sunset hike. My birthday wasn't over yet! Joy could still be mine! Pleasure was still a possibility!

Deep in the east hills above Boonville, in the middle of literal nowhere, a dog the size of a small bear suddenly appears. Bear-Dog charges straight at Perro. Perro's not very smart, and he's no fighter. He sticks around like he's just met a new friend. Bear-Dog barrels into Perro, locking onto his head, and the dogs are immediately locked in mortal combat. Perro is quickly up on his hind legs fighting a rear guard action. The lady with Bear-Dog is tiny. She tries to separate the animals. Even if she weren't tiny, and even if I weren't mesmerized by the fight raging around us, both of us together couldn't get the dogs apart. Perro is very strong. Bear-Dog is even stronger. I impotently wave my walking stick around as if it's a magic wand through whose frantic thrusts and parries I can restore order, but it looks like my dear dog, the only dog I've ever owned — the only animal I've ever loved — is going to die.

By now Perro is fighting for his life. He's got to fight because Bear-Dog is trying to kill him. Perro's got about half of Bear-Dog's huge head locked in his jaws, but Bear-Dog has his mammoth jaws sunk bone deep in Perro's bad leg, and Perro's tiring.

The combatants tumble down an embankment in a furious jumble of deep growls and flying fur and into a stream. The tiny lady follows them, still bravely trying to grab her Bear-Dog's collar. Bear-Dog probably has fifty pounds on her. But she tries. I remain literally above the fray on the road above and resume inanely waving my walking stick.

Bear-Dog tires. He's old, fortunately. If he were young Perro would have been a goner three minutes ago. Bear-Dog un-jaws Perro. Perro un-jaws Bear Dog. Perro runs off on his three functioning legs as Bear-Dog sucks in restorative oxygen, watching Perro go, panting, exhausted, but looking like he'll resume the chase as soon as he gets his wind back.

I catch up with Perro and hide him in a copse of young fir from which both of us peer apprehensively out back down the road. Bear-Dog, who is already jogging in our direction, but hasn't yet seen us. Bear-Dog clearly wants another round. I have the insane thought that maybe Bear-Dog doesn't like dogs with Mexican names. Perro and I are well-hidden and we're still a couple hundred yards away. Bear-Dog can't see us. Bear-Dog is looking hard in our general direction but he can't see us. I've got a fifty-pound rock ready for his relentless head if he does spot us, but Bear-Dog turns around and jogs off towards his apologetic owner who is crying out, "Sorry. Sorry, wherever you are." Perro's beat up pretty good. Bear-Dog is beat up, too, especially his face. Perro's done. I have to lift him into the truck and we drive home where Perro immediately goes to sleep as soon as I un-lift him from the truck. I head for the freezer for some birthday ice cream.

There's no ice cream.

The next day I call the Press Democrat's corrections desk. "That wasn't me in yesterday's paper," I inform the lady who answered the phone. "That was a child molester."

She laughs.

"Are you sure?"

I can get a positive ID from my wife again if you want, I reply.

She laughs again.

"We'll certainly print a correction," she says.

For the next five days I look for the correction. The correction finally appears on the fifth day after my name had appeared beneath the perv's picture.

The "correction" said: "A photograph accompanying a story about Anderson Valley Advertiser publisher Bruce Anderson that ran in Tuesday's Empire section was misidentified as Anderson. The photo was supplied by the Los Angeles Times."

They blame the LA Times for something like this?

That very day I happen to encounter a PD staffer. PD people are under strict orders not to be seen with me, not to communicate with me, not to associate themselves with me in any way. I'm a one-man no-go zone, and may the newspaper gods keep it that way. But PD reporters often communicate with me on the q.t. This one says, "I heard that photo was a picture of some guy we took at the California Newspaper Publisher's Association meeting."

I'll stay with the perv jacket, thank you. Newspaper publishers these days are a lot worse than any weirdo I can think of.

Before I left the city, the County of Alameda sent David Mason to live with us in our downwardly mobile tenement on Sacramento Street. We were packing up to head for Mendocino County when Little Dave arrived, just as I was dreaming about the precise route of my exit, just imagining that anyone except me would care and even I was bored thinking about it, but I'd drive west on California, turn right onto Park Presidio and head north for the bridge, on past Mountain Lake where Juan Batista de Anza stopped in 1776 to camp and water his horses before he established Spain's first fort up the hill at Fort Point. Less than 200 years later I was in charge of a small, blonde haired, blue eyed, polite, cherubic, murderous little psychopath named David Mason, who, even as a child, was a conquistador of convention, you might say, the cat-like blue of his unblinking eyes uniquely, given his age, unnerving, the blue reminiscent, I'd find, of several Covelo Indians who had the blue-blue eyes of their Italian grandfathers who'd come to Covelo in the 1920s to mine coal.

"David did that?" people would say, incredulous, the day he tossed a cherry bomb through Andre The Bathrobe's window, a black man of mysterious means who would have been unrecognizable in any other garment. Andre The Bathrobe had come charging upstairs to my place. "I don't care how old that little bastard is, he fucks with me one more time and I'm going to beat his ass good."

Yes, yes. The boy was difficult. He liked Boonville, though, and probably should have stayed there. Sure he torched a few cats and had a disconcerting propensity to laugh at other people's physical pain, but at that point, as a kid, he wasn't all that removed, psychologically considered, from the childhood mental make-up of the average cop. Or NFL football player. Or most of us, if we fess up. But after a year's rustication in Mendocino County, Alameda County decided David was "ready to go home."

A few years later, David was described as "a 27-year-old San Lorenzo man who authorities say manifested a lifelong desire to destroy himself was ordered yesterday to be executed at San Quentin Prison." Which he duly was, right there on San Quentin point where, some scholars think, Sir Francis Drake put in, where the Miwoks hunted and fished in the tidelands, telling a reporter that he was an environmentalist and that his favorite writer was Stephen King. I like to think that his Boonville interlude turned Dave green, so green he carried out his own population control exercises.

"David Edwin Mason expressed no emotion when Alameda County Superior Court Judge Jacqueline Taber formally sentenced him to die in the gas chamber for killing four elderly Oakland residents and a cellmate in the courthouse jail. The only good thing Taber had to say about Mason was that 'he conducted himself in a respectful, controlled manner during his long and gory trial.' 'The totality of the criminal conduct of the defendant is awesome,' Taber said. She spent more than an hour detailing his crimes, which included an uncharged murder and six armed robberies in addition to the five homicides. Before his arrest, Mason confessed the crimes in a tape recording titled 'David Mason — Epitaph.' His brother turned it over to police. Between March and December 1980, Mason strangled and robbed Joan Pickard, 69, Arthur Jennings, 83, Antoinette Brown, 79, and Dorothy White, 72. He also garroted Boyd Wayne Johnson, his cellmate, on May 9, 1982, and admitted murdering his homosexual lover, Charles Groff, in Butte County.

Little Dave Mason was the fourth of eight children born to a devout middle-class couple who moved to the Bay Area from Georgia. "The children had more than a fair start in life," Judge Taber said. Probation officers reported that Mason had always been considered a "black sheep" by his Pentecostal family. He rebelled against their beliefs, which forbade watching television, dancing or drinking. "David's behavior was very weird, to say the least," his mother was quoted as saying. "He has tied himself up, kidnapped himself, cut himself, wrote threatening letters to himself and cut crosses on his forehead and hands." He became a "problem child" after falling and striking his head, she said. When he returned home late from school, he was switched once for every minute of tardiness, and when the discipline failed to produce the desired results, he was locked in his room, sometimes for several days.

"Death by strangulation seemed to be a fascination for David Mason," Taber said. At age 10, he strangled himself so severely that he had to be rushed to a hospital to be revived. His teachers considered him a "social misfit." He jabbed girls with pins and tripped fellow students. He set fires at home and at the family church. He ran away from a reform school — Boonville? — and lasted only two and a half months in the Marine Corps. "Medical personnel recognized that he needed help as early as age 8, but he never got any, probation officers said."

Which is not true. The diminutive nutball did alright in Boonville for the year he lived in Mendocino County. If he hadn't had the empathy beaten out of him as a child he probably would have grown up to be not all that much crazier than most of us. He might have been just another non-lethal weirdo wandering around Northern California, not that much different, historically considered, than the hard, ruthless men who landed on the Indians with the Gold Rush.

Right around the time of the Summer of Love, embattled authority began to notice that delinquents as young as nine were becoming much more ruthless, much more irredeemable, much less child-like, much more comprehensively dangerous than they'd been pre-hippie. And that was long before estranged youth organized itself into armed gangs and commenced killing each other in drive-bys. Nobody knew what to do, but everybody went right on pretending they were "just kids." 925 Sacramento Street wasn't much to look out but it was our home then, home, too, to Little Dave, who'd grow up to die at San Quentin by the midnight needle.

The Indians didn't have aberrant children, and they shunned their aberrant adults, not killed them.

The Chronicle recently featured a series of tired reminiscences about The Summer of Love from the same old Summer of Lovers — Wavy Gravy, Grace Slick, Country Joe and other A-Group Hippies. The fairest assessment I've read of that dreary, foggy summer of race riots and prevalent bad urban vibes, comes from a fellow survivor named James Pendergast of Sonoma: "The Summer of Love per se may not have had much meaning, but many features of the counterculture had a great effect that is still powerful today: the organic food movement, the peace movement, sustainable agriculture, back-to-the-land, protecting the environment, 'living lightly on the earth,' 'small is beautiful' and more. On the other hand, I witnessed many transcendent examples of ignorance, naiveté, mindless hedonism, venality, and plain old American stupidity. And drugs ruined many promising things. As David Crosby said later, 'We were wrong about drugs; we were right about everything else'."

Robert Oswalt died recently — 2007 — and a man is gone whose preservation of Pomo language, songs, stories, and histories comprise a very large part of what is known about the ingenious people who lived successfully in Mendocino and Sonoma counties for 12,000 years before us, the destroyers. Much of Mr. Oswalt's important legacy is found in his 1964 book, "Kashaya Texts." He died at his home in Kensington at age 84 and, apparently, was still at work on dictionaries of three Pomo dialects, when he went. It is to be hoped that scholars will complete Oswalt's life's work.

Henry Meiggs was among San Francisco's founding capitalists. And crooks. Mendocino County's, too. A tireless entrepreneur, Meiggs was a member of San Francisco's city council whose offices he would use to swindle his fellow entrepreneurs out of so much money he'd have been killed if he'd remained in the city; Meiggs' vaunted Mendocino holdings — the first sawmills on the Mendocino Coast — were under-capitalized, not that Meiggs ever stopped borrowing huge, for the times, sums of money on them.

Meiggs convinced German bankers that with another $20,000 he could build a sea-going tugboat to tow his lumber ships on into San Francisco Bay. The Germans were persuaded because their loan to the Mendocino timber man seemed to be secured by mortgages on San Francisco real estate and by warrants issued by the city government.

Meiggs, fresh capital in hand, disappeared, and was next known to be in business in Chile, then in Peru, far from the short reach of both German and American law. Meiggs had owed a lot more money to a lot more people than either his American or German creditors knew — more than a million dollars. The German bank in San Francisco went broke, Meiggs' mill and timber holdings in Mendocino wound up in new hands but Meiggs became one of the wealthiest men in South America, not quite wealthy enough to buy his way back to San Francisco. He'd partially repaid some of his creditors, and he'd spread enough of his Latin American fortune around Sacramento to persuade the California legislature to pass an amnesty act for him, the amnesty was vetoed by the governor, and Meiggs lived out his life in Peru.

A friend commented the other day, "I sometimes walk six miles to avoid taking Muni." Depending on how my legs feel, I'll walk the six miles from the Inner Richmond to the bay, sometimes passing through Pacific Heights where Meiggs once lived, thinking much of the way about how much speeded-up history lies beneath my feet, how thin the veneer of industrial civilization lies over four hundred years of honest murder. I'll take Muni back out to the dunes, not that I ever click my heels in anticipation of the ride.

Muni is invariably unpleasant in ways large and small, from buses with windows blacked out with advertising so passengers can't enjoy the passing parade on the streets (which says it all about management's regard for its customers), to constant mechanized voices reminding us to "hold on," to feral co-passengers, to drivers who range from the verifiably insane to the merely rude and stupid to the saintly.

I had a minor run-in with both the driver extremes the other day at the foot of Market Street. I'd been down at the ball park, then into the Ferry Building for a cup of Peets and an hour of people watching. (It's time for a national dress code, but that's a subject for another time.) I crossed the Embarcadero to Market where, as I approach, I am delighted to see a 2 Clement at the bus stop, just sitting there with its door open, its engine idling, its driver, an obese white man, at the wheel. All for me! Me! I silently exult. I bound up the buses' three steps, flashing my wife's senior pass at Fatso who startles me by half rising out of his seat to shout right in my face, "Out of service! Get off. Can't you see I'm out of service?" Of course. Silly me. A bus idling at a bus stop with its door open and its driver at the wheel. How blind could I be?

"Why don't you close the door if you're out of service?" I ask him. Fatso stares back at me. He looks peeved, very peeved at my impertinence. I dismount and stand on the sidewalk a foot from the open door of the bus. A black female driver appears She and Fatso exclaim pleasantries. Fatso, his jello-like bulk seeming to move in sections, manages to squeeze out from behind the controls. He shoulders past me and rolls off towards the Ferry Building, his bulk blotting out lower Market Street. I supposed he was on his way home to power trip Mrs. Fatso for another eight hour shift.

The new driver says to me, "You can sit down on the bus if you want, but I can't leave for another fifteen minutes because of the schedule." I thanked her and got back on, so pleased with her graciousness I wrote down the bus number and called in a commendation to the bus barn on Presidio.

"I had one bad driver, one nice one," I said to the woman who answered the phone. "But the driver ahead of the nice driver, I'm sorry to have to tell you, asked me if he could see my private parts. I'm a senior citizen from Mendocino County, and I think that's totally inappropriate, as we say up there. I hope you can talk to your drive about it."

The lady on the other end of the line paused before she said, "We'll make a note of that, sir. Thank you for calling."

Marie the mystery woman was so much the mystery woman it was hard to find out her last name, but it's. It's Helmey, Marie Helmey. Still don't know her, do you? How about the old lady who always wore a long black coat and lived in the Mannix Building? The old lady who drank one small beer every afternoon in the

Boonville Lodge? Now you remember, don't you?

She lived in Boonville for a long time, maybe as long a time as twenty years, which is a long time in a transient little town in a transient time. Before Boonville, Marie lived in Ukiah, also for a long time. She was a hot lead typesetter and linotype operator from the old days of newspapers when typesetters plucked each letter of each word out of overhead cases containing all the letters of the alphabet in many type faces and sizes to make every word that went onto every page of the newspaper, when newspapers were composed by hand, one letter at a time. When the Ukiah paper went from hot lead to cold type technology in the 1960s, Marie moved to Boonville where Homer Mannix continued to make his paper the old fashioned hot lead way — one letter, one word, one page at a time. Homer's handcrafted weekly would have been impossible without Marie Helmey, the last working hot lead typesetter in California, maybe the last hot lead press operator in the United States.

Homer Mannix worked out a deal with Marie; she would live upstairs in one of his apartments and work downstairs every Tuesday when Homer's Advertiser was put together on an antique hot lead linotype machine. The deal was good for more than twenty years.

From the service counter on paper days you could see a dim figure moving very fast from task to task in the rear of the shop, the ancient machinery wheezing and clanking around the mysterious dervish whirling at its center. Stepping behind the counter and peering into the mechanical murk, there was Marie in her long, black coat, fingers flying at hummingbird speed, blindly but unerringly plucking letters from their overhead cases, placing them exactly where they had to go to make a word, then a complete story, then a full page of stories.

Boonville people who didn't know how the paper was produced every week, only remember Marie as the tall-ish, spare, spry elderly woman who always wore that long, black dress coat even if it was a hundred degrees outside, one-ten inside. Most people also knew Marie had some sort of function at the newspaper although they didn't know what that function was. And they knew she lived upstairs in the Mannix Building.

Vivid in her interminable black coat, Marie was part of Boonville's human panorama, as eccentric as the rambling, pre-code Mannix Building itself. She walked like a bird, a few quick head-down steps, pause, look around, then a few more quick steps, gingerly, haltingly but somehow briskly making her way to the Boonville Lodge or the Horn of Zeese where she took most of her meals. Marie had no family that anybody knew of, no friends, belonged to no associations, never ever was seen at community events. But up close, Marie always looked amused, happy even, her eyes twinkling. She got along just fine outside the social ramble.

At the Lodge where she stopped in every day, Marie would linger over her one short late-afternoon beer, smiling to herself, nodding to the regulars who greeted her. She was locally famous for continuing to sip her Miller's the day a woman was shot to death a few stool's down by a jealous husband. Marie had looked on impassively, finished up her drink and walked her stutter-stepping blackbird's walk on home to her front bedroom in the Mannix Building, bathroom down the hall. Nothing got in the way of her daily beer, and the Lodge in those days, even before nightfall when it could become positively thrilling if not life-threatening, could be an extremely distracting establishment. It was no place for a lady, and certainly no place for a senior citizen lady, not that there weren't ladies, senior and junior, among the bar's regular customers. But the Lodge wouldn't ever be confused with the Unity Club whatever the gentility quotient among its female patrons.

The occasional afternoon mayhem never bothered Marie. On another ultra-violent afternoon she was downing her daily mini-Miller's when a little guy broke off a cue stick and stabbed it deep in a big guy's back. The matador then ran for his life out onto the middle of 128 where he pivoted south and kept on running towards Cloverdale, his bull right behind him, the shattered cue stick sticking out of his back, blood running down into his Levis.

Unfazed, Marie would be back the next afternoon right about four. If the venue got a little rough sometimes, so what? There she was every afternoon except paper day, the day her flying fingers worked their obsolete hot lead press magic in Homer Mannix's living history newspaper museum, Boonville, California.

Marie spent her long Boonville life in that austere upstairs room in the Mannix Building where she was the beneficiary of many kindnesses from the Mannix family. Homer's wife Bea gave Marie clothes because Marie spent very little money on herself and always refused the raises Homer tried to give her because she was afraid the extra money would reduce her pension and social security income. She had a lot of money salted away, it was said, as it's always said about reclusive, mysterious figures.

Marie's one-day-a-week job with Homer's Advertiser ended with the sale of the paper and the technology upgrade brought to the operation by the new owners, Marie went on living in her room upstairs over the print shop, went on walking down the pitted margins of Highway 128 to the Horn of Zeese and, every afternoon, to the Boonville Lodge, for her one beer. When she began to fail, a nephew appeared from somewhere and took Marie away, and Marie left town like shed arrived — not a word to anybody.

Mike Mannix, Homer's nephew, remembers Marie this way: "She was about the same age as the old linotype machine. I had the impression that she drank a lot. All week long nobody saw her, but she'd come down on paper night and work her miracle with that cranky old Merganthaler, c. 1898, and make it happen. Things would start sparking and arcing and jamming up, but she never lost her cool. She always wore that long, black coat. Homer would say to me, 'Just stay away from it. She can make it happen.' I remember her fingers flying in and out of the type boxes. When something happened, something went wrong, Marie would know just what to do. She didn't seem to have a life other than those Tuesday production nights. Now that you mention it, she was dark like an Indian, with a sharp-featured, angular face."

The one time I tried to talk to Marie in the Lodge she'd said, "Sorry, gotta go," and got up and went. Someone told me that Marie was an Indian, not that that was a question I would have asked her. But I was hoping to get to know her a little bit so she'd volunteer some personal bona fides. Nope. Sorry, I gotta go, she'd said, making it clear that she'd always be gotta be going if I should ever try to get to know her again.

I knew an Indian in Covelo who'd been trained as a hot lead printer at an Indian school in the 1940s. He told me that Mendocino

County Indians were often taken away to Indian schools up through the 1950s to get them out of their Indian-ness; the government viewed Indian-ness as incompatible with consumer capitalism. These abductees, my Covelo friend told me, often took advantage of the Indian school's vocational emphasis on the print technology of those times. I thought maybe Marie had learned her amazing trade at an Indian school. Because she looked like an Indian I thought she probably was one.

With the help of a San Francisco researcher, I was able to track the mystery woman to Wayland, Michigan, where she died, at age 85, on December 16th, 1989; her date of birth was listed as February 4th, 1904.

Irvin and Helen Helmey owned and operated the Wayland Globe, a weekly newspaper, until 1986. It had been founded by the Helmey family in 1884. It is safe to say that the Helmeys were also Marie Helmey's family.

"My great uncle, Irv Helmey," writes Lisa Dye, "owned the Wayland Globe, a weekly newspaper in Wayland, Michigan. He had a sister named Marie. He also had a sister named Audrey, who was my grandmother. I never knew Marie, but she was a favorite of my dad's. My name is Lisa Marie in honor of Aunt Marie. I don't know if this is the Marie Helmey you are looking for, but it makes sense that she may have come back to live with her brother, my great uncle, Irv Helmey, before she died. I think Marie was a single lady; I vaguely recall that she was considered adventuresome and somewhat eccentric. She'd had mental problems, and had been put away when she was a young woman for a few years. There was talk of her running naked through the streets, a great scandal for that time. The family never talked about it, and when she went out to California life in Wayland went on without her. My people on Marie's side immigrated from Norway to settle originally in the Dakotas. My grandmother was reportedly born in a 'soddy,' a sod hut the settlers built for lack of lumber. I wish I had been older when this generation was lost. I'd love to know more about them."

The hot lead Anderson Valley Advertiser, Homer Mannix, Marie, the Mannix Building, and all the museum-quality equipment used to publish the paper are gone, as is much of old Boonville, a distinct place with vivid personalities to match, a town now so changed, so blanded down, it's as if there's been a population transplant and the history of the place destroyed.

Pretty soon we'll be gone too, but this beguiling place of big trees and sea shore, golden hills and ghost dances, will go on, its laughter and its great sorrows all the way back to the first people, folded into its beauty as if none of it had ever happened.